GREEK SPORT AND SOCIAL STATUS

 The Fordyce W. Mitchel Memorial Lecture Series, sponsored by the Department of History at the University of Missouri–Columbia, began in October 2000. Fordyce Mitchel was Professor of Greek History at the University of Missouri–Columbia until his death in 1986. In addition to his work on fourth century Greek history and epigraphy, including his much-cited *Lykourgan Athens: 338–322*, Semple Lectures 2 (Cincinnati: 1970), Mitchel helped to elevate the ancient history program in the Department of History and to build the extensive library resources in that field. The lecture series was made possible by a generous endowment from his widow, Mrs. Marguerite Mitchel. It provides for a biennial series of lectures on original aspects of Greek history and society, given by a scholar of high international standing. The lectures are then revised and are currently published by the University of Texas Press.

Previous Mitchel Publications

Carol G. Thomas, *Finding People in Early Greece* (University of Missouri Press 2005)
Mogens Herman Hansen, *The Shotgun Method: The Demography of the Ancient Greek City–State Culture* (University of Missouri Press 2006)

Greek Sport
and Social Status

by Mark Golden

UNIVERSITY OF TEXAS PRESS
Austin

This book has been supported by an endowment dedicated to classics and the ancient world and funded by the Areté Foundation; the Gladys Krieble Delmas Foundation; the Dougherty Foundation; the James R. Dougherty, Jr. Foundation; the Rachael and Ben Vaughan Foundation; and the National Endowment for the Humanities.

Requests for permission to reproduce material from this work should be sent to:
Permissions
University of Texas Press
P.O. Box 7819
Austin, TX 78713-7819
www.utexas.edu/utpress/about/bpermission.html

♾ The paper used in this book meets the minimum requirements of ANSI/NISO Z39.48-1992 (R1997) (Permanence of Paper).

Library of Congress Cataloging-in-Publication Data

Golden, Mark, 1948–
    Greek sport and social status / by Mark Golden.
        p.   cm. — (Fordyce W. Mitchel Memorial Lecture Series)
    Includes bibliographical references and index.

    1. Athletics—Greece—History.   2. Athletics—Greece—Social aspects.   I. Title.
    GV21.G65   2009
    796.0938—dc22
                                                    2008005217
    ISBN 0-292-72153-6
    ISBN 978-0-292-72153-1

For J. D.
My Prairie Vole

CONTENTS

PREFACE

This short book has been a long time in the making. When Ian Worthington invited me to give the first Fordyce W. Mitchel Memorial Lectures at the University of Missouri at Columbia in 2000, I was a little intimidated—Mitchel's own 1968 Semple lecture at Cincinnati set a high standard—but of course I was very pleased to accept.[1] I could not, however, promise quick publication: I had already committed myself to other book-length projects. In any event, these took even longer to complete than I had expected. My tardiness was fortunately more than matched by the energy of others, and I have consequently been able to make use of a spate of first-class work that has become available in the interim. Of particular benefit: that of Nigel Nicholson on jockeys, charioteers, and trainers; Jason König, Tom Scanlon, and Onno van Nijf on Greek athletics under Roman rule; Michael Carter on gladiatorial spectacles in the Greek east; and the surveys and syntheses by Don Kyle and Stephen Miller. The collection of Nigel Crowther's many shorter pieces on Greek sport (along with the author's updates) has also been most helpful. Nevertheless, I have tried to reproduce something of the flavor of the original lectures: readers may find the occasional reference to current events and a few good stories told more than once.

This book is to some extent a continuation of an earlier one, *Sport and Society in Ancient Greece* (Cambridge 1997). There I identified a "discourse of difference": Greek sport afforded "a field for the creation and reinforcement of divisions among groups and the ordering of these groups into hierarchies" (176). The phrase does not recur here—"discourse" is used only to denote a circular object, thicker in the middle than at the edges, thrown in the ancient pentathlon—but some of the same concerns do.

In Chapter One ("Helpers, Horses, and Heroes: Contests over Victory in Ancient Greece"), I discuss the importance elite Greek males attributed to competitive success and the means they used to ignore or deny any claims others—jockeys, charioteers, coaches, women—might make to share the status based on it. Recent papyrus finds, especially "the new Posidippus," enable us to trace these tactics into Hellenistic and Roman times; in this respect too this book extends *Sport and Society,* restricted as that is for the most part to the archaic and classical periods.

Chapter Two ("Slaves and Ancient Greek Sport") takes up the intersections of sport with another defining characteristic of Greek society: slavery. Though sport was one of the means by which Greeks separated themselves from barbarians and free citizens from slaves, competitors put themselves under the control of referees and other officials and could suffer the indignity of corporal punishment. Moreover, one term used for slaves associated with athletics, *palaistrophylax, "palaestra* guard," also came to be used for free citizens of some distinction in Greco-Roman Egypt.

Chapter Three ("Greek Games and Gladiators") begins with the stock—and stark—contrast between the glories of Greek festival competition and the base brutality of the gladiatorial spectacles of the Romans, only to argue that Greek spectators thronged amphitheaters and similar venues, that Greek gladiators sought to raise their social status by representing themselves as athletes, and that the Greek elite saw gladiatorial shows as a legitimate means to enhance their own standing in the community. In the end, I conclude that gladiatorial combat has a valid claim to be considered sport.

In Chapter Four ("Olive-Tinted Spectacles: Myths in the Histories of the Ancient and Modern Olympics"), I bring the

story of the use of Greek sport to enhance status up to the present day. The modern Olympic movement used links with antiquity as a source of legitimation and prestige from its very
start and has never ceased to do so. But, as is so common when
we invoke the past for present purposes, these claims have often
been based on mistakes and misrepresentations. For example,
the ancient Olympics were never restricted to amateurs, and
wars did not stop during the festival. Myths such as these have
hindered our understanding of ancient Greek sport. What is
worse, they have caused harm in the present and (in the case of
the Olympic truce movement today) may prevent us from doing as much good as we can in the future. If we want to change
the world, we must base our arguments on what we believe is
right and not seek to raise their status or limit our aims according to what the Greeks did or did not do.

No part of writing a book is more welcome than acknowl-
edging the help of others and not just because it means the job is
almost done. The generosity of the Mitchel family made my visit
to Missouri possible; it was a pleasure to meet them all (all the
more because the occasion revealed a tie to Winnipeg that had
previously been hidden from history). Hugh Grant provided the
refuge where I wrote the original lectures. Ian and Tracy Worthington and their son Oliver generously opened their home in
Columbia to me and Max, age ten at the time. ("I'm tired," Max
told me after playing with Oliver for a while. "Two year olds
are a lot of work.") Ian's colleagues in the Departments of History and Classics shared the burden of entertaining us. After our
return from Missouri, Michael Carter, Kelly Joss, Jason König,
Don Kyle, and Pauline Ripat read chapters of this book in draft.
I sought advice from many others, including Sinclair Bell, Martin Cropp, Pauline Greenhill, Nigel Kennell, the late Victor
Matthews, Nigel Nicholson, John Oakley, David Roselli, Tom
Scanlon, Josh Sosin, Onno van Nijf, Michael Wahn, and Rob-
ert Weir. Sinclair Bell compiled the indexes. Jane Cahill, Craig
Cooper, Lou Lépine, Iain McDougall and Pauline Ripat—my
colleagues in the Department of Classics at the University of
Winnipeg—continued to offer the friendship and models of

commitment to our work that have made this an ideal academic home for the past twenty-five years. In addition, Lou Lépine typed every word with her usual remarkable competence and good humor and never once complained about my handwriting. (Students take note.) Heather Mathieson and Lynne Schultz of our library's interlending department fulfilled my every request, no matter how unreasonable. At the University of Texas Press, Nancy Moore saved me from many errors and obscurities and helped me slay the Wicked Which (that, I know). But my deepest debt of gratitude is owed to the subject of this dedication, the modest prairie denizen who has made the whole of each year since I began work on this book feel like Volentine's Day.

All translations are my own, unless otherwise indicated. Abbreviations for ancient authors and works follow the usage of the *Oxford Classical Dictionary* or of H. G. Liddell, R. Scott, and H. Stuart Jones, *A Greek-English Lexicon* and its supplements.

SOME IMPORTANT DATES

Note: many dates are approximate or conjectural.

ARCHAIC PERIOD (GREECE)/REGAL AND REPUBLICAN PERIODS (ROME)

776 BCE	Foundation of Olympic games (Hippias' date)
753	Foundation of Rome (traditional date)
750	Homer, *Iliad*
725	Homer, *Odyssey*
704	Foundation of Olympic games (Mallwitz' date)
680	Olympic four-horse chariot race
594	Solon's legislation at Athens
564	Arrichion's third *pankration* victory and death at Olympia
536	Milon's first adult wrestling victory at Olympia
520	Olympic race in armor
520–470	Simonides' poems
509	Expulsion of last king of Rome/establishment of Roman Republic
498–446	Pindar's poems
490	Persian invasion of Greece/Battle of Marathon/Pheidippides
484	Prime of the trainer Menander
482	Hieron's first horseracing victory at Delphi
480	Astylus' three victories in footraces at Olympia

CLASSICAL PERIOD (GREECE)/ REPUBLICAN PERIOD (ROME)

479	Battle of Plataea/end of Persian Wars
480–450	Bacchylides' poems
476	Alexander I of Macedon's competition at Olympia
468	Fifth day added to Olympic festival
460	Thirtieth panhellenic victory for the trainer Melesias
456	Completion of Temple of Zeus at Olympia
450	Building of Stadium III at Olympia
431–404	Peloponnesian War
420	Lichas' chariot victory at Olympia
416	Alcibiades' chariot victory at Olympia
415	Euripides, *Alexandros*
408	Olympic two-horse chariot race
400	Compilation of Hippias' list of Olympic victors; Damonon's stone list of his competitive successes
399	Execution of Socrates
396	Cynisca's first chariot victory at Olympia
384	Olympic four-colt chariot race
380	Panathenaea prize list
372	Troilus' chariot victories at Olympia/judges henceforward banned from competition
364	Arcadians and Eleians wage war at Olympia
356	Philip II of Macedon's horseracing victory at Olympia
338	Battle of Chaeronea: Philip defeats Greek alliance
323	Death of Alexander the Great

HELLENISTIC PERIOD (GREECE)/ REPUBLICAN PERIOD (ROME)

314	Ptolemy I's chariot victory at Delphi
300	Athenodorus' Nemean boxing victory/request for assistance from Ephesus
284	Chariot victories of Ptolemy I, Berenice I, and Ptolemy II Philadelphus at Olympia

IMPERIAL PERIOD

MODERN PERIOD

GREEK SPORT AND SOCIAL STATUS

One HELPERS, HORSES, AND HEROES

Contests over Victory in Ancient Greece

On March 7, 2000, a judge of the U.S. Seventh Circuit Court in Chicago ruled on the case of Ford Olinger. Olinger, then 33, suffered from bilateral vascular necrosis of the hips, a condition that made walking both difficult and painful. Under the Americans with Disabilities Act, he sought to force the U.S. Golf Association to allow him to use a golf cart in qualifying rounds for the U.S. Open golf tournament. The judge, however, ruled against Olinger. The next day, another judge of another court, the U.S. Ninth Circuit Court in San Francisco, delivered a judgment in the matter of Casey Martin. Martin, a twenty-seven-year-old professional golfer and former college roommate of Tiger Woods, had Klippel-Trenaunay-Weber Syndrome, a rare circulatory disorder. This affected his right leg and made walking difficult and painful for him as well. He too invoked the Americans with Disabilities Act, in his case to use a golf cart on the Professional Golf Association (PGA) Tour. After his request was granted by a lower court, the decision was appealed and then reviewed by the Ninth Circuit Court. On 9 March, that court decided in favor of Martin: the PGA Tour was required to let him use a cart in its competitions.

In the end, it took the U.S. Supreme Court to resolve the difference of opinion, though only by a split decision. In May 2001, seven of the nine justices upheld the lower court ruling in Martin's favor (and sent Olinger's case back to the Seventh Circuit for reconsideration). Martin went on to play for several years on the PGA Tour, finishing as high as a tie for twenty-third at the U.S. Open and winning some $500,000; he retired from competitive golf in 2005 and later became golf coach at the University of Oregon in his home town. A happy ending. Meanwhile, just a week after the Supreme Court delivered its decision, an autistic nine-year-old was refused entry into a Greater Tampa Junior Golf Association tournament because he could not keep score on his own. . . .

It is tempting to regard all this as unique to the wonderful world of golf. In what other sport do manufacturers spend $250 million to come up with a better ball, or players spend $500,000 for membership in a Japanese club and $67,000 for a shed-sized Full Swing Golf Simulator device? What other sport has spawned anything like No-Golf Day (29 April) or the Global Anti-Golf Movement, the first recorded benefit of globalization? Golf also makes a cameo appearance, along with a game called knipsbrat, in Miriam Toews' award-winning novel of Mennonite life in southern Manitoba, *A Complicated Kindness*.[1]

> It was one of the few games we were allowed to play.
> Golf was another one because it consisted of using a rod
> to hit something much, much smaller than yourself and
> a lot of men in this town enjoyed that sort of thing.

But in fact the Olinger and Martin cases raise several issues of interest for students of sport in general.

The first concerns the credit for victory. No one (as we are all too aware from the speeches at the Academy Awards) wins entirely on his or her own. But what kind of assistance is acceptable? And to what extent do acceptable aids diminish the glory of the victory and undercut claims to distinction that may be based on it? The Olinger and Martin cases turn on the use of golf carts. It is interesting to note, however, that other forms of assistance in golf are not the subjects of controversy, let alone litigation. Caddies, for instance. However athletic professional golfers may be—an issue we will take up in a moment—it is their caddies who carry their clubs (which may weigh forty pounds) and whose advice is often crucial for their success. Yet until very recently they were virtually as invisible on the course as they are in the courts, taken for granted as much as golf tees. Perhaps Martin and Olinger should simply have gotten their caddies to carry them around the course.

The irony is that the golf tee—another necessary ingredient in a golfer's success—was invented by a Black American, George Grant, in 1899. This was sixty years before the PGA Tour lifted its Whites-only policy (in 1961) and almost one hundred years before a non-White player first won a major U.S. golf tournament (in 1997). In the intervening years, the only Blacks to be seen on championship courses were caddies, often richly rewarded by the grateful and generous professionals whom they helped to win, to be sure, but almost entirely left out of the public and official versions of victory.[2] Golf clubs may often have been the Black man's burden; golf itself was a White man's game, and he did not share the fame that followed success. Now the caddies have arisen, fueled in no small measure by the extraordinary popularity of golf as a spectator sport. (Among its unique attributes, golf is the only sport to enjoy its own TV channel.) Among the most prominent, Steve Williams, long Tiger Woods' caddy, was jokingly referred to as the best-paid athlete in New Zealand until his countryman Michael Campbell won the 2005 U.S. Open. No caddy is likely to bag Campbell's $1,700,000 purse. Standard wages, however, now run from $500 to $1,000 a week plus a percentage of the winnings, perhaps as much as ten percent in the case of a victory, and a Professional Caddies Association has been organized to negotiate on such benefits as medical insurance for its 2,000-plus members. Predictably, some golfers resent the caddies' new perks and prominence. "When it becomes news that caddies are being hired and fired, we have to step back and take a look at our priorities," says Curtis Strange, himself twice a winner of the U.S. Open. "I don't know a single caddy who will win or lose a tournament."[3]

Golf carts are not the only conveyances to cause controversy in the sporting world. In 1997, Colorado Rockies outfielder Larry Walker had a great season, hitting .366 with forty-nine home runs, stealing thirty-three bases, and throwing out twelve runners. It was one of the best all-round years ever, without question the most successful by a Canadian, and earned Walker recognition as the National League's Most Valuable Player. Yet it did not win him the Lou Marsh award as Canada's outstanding athlete. Instead, voters (narrowly) selected Jacques Villeneuve, world champion in F1 auto racing (and a previous recipient, after winning the Indianapolis 500 race in 1995). The choice provoked an outcry. Walker, it was protested, had achieved his distinctions on his own; Villeneuve (however fit, skillful, and courageous he might be) was only as good as his car.[4] Villeneuve's partisans responded that he excelled at a sport of worldwide scope and interest, unlike baseball, whose "World Series" is confined to North America. Furthermore, Walker's numbers, impressive as they seemed, were not entirely his own doing: they were assisted by the run-rich period and park in which he played. Anyway, winners in the award's seventy-year history have included equestrians, jockeys, sulky drivers, and, in 1980, Terry Fox, a young cancer victim who captured the country's admiration by setting out to run across Canada on his one good leg. (To say nothing of three golfers.) After the dust settled, Walker did go on to win a Lou Marsh award, in 1998, and Villeneuve's career sputtered and stalled with the motors of his Williams and British American Racing (BAR) racecars.

A similar furor erupted in 2004, when wheelchair racer Chantal Petitclerc shared Athletics Canada's two awards for the top track and field competitor with hurdler Perdita Felicien. Petitclerc had won five races at the Athens Paralympics, setting three world records in the process, plus a demonstration event in the Olympic stadium, the only time Canada's anthem was played there during the games. Felicien, for her part, was the world indoors titleholder at 60 meters, but she had fallen over the first barrier and failed to finish her race at the Olympics. Athletics Canada's explanation—it wanted to honor two athletes without making a tough choice—did not help matters. As one wheelchair racer put it, "Chantal had one of the most incredible performances, and it was downgraded to make her co-recipient with someone who crashed."

Petitclerc too later found vindication, being named female athlete of the year at the 2004 Canada Sports Awards and bearing her country's flag at the Commonwealth Games at Melbourne in 2006. Those games integrate events for "élite athletes with disabilities" into the official program and include them in medal tallies—and so raise the further question of why there are separate Paralympics at all. Petitclerc herself noted that when one of Canada's Olympic cyclists needed a tool to fix his bike, he came to her; one wheeled conveyance is much like another.[5]

So much—for the moment—for the help modern athletes are entitled to rely on, and not. The second issue raised by the Olinger and Martin cases concerns nothing less than the definition of sport itself. In the Olinger case, the circuit judge—a golfer—was apparently much influenced by the testimony of Ken Venturi, who won the 1964 U.S. Open in conditions that took a terrible physical toll on all competitors: temperatures of 100 degrees F, 97 percent humidity. In his decision, he referred to Ben Hogan, who won the 1950 Open only one year after a devastating automobile accident that all but left him a cripple. He accepted in the end the U.S. Golf Association's argument that allowing anyone, even a competitor with a disability, to ride was tantamount to taking the dribble out of basketball.[6] With this statement, the judge was demanding recognition of golf as an athletic endeavor, a contest involving strength and endurance, in which walking is an essential element. This conforms to Mark Twain's famous definition: "Golf is a good walk spoiled."

Martin's judge, on the other hand, was not a golfer. He rejected the contention—made by the PGA Tour too—that walking was a fundamental part of competitive golf at the highest level. Instead, he determined that golf was a contest in making the shots and not a matter of physical fitness. It was closer, in other words, to a sport of skill and self-control, such as pistol shooting or archery, than to track and field. Consistent with this perspective is the rule of golf that says the game "consists of playing a ball . . . from the teeing ground into the hole" and makes no mention of walking.[7]

JOCKEYS AND CHARIOTEERS

We will return to definitions of sport in Chapter Three in the context of the relationship between athletic and equestrian competitions and gladiatorial spectacles in the Greek lands east of the Roman Empire. Now I want to focus on the question raised by the caddies, the role of those who helped heroes achieve their triumphs in ancient Greece and their recognition. I will first discuss jockeys and charioteers—yes, I've put the golf cart before the horse—and then move on to athletes' trainers and coaches.

Demaratus of Sparta, Hieron of Syracuse, Philip of Macedon, Attalus of Pergamum, and the Egyptian Ptolemies ruled widely separated sections of the Greek world over a period of several hundred years; nevertheless, they shared one ambition at least: to have their horses triumph. Then as now, equestrian competition was the sport of kings. Indeed, among the new festivals of the Hellenistic period, equestrian events were restricted almost without exception to those founded by monarchs.[8] Their rivals might only rarely be royal, but they were always rich. How could it be otherwise in a society in which even owning a horse—costly, skittish, less surefooted than a mule or a donkey, too small to carry or pull heavy loads—was of limited practical use?[9] To buy or breed horses merely for the pleasure or prestige of racing them was beyond the means of any but the wealthiest. This was truest in panhellenic competitions, where the costs and risks of transporting horses made up an extra burden.[10]

The only counter-indications I know combine in a scandal surrounding the Athenian playboy politician Alcibiades. Alcibiades, we are told, was asked by a friend to help him purchase a likely-looking chariot team owned by the Argives. Teams from Argos had won at Olympia in 480 and 472; such community-owned entries were the only way ordinary citizens could compete in equestrian events, an exception to the general rule. In any event, Alcibiades bought the team for himself, and it went on to bring him victory at the Olympic festival of 416 BCE.[11] Alcibiades was later sued for the purchase price by his friend (or an associate), identified by one of our ancient authorities for this squabble as a man of moderate means.

We should hesitate to take this designation at face value. It occurs in one source only, and that source, the fourth speech ascribed to Andocides, is almost certainly a forgery, a literary exercise written long after the events in question, perhaps in the later fourth century ([Andoc.] 4.26). It is true that chariots were still raced at the time and that the forger might therefore feel some obligation to reflect current assumptions about the financial capacities of competitors. More compelling, I imagine, was his desire to denigrate Alcibiades, by portraying him as a man who would defraud a fellow citizen. He would also be reluctant to have this dispute appear merely as a reflection of the lifestyles of the super-rich, a tempest in a silver tea service with a family crest. Conclusive here is the sum in dispute; this is variously given as five or eight talents, in either case well beyond the means of any but "the most fortunate."[12]

Naturally enough, those who were winners in equestrian competitions—horse, chariot, and mule-cart racing—tended to represent this win as the pinnacle of sporting success. Victors in any event (and not just equestrian ones) liked to celebrate and advertise their good fortune. Many dedicated statues to the gods whose festivals provided the platform for their performance or commissioned praise poets—Simonides, Pindar, Bacchylides—to write songs in their honor; some had the power to strike commemorative coins. It was equestrian victory, however, that inspired the most spectacular displays. The chariot victory of Gelon, tyrant of Syracuse, at the Olympics of 488 BCE was marked by both a bronze monument at Olympia and the addition of a crowned image of Nike to his city's coins.[13] When his brother and successor Hieron won the horse race at Olympia in 476 BCE, he commissioned victory songs from both Pindar (*Olympian* 1) and Bacchylides (5).[14] Another western potentate, Anaxilas of Rhegium, won the mule-cart race (*apēnē*) in 484 or 480 BCE. He too minted coins as a result and may have used some of them to pay Simonides: the story goes that the poet initially thought mules beneath his dignity

and accepted the commission only after Anaxilas raised his fee
(Arist. *Rh.* 3.1405b24).

Special achievements clearly required exceptional efforts, and
equestrian victory was a crowning glory even for those who already wore crowns. So it is said that Philip II of Macedon got
three pieces of great news on the same day in 356 BCE: his army
had won, his son Alexander had been born, and his racehorse
had won at Olympia (Plut. *Alex.* 3). The cachet of equestrian
victory was widely recognized: it motivated the size of the prize
for the chariot race at the Athenian Panathenaea in the early
fourth century, much larger than that for any other event, and
the Hellenistic scholars who placed songs for equestrian victories first in their collections of Pindar's poems for champions at
each of the four great panhellenic festivals.[15]

Quite aside from Simonides' reservations, the claim did
not go uncontested. This should come as no surprise. Today
too opinions differ on the primacy of events. Who is the fast-
est man alive? North American sources generally nominate the
winner of the Olympic 100-m dash, often American or Canadian or Caribbean. They make this nomination despite runners
in the less glamorous 200 m reaching a higher average speed:
the world record at 200 m is less than double that for 100 m.
Claims for the winners of still other races garner more attention in other parts of the world. The mile or the "metric mile"
(1,500 m) are as steeped in lore as any sprint and require a mix
of speed and endurance; the longer races, the marathon above
all, are punishing tests of fitness. Perhaps predictably, these arguments weigh especially heavily in North Africa, Ethiopia,
Kenya—the homes of the world's greatest middle- and long-
distance runners. Of course, the prominence of track in this account is itself shaped by local conditions: it is Olympic wrestlers
and weightlifters who attract the most attention in places such
as Turkey, Bulgaria, or Iran; boxers, in Cuba. And where except in Canada would curlers, no matter how successful, whatever their coolness under pressure, however much their thigh
muscles rival those of porn stars, receive honorary degrees from
a university?

So in antiquity, Exaenetus of Agrigentum celebrated his second Olympic victory, in 412 BCE, as lavishly as any ruler, entering the city in a procession that included three hundred chariots, each drawn by two white horses.[16] But Exaenetus won the *stadion* race, not an equestrian event: his display was meant to portray his achievement as second to none.

A rivalry between equestrian and athletic events runs throughout the history of Greek sport. It is most strident, as so often, in a sentiment attributed to Alcibiades by his son; he disdained athletic competition with those "of low birth, from small towns, poorly educated" and instead devoted himself to an unprecedented degree to chariot racing, as shown by his entry of no fewer than seven teams at Olympia in 416 BCE (Isoc. 16.33–34). This rivalry may even, more subtly, have had some influence on the traditional version of the development of the ancient Olympic program. It is at any rate striking that the customary account of the festival's earliest years insists, despite circumstantial evidence to the contrary, that only footraces were held until 708 BCE and that chariot racing was not introduced before 680 BCE, almost one hundred years after its founding. I have suggested elsewhere that Hippias, the Eleian polymath generally credited with drawing up the first comprehensive list of Olympic victors at the turn of the fifth century BCE, had no definite data to draw on and gave pride of place to running in response to—and in reaction against—the addition of the two-horse chariot race to the program shortly before, in 408 BCE.[17]

Equestrian events shared a number of characteristics to make them a more attractive avenue for those among the élite who sought competitive distinctions. The pool of rivals was restricted, and success correspondingly more likely. This was all the more so because the wealthiest or most ambitious could field multiple entries, as Alcibiades did, and so improve their odds. On top of all this, competitive careers in equestrian events easily outlasted those of athletes, unimpeded as owners were by the infirmities of age at either extreme.[18] Runners and fighters could not hope to hold their own against youthful opponents indefinitely, whereas Greek patterns in the transmission of property ensured that equestrian competition tended to begin in earnest when physical strength faded and continued much longer. A paradigm: when Empedocles of Agrigentum won the Olympic horse race in 496 BCE, his son Exaenetus succeeded in an athletic competition (perhaps the boys' *stadion* race or wrestling).[19]

But some of these advantages had their drawbacks. In particular, the same practice that permitted owners to enter more than one animal or team at a time (they were not required to appear in person) imperiled the standing of equestrian victory as a signifier of preeminence among the male élite. First, owners risked sharing the credit for their crowns with another man, the jockey or charioteer who actually rode or drove their horses and mules to triumph. Second, women could win as well. This was so even at the Olympics, the most prestigious festival of all, where the attendance of married women (at least) was prohibited.[20]

Equestrian victors drew upon a range of strategies in meeting these challenges to their status. The meaning or value of women's successes, for example, could be contested. Most famous in the classical period were those of Cynisca, a member of one of Sparta's royal families, in the Olympic four-horse chariot races of (likely) 396 and 392 BCE.[21] Cynisca herself made sure of her renown, dedicating two grandiose memorials for her victories at Olympia—at a scale and expense greater than any earlier Spartan victory monuments—and trumpeting her attainments in an epigram much like those of other, male victors in tone:[22]

> Sparta's kings were my fathers and brothers,
> And having won with my chariots of swift-footed
>   horses, I, Cynisca,
> Set up this statue. Alone, I say, of the women
> Of all Greece I won this crown.

The references to fatherland and pedigree are standard in such texts, as is the care to specify the event, here placed in a prominent position at the beginning of the second line. Cynisca likewise echoes male victors in taking pains to present her victory as special. On the face of it, then, Cynisca has done both herself and her people proud. Pausanias, writing over 500 years after the fact, and perhaps having no evidence beyond this epigram, says she was exceedingly ambitious, the first woman to breed horses as well as to win at Olympia, and he adds that no woman who won after her matched her in distinction (Paus. 3.8.1, 15.1).

But a contemporary source sketches a very different background for Cynisca's victory. According to Xenophon, it was Cynisca's brother, King Agesilaus, who induced her to breed chariot teams, and Xenophon knew him well. The king's motive was to show that rearing horses was a mark of wealth rather than manly merit.[23] This version too equates Cynisca's victory with a man's but only by demeaning both. What real man would care for a crown a woman could bear? Building on this account—the best available evidence—Don Kyle has outlined an attractive scenario in which Cynisca's equestrian excellence figures as a slap at Elis, Sparta's rival and enemy for much of the later fifth century and after, and a riposte to Alcibiades' unprecedented display in 416 BCE. Condemned to death in his native city, Alcibiades later lived for a spell at Sparta, but he was forced to flee after cuckolding King Agis. It would be difficult and pointless for any Spartan male to try to outdo what Alcibiades had done at Olympia, and so Agesilaus encouraged Cynisca and got revenge "by, in effect, emasculating the Olympic chariot race."[24] Who or what motivated Cynisca's entries cannot be safely ascertained today. That she won twice implies (at least to me) that no mere object lesson was at stake; one victory would have satisfied Agesilaus, but Cynisca was more ambitious. Moreover, the hero shrine erected in her honor at Sparta indicates that Cynisca was not the only citizen to find her triumphs worth a fuss (Paus. 3.15.1). Located as it was near the center of the city, the shrine may have proclaimed Cynisca as a model to be emulated by Spartan girls who exercised nearby. (One, Euryleonis, triumphed with the two-horse chariot at Olympia in 368 and dedicated a statue in a still more prominent place, the acropolis [Paus. 3.17.6].) We may note too that, whatever

Agesilaus' own opinion of chariot racing, neither it nor Cynisca's victories prevented male members of the Spartan élite from winning chariot races at Olympia immediately afterwards, in 388 and 384 BCE. In any case, it is clear from what Xenophon says that a woman's equestrian victory could be used by men in a manner that depreciated its worth.

Let us now take up the problems posed by jockeys and charioteers.[25] These were easier to deal with in ancient horse racing. There seems to have been no expectation that the élite owners would ride for themselves—for one thing, Greek racehorses were much smaller than ours—and jockeys were too young to be important and likely outgrew their mounts too fast to make a name for themselves.[26] In fact, none is named in any victory monument or song.[27] It is significant that the victor in the horse race was said to win "with a horse," *hippōi,* and not with a jockey. Significantly too we do know the names of several horses. Bacchylides celebrates the success of one of them, Hieron's horse Pherenicus, "victory-bearer" at Delphi in 478 and Olympia in 476, describing his "dustless" victory—and so using a term applied for athletes who won in walkovers—and saying he went like the wind, like a runner in another poem (Bacch. 5.39–45, 10.21–26). There is no role for a jockey here.

Sculptors too tend to depict horses rather than the boys who guided them, as if the boys' skill and encouragement made no contribution to victory. The story of Pheidolas' mare expresses the wish to elide the input of humans who helped the élite to equestrian glory: the mare threw her rider but won Pheidolas the Olympic victory all the same.[28] No mere one-off, the theme of the mare throwing her rider also occurs in a poem attributed to Parmenon and dated to the third or early second century BCE (*Anth. Pal.* 13.18). This poem supplies the mare with a motive: her boy (*paida*) jockey goaded her, so she threw him and went on to win, perhaps at Sparta.

Charioteers (and mule-car drivers) were harder to ignore. In their events, owners did occasionally compete in person. No less a figure than Hieron, tyrant of Syracuse, is said to have driven his own horses to victory at the Theban Iolaeia (Pind.

Pyth. 2.1–9). His age and eminence have given rise to doubts, but hippic hyperskepticism is unwarranted here.[29] A local contemporary, one Herodotus, also drove for himself at this festival and met with success (Pind. *Isthm.* 1.55–56). Perhaps it was the custom: Iolaus, the festival's honoree, was his kinsman Heracles' charioteer. A century later, Damonon boasted of forty-three chariot victories at home in and around Sparta, all won with horses he bred and drove himself.[30]

Even though Herodotus won at Isthmia too (Pind. *Isthm.* 1.15), few owners would be capable or confident enough to handle the reins at prestigious panhellenic competitions. Fortunately, Homer offered alternative models for those who sought to rival the epic heroes: the great warriors drove for themselves in the funeral games for Patroclus in *Iliad* 23. But those were two-horse chariots. The four-horse team sent by Neleus to compete in Elis, perhaps an echo of Olympic contests, was accompanied by a charioteer (*Il.* 11.698–702). Some might have family members or friends to whom they could turn to drive. For example, the prominence of Thrasybulus in Pindar, *Pythian* 6 and the poem's interest in the relationship of Antilochus and his father Nestor in the chariot race of *Iliad* 23 combine to suggest that Thrasybulus drove his own father Xenocrates' team to a Pythian victory in 490 BCE (Pind. *Pyth.* 6.19). Because they would enjoy the same social standing, or something close to it, their involvement would not threaten the belief that an equestrian victory indicated élite superiority. But hirelings or slaves were different and less easy to overlook than jockeys. They did a dangerous job—chariot crashes were eagerly anticipated, much like those in motor sport today—and a difficult one, controlling two or four powerful and high-spirited animals rather than a single horse.[31] Anacreon plays on the contrast between the subordinate status of a charioteer (not necessarily in competition) and his control over those who are more powerful in a famous poem (Page, *PMG* 360):

> Boy with a maiden's look,
> I court you but you don't listen,

Not knowing that it's my
Heart whose reins you hold.[32]

The beautiful boy is in the driver's seat but his care and capacity
are alike open to question: love (like charioteering) can end in
disaster. It was correspondingly less convincing to suppose that
it was the animals that were really responsible for the outcome.
Our sources' silence on the involvement of charioteers (like
jockeys) in the procession from Elis to Olympia may be telling
here (though we know too little of this to be sure). Likewise the
conclusion of the Olympic chariot race of 420 BCE. As his native city of Sparta was barred from the festival because of a dispute regarding the truce, Lichas entered his chariot in the name
of the Thebans and won. He then made a point of stepping onto
the racecourse to bind a victory ribbon around the charioteer's
head to show that the team was really his.[33] The implication is
that drawing attention to the charioteer's contribution in this
way was unusual and was meant to be noticed.

Tensions around the role of the paid or purchased charioteer
inform the story of Pelops and Hippodameia, a Greek version
of a widespread folktale.[34] Hippodameia was the daughter of
Oenomaus, king of Pisa, who offered her to the first suitor to
defeat him in a chariot race to the Isthmus of Corinth. Many
tried but lost, overtaken by Oenomaus and his horses begotten
by the winds despite a head start. Finally, Pelops, a foreigner
from the east, prevailed, winning not only a bride but a kingdom after Oenomaus crashed and was killed. The start of this
race was depicted on the east pediment of the great temple of
Zeus erected at Olympia in the mid fifth century BCE;[35] its
outcome led directly, according to one etiology, to Pelops' in-
auguration of the Olympic festival. The original folktale appears to have included "a character . . . who had something to
do with chariots."[36]

Our Greek sources ring changes on this character, producing
three identifiable strains that express divergent ways of thinking
about the assistance needed to win a chariot race. One variant is
followed by Pindar in *Olympian* 1, written in honor of Hieron's

victory in the Olympic horse race of 476 BCE, looking forward to his eventual chariot victory in 468 BCE and back to the
games' legendary origins, as befitted the first festival after the
Persian wars. It is at least as old as the Chest of Cypselus, an object from about 570 BCE described by Pausanias (5.17.7). Here,
Pelops' victory is ascribed to his love affair with Poseidon and
to the golden chariot and winged horses given him in gratitude
by the god: we are in the world of aristocratic gift exchange,
where equals forge and affirm links through favors of various
kinds. He drives his chariot himself.

A second strain, attested in the fifth-century mythographer
Pherecydes and widespread thereafter, ascribes Pelops' success
to a charioteer, but not his own. Oenomaus' driver, Myrtilus, betrayed his master, persuaded by Hippodameia herself or
bribed by Pelops (in some stories, by the offer of a night with
the bride he hoped to win). It was due to Myrtilus that Oenomaus' chariot crashed: Myrtilus failed to secure a wheel. Myrtilus jumped free of the chariot as it went out of control, but the
king perished (or was killed by Pelops). In the Pindaric version,
Pelops is his own charioteer. He does get help with his chariot,
but it is help of the best kind, the kind necessary for success
in any endeavor, the favor of a god. This can only add to his
stature. In Pherecydes' treatment of the tale, Pindar is aided by
the charioteer of his rival: Oenomaus' dependence has a base
motive—he needs his spear hand free to cut down the suitors
as he overtakes them—and an ignoble end. Nor does Myrtilus'
betrayal go unpunished: he reminds Pelops of their bargain or
assaults Hippodameia or otherwise incurs the hero's wrath and
is himself disposed of.

So far the situation is straightforward. One competitor drives
for himself and triumphs with a god's help, the other (a tyrant
and an ogre) relies on a hired hand and pays the price he deserves as he is essentially outbid for the charioteer's services.
But in fact things are not so simple. There is a third strain in
Greek treatments of this folktale, and in this version the role
and reputation of the charioteer are more ambiguous. Pelops,
it turns out, did have a charioteer of his own, but this man,

Cillus, died near Lesbos in the eastern Aegean on the way to the race with Oenomaus. In this tradition (found in the fourth-century historian Theopompus), Cillus is someone important to Pelops:[37] he mourns him deeply and is eager to comply with a dream vision in which Cillus' ghost asks for a funeral. He even founds a temple to Cillaean Apollo and a city in his memory. In recompense, Cillus—dead though he is—helps Pelops defeat Oenomaus; another source suggests that the ghost's help involves advising Pelops to sacrifice to Apollo.[38] In this strain, Poseidon is replaced as Pelops' intimate by Cillus and as his divine benefactor, by Apollo. The charioteer Cillus is clearly a main factor in Pelops' victory, despite his absence. This absence may recall Myrtilus' defection from Oenomaus, but the team of Pelops and Cillus also echoes and inverts the standard situation in Greek chariot racing, in which an absentee owner can claim credit for what his driver has done.

POSIDIPPUS AND THE PTOLEMIES

A papyrus permits us to follow this theme into the Hellenistic period. Macedon's monarchs were sensitive to the political value of panhellenic festival competition long before Philip II.[39] Alexander I entered the *stadion* race at Olympia (perhaps in 476 BCE) partly to establish a claim to be Greek: admitted by the *hellanodikai,* "judges," over the objections of other competitors, he finished in a dead-heat for first.[40] Towards the end of the century, Archelaus won four-horse chariot races at both Olympia and Delphi (Solin. 9.16). As part of his campaign to move Macedon from the barbarian margins of Greek life—he also invited the tragedian Euripides to his court—Archelaus founded the first of what would be many parallel Olympic festivals, at the city of Dion.[41]

Philip himself won both horse and chariot races at Olympia in the mid fourth century and broadcast his triumphs by minting coins in the manner of other faraway leaders, the Sicilian dynasts of the early fifth century.[42] He marked his settlement of the Third Sacred War in 346 BCE by presiding over the Pythian festival—faraway no more because he now was the center of an important panhellenic institution in central Greece (Delphi)— and unified Greece in his League of Corinth in the wake of the Battle of Chaeronea in 338 BCE. The council of the league was to meet in peacetime at each of the four major panhellenic festivals. Philip then began work on the Philippeion, the first structure at Olympia named for a mortal benefactor. Including statues of Philip's family, this was completed by his son Alexander the Great, Philip having provided sufficient proof of his mortality by being assassinated. Alexander disdained competition.[43] ("Will you enter the *stadion* race at Olympia?" someone is supposed to have asked him. "Yes," he answered, "if I would have kings as my opponents" [Plut. *Alex.* 4.10–11].) He too, however, made use of the Olympic festival for propaganda purposes, having an envoy announce amnesty for political exiles at the games of 324 BCE (Diod. Sic. 18.18.3–5). The rulers of the successor kingdoms, themselves members of the Macedonian élite or eager to be thought so, revived the tradition of active involvement. Long outsiders, only very recent conquerors, they were aware that many of their new subjects were not Greeks at all and so were keen to demonstrate their superiority in the time-honored Hellenic way.[44] Attalus, son of the founder of the royal house of Pergamum, won an Olympia chariot race for colts between 280 and 272 BCE; his grandsons, including King Eumenes II, were victors at the Panathenaea about a hundred years later.[45]

Nowhere was equestrian victory more valued than among the Ptolemies of Egypt, from Ptolemy I, who won the first chariot race for a pair of colts at the Pythian festival in 314 or 310 and also triumphed at Olympia, to Ptolemy XII, chariot champion at the Basileia at Lebadeia in the late 70s or early 60s BCE.[46] Ptolemy II won at Olympia (in 284 BCE), and Ptolemy V and VI were both Panathenaic victors in the mid second century BCE.[47] The prominence of female contestants in this royal register is still more striking. Even before our new evidence, we knew that Berenice II had won at Nemea, and Cleopatra II joined Ptolemy VI as a Panathenaic victor. The most intriguing example, however, is furnished by Bilistiche (or Belistiche or Belestiche or Blistichis), one of the mistresses of Ptolemy II.[48] Both Bilistiche's name and origins are disputed. Plutarch calls her a barbarian; Athenaeus, a descendant of Argos' House of Atreus—this is not necessarily a compliment (Plut. *Mor.* 753E, Ath. 13.596E). The Armenian version of the Olympic victor list found in Eusebius' *Chronica* turns her (on *Ol.* 129) into a male, P'ighistiak'os, son of Maketis, apparently a misunderstanding of the Greek ethnic for "Macedonian" (cf. Paus. 5.8.11; *POxy.* 17.2082; and the Armenian addition to *Ol.* 131). There is no question, however, that she was an Olympic victor, in the first running of the pairs chariot race for colts in 264 BCE and in the four-colt race in (likely) 268 BCE (Paus. 5.8.11; *POxy.* 17.2082). An epigram in the *Greek Anthology* makes sport of her success:[49]

> Her purple whip and shining reins
> Plangon has placed on the porticoes rich in horses,
> Having defeated with her racehorse Philaenis, who
> often competes
> When the colts of evening are just starting to neigh.
> Dear Cypris, may you bring her victory's true
> Credit, making this pleasure remembered forever.

On one level, this is a riff on the well-known image of a woman riding a male sexual partner, much like the epigram that follows it in the anthology (Asclepiades, *Anth. Pal.* 5.203). But the competitive element is odd, and the references to Aphrodite, royal purple, the reins of a chariot, and above all the colts guarantee that there is another level too.[50] The poem must refer to Bilistiche, honored already in her lifetime by a cult to Aphrodite-Bilistiche; moreover, it elevates her achievements above those of another woman. Such a rival had recently left the lists: Ptolemy II's dead wife Arsinoe II, who had won all three chariot races at the same Olympics (perhaps those of 272 BCE)—the two for full-grown horses and the four-colt race—but could not yet win that for a pair of colts.[51] It must therefore date to 264 BCE or later. But the poem is not simply a celebration of Bilistiche's success. After all, she appears in the guise of a whore—both Plangon and Philaenis were names of well-known *hetaerae* of the time—and also in that of a jockey. Jockeys, as I have indicated, were generally slaves or at least hirelings (like whores, bought or rented for cash), certainly of low status, and rarely if ever recognized for their contribution to their horses' victories. Thus the epigram acknowledges Bilistiche's achievement at the same time as it undercuts it; the "true credit" of the poem's close is ironical.[52]

Earlier papyrus discoveries brought to light fragments of three poems written by Callimachus to honor victors at competitive festivals. One celebrates Queen Berenice II's Nemean triumph; another, the varied career of Sosibius, a major figure at the courts of Ptolemy III and IV and a runner, a wrestler, and a chariot champion at Isthmia and Nemea.[53] Then in 2001 Guido Bastianini, Claudio Gallazzi, and Colin Austin published a papyrus roll from the late third century BCE that contained 600 lines of 112 poems, in elegiac meter, now generally attributed to Posidippus.[54] A portion of the collection, which was perhaps arranged by the poet himself, is made up of eighteen "equestrian poems," *hippika,* on the theme of victory in horse and chariot races. The roll contributes significant items to our evidence for the equestrian accomplishments of the Ptolemies and their associates. So we learn of Olympic chariot victories by Ptolemy I, Berenice I, Ptolemy II, Arsinoe II, and Berenice of Syria (AB 78, 87, 88), and of further triumphs for Berenice of Syria at Nemea and Isthmia (AB 79, 80, 82); their Macedonian ethnicity is stressed (AB 78.14, 82.3, 87.2, 88.4).[55] The poems also demonstrate continuity with the traditions of archaic and classical epinician poetry and the vitality of one motif in particular, the effacement of the roles of jockeys and charioteers.

Elegiac in meter like Callimachus' poems, Posidippus' recall them in other ways as well. Winners speak for themselves (AB 71, 77, 78, 85, 86, 87, 88), as Sosibius does in Callimachus (384 Pf.). This is a nod to epigrammatic convention, Posidippus' poems being presented as if they accompanied a dedicatory statue. The verb *a(e)thlophoreō,* "I bear the prize," found at AB 76.2 and 79.2, is otherwise known in literature only from Callimachus 384.40 Pf. But Posidippus (again like Callimachus) also makes conscious bows towards the great epinician poets of the past. Some are stylistic, like the traces of Doric dialect (especially in poems with Olympic resonance). Some concern the arrangement of the poems: the first, in honor of Hippostratus' racehorse Aethon, recalls the Olympian ode for Hieron and his Pherenicus, which leads off the collection of Pindar's victory songs (itself organized in Posidippus' period). Here, Posidippus assimilates his victors to the potentates of the past at the same time as he elevates himself to Pindar's level.[56]

As for content, both Pindar and Posidippus revel in earlier triumphs of their subjects and their families; of course, such catalogues are easier to introduce into the epigrams than Pindar's poems, designed as they were for performances at, or closely linked to, one occasion. Each also notes the expense involved in equestrian competition.[57] I am inclined to explain the claim that Ptolemy I drove his own team to victory in the four-horse race at Olympia (AB 78.3–4) in the same fashion, as a reminiscence of Pindar's reference to Hieron's feat, discussed above. The combination of reigning and reining monarch seems less plausible for a top-level international competition than for local festivals. Furthermore, Posidippus' language can hardly be taken literally in every respect: Ptolemy is said to have driven "his horse" (*hippon*) rather than a team, and in the stadium (*epi stadiōn*) at that, rather than in the hippodrome. This last usage is only one of many means by which horses are promoted as actors—and athletes—in these poems and the contributions of their jockeys and charioteers, correspondingly reduced or ignored.[58]

Not only human victors have a voice in Posidippus: horses boast of their success in three poems.[59] In AB 73, Trygaeus' horse races to victory at Olympia without, according to a plausible restoration of the text, need of the goad and carrying a pleasant burden; the jockey has neither wit nor weight in this presentation. In AB 75, four mares took two Olympic wreaths in succession from Zeus the Charioteer for their Spartan owner, as if no mortal had held the reins.[60] A similar effect results from the qualities attributed to horses: not merely speed but light-footedness, tenacity, spirit. Theirs is the responsibility for victories won by a nod or by a head (AB 72, 74, perhaps 76), narrow margins that testify to both the quality of the opposition and the capability of those who defeated them.

Of particular interest is AB 74, one of the two longest of the equestrian epigrams.[61] It seems that Callicrates of Samos, admiral of the Ptolemaic fleet, won the Pythian chariot race of 274 or 270 BCE by a mere nod. At this point, charioteers do make an appearance but only to protest the result, and the judges (or some of them) respond by throwing their staffs of office to the ground, ready to leave the decision to the lot. The tide is turned by the right-hand tracehorse in Callicrates' team, the filly whose nod had already brought his chariot home first: she picks up a judge's staff, "a clever female among males," and elicits a roar of approval from the crowd. They proclaim her the victor. The poem ends with a reference to the statue it is supposed to accompany, depicting the chariot and its driver. But what has gone before seems designed to make the reader ask, "What is *he* doing there?" So too "in speed the chariot of [Berenice's] horses was leaving many a charioteer behind" (AB 79.3–4); the horses come first, literally and metaphorically.

The final pair of equestrian poems brings us back to Cynisca.[62] In AB 87, for Berenice I, the wife of Ptolemy I and mother of Ptolemy II, her accomplishment is challenged directly:

> Mares still, for Berenice of Macedon
> We brought an Olympic crown, Pisatans.
> This possesses a celebrated fame, by which Cynisca's
> Ancient glory in Sparta was taken away.

It is Berenice's mares, victorious in the Olympic chariot race, to whom Posidippus gives these words; the first identifies them. We have already had occasion to note the prominence of horses in these poems. But these horses' female voice also recalls Cynisca's own epigram, the Doric elements in the dialect perhaps her Spartan heritage. The reference is made explicit in the third line, where "Cynisca's" at the end echoes the use of Berenice in the same case as the last word of line 1. So too the reference to Sparta in line 4 parallels the ethnic "of Macedon" in line 2 (of the Greek original). Berenice is the new, improved Cynisca. That her superiority does not depend on equestrian competition only is the burden of AB 88, written to commemorate the Olympic victory of her son, Ptolemy II:

> First and only, at the Olympics we three monarchs
> Are winners with our chariots, my parents and myself.
> I am one, same-named son of Ptolemy and of Berenice,
> Of Eordean descent, the other two my parents.
> To the great fame of my father I add my own,[63] but that my mother,
> A woman, took a victory with her chariot—*that* is great.

Here also there are unmistakable verbal cues to remind us of Cynisca and her epigram. In both, *basilēes,* "kings, monarchs," appears in the same place in the first line; the technical term for winning a chariot race or races, in the second; and forms of *monos,* "only, alone," proclaim the distinction of the victor. In Cynisca's case, we might take the word to insist on her independent agency as well as her unique achievement (though this would not work as well with every instance of the term, e.g., AB 82.5–6, 83.3). Ptolemy, however, aims to stress that his own victory is extraordinary precisely because he shares his accomplishment with his parents. No other dynasty has produced a family like his: if kings should match themselves only with their peers (as in Alexander's demurral), the Ptolemies have reached the top rank. Berenice no less among queens: after all, Cynisca can claim to be the daughter and sister of kings, but Berenice is their wife and mother too.

The Ptolemies' encouragement of equestrian activity by women of their family and court had some practical purposes. It increased the pool of competitors they could claim and also provided the prospect of deniability, a way of insulating them from the dishonor of defeat: the race was not always to the rich. (Dionysius II of Syracuse sent a shipload of horses to the Olympics of 388 BCE, but all his chariots ran off the course or collided [Diod. Sic. 14.109.1–4].) But more than this, it was also consistent with their stress on the family in other contexts, emphasis that led (among other places) to a cult in honor of the infant daughter of Ptolemy III.[64] Ptolemy II's praise of his mother, the climax of Posidippus' poem, conforms to this and to Greek notions about women's place in general. Similarly, the young Berenice of Syria is said to have brought victories to her home, as this is where a girl belongs.[65] Cynisca, we may now feel, speaks for herself because she has no son or husband to speak for her; she is lonely rather than unique. So not only could her victory be used to suggest that equestrian competitors were not real men: Posidippus implies that some were not real women either.

COACHES AND TRAINERS

Athletes of the archaic and classical periods were often drawn from the same élite who engaged in equestrian competition. Pindar praises Thrasydaeus, (likely) victor in the boys' *stadion* race at Delphi in 474 BCE, as a member of a Theban family that could claim Olympic equestrian triumphs in the past (Pind. *Pyth*. 11.46–48). In fact, some horse and chariot owners had been athletes in their youth. Damonon won footraces in and around his native Sparta before going on to equestrian success at numerous local festivals and, on the panhellenic stage, Eubotas of Cyrene won the *stadion* race at Olympia in 408 BCE and the chariot race there forty years later (*IG* 5.1 213; Xen. *Hell*. 1.2.1; Paus. 6.8.3; Ael. *VH* 10.2). A similar trajectory likely lies behind the obscurities of Pindar's third and fourth Isthmian odes: Melissus of Thebes was a successful pancratiast as a young man and is now an equestrian victor at Isthmia and Nemea.[66]

Some athletes clearly moved in similar circles. Lampon of

Aegina commissioned two victory songs for both of his pancratiast sons (Pind. *Nem.* 5, *Isthm.* 5, 6, Bacch. 13), an extravagance paralleled only among the rulers of Sicily. (It seems that
well-off Aeginetans did not race horses competitively.) Others
certainly did not. But how many? David Young has pressed the
case for the involvement of poorer athletes from the earliest
days of organized festival competition in Greece.[67] He points
to a cook, a goatherd, and a cowherd among early Olympians.
Unfortunately, our information on these athletes usually dates
from many centuries after their deaths and it is not always self-
explanatory or reliable. Was Coroebus, the first Olympic victor,
a cook or a cult functionary involved in sacrifice? Is the designation influenced by its source, himself a cook in a work of fic-
tion (Ath. 9.382B)? The unnamed Olympic victor who attracts
Diogenes' scorn as he tends his sheep (*probata nemonta*) in one of
the many anecdotes designed to show the Cynic's disregard for
convention is obviously invoked and invented for the sake of a
pun: "You've made a quick transition from Olympia to Nemea"
(Diog. Laert. 6.49). Significantly, Aristotle (perhaps writing as a
contemporary) notes that one such Olympic champion, a fish-
monger, was exceptional.[68]

We may also wonder (to raise more general considerations)
how poorer athletes could afford the time and expense of training and travel to competitions; these were greatest at Olympia,
not only distant and hard to reach from most of the Greek world
but requiring athletes to spend thirty days at the site before
competition began. Cities might honor victory—as Athens did
in providing free meals for life in the Prytaneion and a substantial cash bonus—and even recruit champions, but they did not
directly subsidize competitors before their success. Public *gymnasia* may have been open to all, but in practice few could have
afforded to while away the hours in conversation, workouts, or
competition. With the exception of Sparta, communities did
not run school systems: forced to choose, most poorer parents
preferred to invest in literacy and letters rather than cultural and
physical education. Furthermore, the few references we have to

provisions that festivals made for athletes would do little to out-weigh disadvantages poorer competitors would face.[69]

Young argues that poorer boys might win local events—natural ability would count most at this age—and use their earnings to finance careers. Certainly prizes might be worth-while: at Athens, the Great Panathenaea rewarded the winner of the boys' *stadion* race with fifty amphoras and the olive oil to fill them, the equivalent of perhaps $50,000 today. Yet few local games can have been as generous as the Panathenaea, itself held only every four years. Other prizes we know of were paltry by comparison.[70] And (to judge by the findspots of Panathenaic amphoras), the more prestigious and valuable the prize, the fur-ther competitors traveled to win it.

A series of documents from the very end of the classical pe-riod is instructive.[71] About 300 BCE, Athenodorus, a young res-ident of Ephesus in Asia Minor, won the boxing event for boys at Nemea and had himself proclaimed an Ephesian. His gesture earned him an upgrade to the citizen status he had enhanced because he had brought honor to Ephesus and its citizens. Some time later, his coach (*epistatēs*) Therippides approached the coun-cil of Ephesus to seek citizenship for two men who had helped defray Athenodorus' expenses to prepare for and journey to the festival and undertook to do so in future. We will return to the role of the coach below. For the moment, it is some of the other implications of this sequence of events that are of interest. First, there is no request for a direct subsidy from the community itself: Athenodorus' athletic career has been underwritten by private benefactors, and this will continue to be the case. Sec-ond, it is tempting to regard this as an example of a poor (or at least less than wealthy) athlete who has proven to be successful, but this cannot be taken for granted. Rich Greeks were accus-tomed to accepting favors from their friends, and in this case, the favor may have been intended to produce just the repayment Therippides intended (and achieved) here: Ephesian citizenship. Finally, let us assume that Athenodorus was indeed too needy to finance his career on his own. We must ask why. After all, an Ephesian resident who triumphs at far-off Nemea must have some local or regional victories to his credit too. They, it seems, were insufficient to supply the head start Young imagines. And indeed, there is no example of an archaic or classical Athenian athlete demonstrably from a family outside the élite among the fifty athletes whose origins can be ascertained.

In any case, however many poor athletes there may have been, athletic competition was ruled by an elitist or at least meritocratic mindset even in democratic Athens:[72] it might be appropriate to select magistrates by lot, but no one would pair athletes like that unless they had already established their capability (Arist. *Rh.* 2.1393b7). Though victors were eager to claim distinctions of every kind, as first of their city or among Ionians to win an event, or first of all competitors to win in three age classes, or twice on one day, none advertises himself as the first of his family or social class. On the contrary: Philostratus observes, "It is human nature to set a higher value on abilities that have been handed down from father to son. Therefore, the Olympic victor who comes from a family of Olympic victors is more glorious" (Philostr. *VS* 611). An aristocratic sentiment. We should not be surprised, then, to find the contributions of trainers and coaches to athletic success ignored or downgraded much like those of jockeys and charioteers.[73]

In our literary sources, trainers are explicitly attested only for combat sports—boxing, wrestling, *pankration*—but images on vases guarantee that they were employed by other athletes as well and by mature men as well as tyros.[74] Pentathletes, for example, had to wrestle. In addition, the long jump, another of the five events that made up the pentathlon, required exceptional timing and coordination, so much so that it was accompanied by the music of the *aulos*. This surely was an event in which advice and hands-on help were essential. Trainers' claim to credit, and the consequent threat to the status of the victor, were all the more strong in that some at least had themselves been successful athletes. Furthermore, trainers, like athletes, had to swear the Olympic oath and attend the games naked (Paus. 5.6.8, 5.24.9; Philostr. *Gym.* 17). It is interesting, therefore, that while modern trainers are sometimes the subjects of books such as R. K. Fried's *Corner Men: Great Boxing Trainers* and a reviewer of that book (G. A. Leyshon) can describe the boxer and his trainer as "united in the brotherhood of struggle," their ancient counterparts rarely attracted attention.[75] Trainers were generally not permitted to have statues of themselves set up at Olympia (Paus. 6.3.6); they are absent from archaic and classical inscriptions honoring victors; they are ignored in extant fragments of the praise poems of Simonides and virtually in Bacchylides' too (he mentions one).

In Pindar, however, four trainers figure in six poems. All work with young victors, whose inexperience may excuse their reliance on others. Their exceptional treatment warrants a closer look all the same. It is notable that Pindar stresses the contributions of the young victor's fellow family members (even Phylacidas' mother figures [metaphorically] as one of the officials who sorted competitors into age classes [*Nem.* 5.5–6]), that he emphasizes the trainers' ability to bring out already inherent natural ability, and that he usually mentions them only at a poem's close. All this suggests that Pindar wants to minimize their contribution. So why say anything about them at all? One reason, it seems, is that he aims to draw a parallel between his own position, as a poet praising patrons, and the trainer's. This explains the description of the trainer Melesias as a "charioteer of hands and strength," a seemingly risky reference to another collaborator most often left out of account (Pind. *Nem.* 6.66). Here, it links Melesias to Pindar and his own chariot of song (6.45–46; cf. 53–54). Though Pindar was commissioned by or for the champions he celebrates, and wrote for pay, he sought to cast his relationship with the élite he served in the mold of the aristocratic ethos of friendship and reciprocal gift-giving; it was represented as a tie of long standing rather than a casual and contingent commercial exchange. Similarly, he represents trainers as models and mentors, not mercenaries—in the image he seeks to construct for himself.

This representation may in some cases mirror the truth: of Pindar's four trainers, one (Orseas) may have been a boyhood

friend of the victor and another (Ilas), his lover.[76] An additional
factor is relevant to the other two trainers of wrestlers and pancratiasts, Menander (mentioned by Bacchylides as well) and Melesias. Both were Athenians: Menander was active in the 480s;
Melesias, about a generation later; and both were highly successful. Menander's athletes won innumerable crowns at panhellenic festivals, often at Olympia (Bacch. 13.193–196); Melesias,
the father of the prominent politician Thucydides and scion of
a "great house," was twice *pankration* champion at the Nemean festival and the trainer of at least thirty panhellenic victors
(Pl. *Meno* 94D; Pind. *Ol.* 8.54–66). Not only were men such
as these too famous to ignore: association with them raised an
athlete's status rather than risking it. Thus, though Pytheas may
have won only at Isthmia, perhaps the least prestigious of the
panhellenic circuit, his work with Menander associates him
with the trainer's Olympic champions. Melesias even gets a
miniature hymn of his own, complete with a victory list, at the
center of Pindar's poem for Alcimedon, winner of the Olympic
boys' wrestling in 460.[77] If a modern parallel is in order, aspir-
ing recording artists sometimes insist on the role of big-name
producers (Quincy Jones, Mutt Lange) when they market their
work. What did the trainers themselves think? Just as few Athenian artisans and craftsmen are likely to have accepted everything Plato or Aristotle said about their base, manual skills, so
too some trainers at least took public pride in their profession.
Indeed, it is possible that it was they who commissioned some
of Pindar's poems in praise of young champions (another explanation for their presence in his texts) or made inclusions in them
a condition of their engagement. Certainly Mycon dedicated a
statue for a Samian boxer he trained (Paus. 6.2.9). Pindar's parallel holds, it seems: trainers could be as eager for renown as the
poet himself.[78]

The papyrus of Posidippus' poems permits us to trace tensions concerning the contributions of jockeys and charioteers
towards equestrian victory into the Hellenistic period. In contrast, the representation of trainers and coaches seems to change
over time. The story of Athenodorus set out above may be taken

as symptomatic. It is his trainer Therippides who appears before the council of Ephesus on his behalf, not the young athlete himself or a family member. (A father brings a similar petition in another, contemporary document, though that is too mutilated for us to tell precisely what is at issue: *IEph.* 1416.) Of course, there are many possible explanations. Athenodorus' father may be ineligible as a noncitizen to address the council. Perhaps he is dead. Or Therippides (unknown though he otherwise is to us) may be another superstar trainer, a man whose presence carries exceptional weight. In any case, the prominence of a trainer on this occasion finds many parallels in a range of sources from the Hellenistic period onward. We know about the ban on trainers' statues at Olympia only because Cratinus of Aegeira got special permission to set one up after winning the boys' wrestling (perhaps in 272 BCE; Paus. 6.3.6). M. Aurelius Agathopous of Aegina, who earned the traditional sobriquet "best of the Greeks" by winning the race in armor at the Plataean Eleutheria in the late second century CE as well as sixty-some other crowns (including two for the *stadion* race at Olympia), made a point of identifying his trainer, Areius of Alexandria.[79] Another trainer, one Pythodorus, figures in a monument set up for a runner and pentathlete successful in fifteen panhellenic crown festivals in the early Roman Empire.[80]

But trainers and coaches nowhere come in for more credit than in *Gymnasticus, On Athletic Training,* a work written in the early third century CE by L. Flavius Philostratus.[81] Here we find a section devoted to some of the most famous of all Greek athletic anecdotes, each attesting the trainers' ingenuity and inspiration and their impact on the success of athletes at the highest level (Philostr. *Gym.* 20–24). In his youth, Glaucus once straightened a plowshare with a blow of his right hand: a timely reminder of this deed by his coach Tisias turned defeat into victory in a boxing match at Olympia. Arrichion sought a third Olympic crown in *pankration* but was on the brink of conceding when Eryxias encouraged him to fight until the end. He persevered and was crowned, even though the effort killed him. Next, Promachus of Pallene: his trainer saw that he was in love and told him that the girl he fancied had promised to accept him if he won at Olympia. On the strength of this fabrication (the trainer had not contacted the girl at all), Promachus beat no less a pancratiast than Pulydamus. Philostratus himself heard another pancratiast, Mandrogenes of Messenia, ascribe his fortitude to his trainer, who had praised it to his mother; Mandrogenes could not disappoint her. Finally, his trainer's willingness to post a large bond allowed Optatus to win the race in armor at Plataea for a second time—and (says Philostratus) the faith he showed was as significant in the victory as the money.

Some of the credit accorded to these trainers must stem from Philostratus' own agenda, such as the important role he attributes to training in the development of the Olympic program and the criticisms he levels at corrupt trainers for their contribution to the decline in athletic ideals (*Gym.* 13, 45). As Jason König has demonstrated so masterfully, Philostratus was engaged in a debate about the role of festival competition and training of the body in which the famous physician Galen was a particularly vigorous exponent of a different view.[82] Galen, anxious to establish medicine's understanding of the body against alternative paradigms and his own eminence against that of other physicians, inveighs against trainers and their charges. Far from leading to health and happiness, intensive training—the kind needed for success—makes the athlete the most miserable (*athliōteron*) of men (Gal. *Protr.* 12 = 1.31 K.). Galen recommends physical exercise based on activities excluded from festival competition: ball play, hoop rolling. It is against this background, and perhaps in direct response to Galen himself, that Philostratus writes, offering a contrasting image of the trainer as a repository of traditional Greek wisdom and of his expertise as a pathway to the glorious past.[83]

Nevertheless, there is more in play here than one author's idiosyncrasies. Other texts too depend on the trainer's wit and wisdom. Hearing a tall man with a long neck praised as a boxer, the *aleiptēs* Hippomachus replied, "Sure, if the crown were hung up and won by reaching" (Plut. *Mor.* 523CD). And some of the stories Philostratus tells occur elsewhere. Our other sources may present them in significantly different forms; for example, Pausanias credits Glaucus' father with the inspirational reminder of the plowshare (Paus. 6.10.1–2). More pertinently, I think, though the tales concern athletes of the distant past (except for Philostratus' contemporary Mandrogenes), the sources are all much later. I suspect that they were invented long after the archaic and classical periods in which they are set, or at least gained wide circulation only when the role of the trainer was less controversial for victors, whatever a critic like Galen thought. Indeed, the very vehemence with which Galen attacks trainers must indicate that they were widely used and respected and so a genuine threat to his own status.

There are further traces of the esteem in which some (at least) were held in the Hellenistic and Roman periods. Epictetus, the stoic philosopher from Asia Minor who wrote in the mid first or second century CE—Galen's lifetime—styles himself a trainer: his athletes are those who struggle against temptation.[84] Real trainers were brought in from abroad—one traveled from Teos in Asia Minor to what is now Albania—and (at Delphi) were rewarded with citizenship and honorary membership in the council.[85] They held office in the associations that lobbied for active and retired competitors, the athletic guilds (e.g., *P London* 1178); an Ephesian *aleiptēs,* styled "my friend" by the triumvir Mark Antony, negotiated on their behalf (*P London* 137 = S. G. Miller, *Arete,* no. 209). They attended festival banquets along with their athletes (as doctors did too; *IPriene* 111).

The term "Hellenistic and Roman periods" covers hundreds of years in a geographical area stretching from Sicily to Mesopotamia: any characterization of such a vast and varied extent of time and space must be approximate only, and each piece of evidence is of course subject to local and perhaps short-lived conditions of which we now know little or nothing. Still, impressionistic as it is, the material does invite the conclusion that athletes shared credit for their victories with coaches and trainers more readily than they had before. Can we explain why?

POORER ATHLETES?

One plausible cause, a large-scale shift in the social origins of athletes, can probably be rejected. We might well expect there to have been more poor or middling competitors in the Greek east during this era in wake of the agonistic explosion (discussed below in Chapter Three). Local, regional, and panhellenic festivals abounded as new foundations took their place alongside those established in the archaic and classical periods. Pleket can even refer to "mass-sport" in the Greek cities of Asia Minor, "a society which was permeated by sport in a way somehow comparable to our world."[86] The increase in the number of local and regional contests offering prizes of value was especially dramatic because these might be introduced and financed by private benefactors as well as by community initiatives. There was therefore plenty of opportunity to pursue the trajectory delineated by Young. Victory as a boy or youth at local games might provide the wherewithal for further successes and greater earnings at regional events, themselves the springboard to the great panhellenic crown games; victory in these brought financial rewards and privileges throughout the Greek world.[87]

We can certainly trace some athletic CVs that might conform to this pattern. For example, an inscription introduces us to Photion, a boxer from Laodicea on the Lycus (near Ephesus), who began his career with victories at the Epheseia and other nearby festivals as an *ageneios,* "beardless youth," in the 160s CE.[88] By chance, a papyrus dating about twenty-five years later reveals that in retirement, Photion had become an official of an athletes' association but only after he had triumphed at Olympia (*P London* 1178). A series of inscriptions allows us to follow the similar progress of L. Septimius Flavianus Flavillianus of Oenoanda, a wrestler and pancratiast with significant success at local games in the early third century CE. He returned home to compete in the Meleagria, which had given him his start, after five crowns at panhellenic festivals.[89] Unfortunately, we cannot tell whether Photion needed his winnings close to home to fulfill his athletic ambitions or if he was a son of a well-off family to begin with. Flavillianus' father, on the other hand, was a regional official, and his aunt, an aristocrat who proudly carved her family lineage onto her tomb: his is no rags (or even synthetic fibers) to riches tale.[90]

Yet it is clear that there were some athletes who did not belong to the upper reaches of the élite. Winners in local competitions at Sicyon in the third and second centuries BCE do not overlap with the rich contributors to fund-raising campaigns.[91] The social status of local participants in athletic events at Balboura in Asia Minor was generally high, but there may have been exceptions.[92] A valuable but puzzling piece of evidence is Artemidorus' discussion of dreams in which a mother gives birth to an eagle (Artemid. 2.20). This evidence points to a poor son who will rise in the ranks to command a military camp; among the rich, an emperor. A third boy, from the moderate or middling class (*metrios*), will become a famous athlete. What does Artemidorus mean by "middling" here? Clearly not the top stratum of the population of the Roman Empire. Pleket understands the term to include the most successful artisans and intellectuals, physicians and lawyers, as well as members of local councils who did not hold high office.[93] Artemidorus' explanation of dreams in which a father eats a son's shoulders or feet—he will profit from the boy's earnings as a wrestler or runner—seems consistent with this (Artemid. 1.70; cf. 5.74). It is possible, however, that the "middling" group he has in mind extends as high as the "curial order," the local élites of the many small and medium-sized cities of the Greek east.[94] As for individuals, Nigel Crowther suggests that a Phorystas of Tanagra, victorious herald at an unidentified "noble contest of Zeus" in the mid third century BCE, was an athlete as well, citing evidence that he boasts of other victories won with his winged feet, *ptanois posin*.[95]

With Crowther, I accept that competitions for heralds (as for trumpeters) were less prestigious and their competitors of lower status than others. Few members of the élite would wish to submit themselves to the subjective judgment of their peers, or inferiors, and merely for the privilege of announcing the athletic and equestrian successes of others. Evidence that heralds might compete and win in athletic events would therefore be welcome. Unfortunately, I do not think Crowther's inscription qualifies. The "feet" mentioned here must refer to passages heralds proclaimed without stopping for breath, a usage we find in Galen, Lucian, and Pollux; that they are winged is a claim to the status of another oral performance, Homer's winged words.[96] More likely candidates for lower rungs of the social scale include an Olympic champion in *pankration* in (?)129 CE, whose cognomen Domesticus hints at servile origin for his family, and a late second-century CE Egyptian boxer and priest of an athletic guild, nicknamed "the dummy," who was illiterate.[97] Even these examples are uncertain, however, given the unreliability of names' semantic content as indicators of social status and disagreements as to the extent of ancient literacy.[98] Another may lurk, generally unnoticed, among the fragments of Plutarch (fr. 176 Sandbach = Euseb. *Praep. evang.* 11.36.1). Here we learn of a certain Nicandas, seemingly a Boeotian contemporary of Plutarch's and a shoemaker who had nevertheless spent some time at wrestling schools (*en palaistrais*). There is nothing to say that he used what he learned there in festival competition.

RICHER COACHES?

Of course, the presence of such athletes need not mean that the élite no longer took part in festival competition. Some scholars have in fact reached just that conclusion, arguing that wealthy boys and men shunned the dangerous and disfiguring heavy events or even virtually retired from festival athletics in favor of another arena for amassing social capital, the study and practice of rhetoric.[99] As Maud Gleason put it in an important and influential book, "Manliness . . . was something that had to be won. Perhaps physical strength once had been the definitive criterion of masculine excellence . . . but by Hellenistic and Roman times the sedentary élite of the ancient city had turned away from warfare and gymnastics as definitive agonistic activities."[100]

But such conclusions are exaggerated. Sosibius and Aratus, the Achaean leader who was a successful pentathlete in his youth and then a chariot winner at Olympia (perhaps in 232 BCE), join earlier athletes who belonged to the equestrian élite.[101] In most other cases, we know too little to be confident that an athlete's honorary citizenships, magistracies, even military commands are a concomitant of élite birth rather than the rewards of competitive success.[102] The surest indicator is the social status of other family members, such as Flavillianus' father and aunt or Mandrogenes' "well-born" mother (Philostr. *Gym.* 23). The wrestler Hermesianax, whose father and uncle contributed 400 drachmas towards building a wall at Colophon about 300 BCE, must also come from a family with means (*SEG* 49.1504). The Tean trainer mentioned above may have helped the son of a prominent local family to win the Olympic *stadion* crown in 136 BCE. Despite the difficulties, studies of particular communities and groups of athletes consistently find a preponderance of the élite among those competitors whose social origins can be ascertained. So for winners at the Plataean Eleutheria and at the Meleagria at Balboura.[103] So at Aphrodisias, Aezani, Oenoanda, throughout Lycia.[104] And far from being avoided, victories in the heavy events seem to have been the most sought after.[105] Otherwise, why would pancratiasts make up far and away the largest number of xystarchs, the leaders of athletes' associations? Why are combat athletes—again, pancratiasts in particular—so prominent among known Pythian victors during this period?[106] We may compare the dueling scars of exclusive Grecian fraternities or, closer to home, the use of steroids by today's professional athletes despite the toll they take on the body. Or—of more immediate relevance—the panhellenic cultural renaissance of the eastern Roman Empire and the fascination with rhetoric which Gleason has done so much to illumine. This renaissance has long gone under the name of "the Second Sophistic." But festival competition by no means lost its allure for the Greek élite of the time, and, as Onno van Nijf remarks, " 'Second Athletics' is as appropriate a label."[107]

Nor do I think the new prominence of trainers attests to a

rise in their own social status.[108] As before, some first-rate competitors took up coaching after their athletic careers came to
an end. (Plutarch says that someone who prepares young men
for civic affairs can still take part himself, unlike an *epistatēs*:
Plut. *Mor.* 795E [as emended]; cf. 783B.) One such, an Ephesian, was a *periodonikēs,* "a winner at each of the great panhellenic games," and twice "best of the Hellenes" as a runner and
then treasurer of an athletes' association as a coach.[109] Another
trainer, P. Aelius Tertius, served as a councilor at Smyrna and
so was likely a member of the local élite (*ISmyrna* 246). These
were presumably freelancers, able to pick and choose their athletes (as Philostratus hints: *Gym.* 28) and to set their fees as they
wished. (Hippomachus, the famous fourth-century BCE trainer
who figured in the anecdote recounted above, is imagined by
one of Philostratus' contemporaries as charging a retainer of
100 drachmas. The sum is scoffed at by a high-class hooker, but
it is a substantial amount all the same: Ath. 13.584C.)

Many of the trainers who gain credit in inscriptions were
wageworkers, civil servants hired for the year or for life by
the community-run *gymnasia* that were a distinctive feature
of Greek cities. Their job was thought to be important, but it
was a job for all that, far below the level of the gymnasiarchs
or other local notables to whom they reported. Public trainers
were comparable in prestige and pay to instructors in literature
and the arts. At Teos in the third-century BCE, for example,
two *paidotribai* each earned 500 drachmas a year, whereas *grammatodidaskaloi,* "teachers of letters," at three different levels got
600, 550 and 500, and a music teacher 700 (*SIG*[3] 578). Fifty to
one hundred years later, *paidotribai* at Beroea in Macedonia also
earned 500 drachmas annually, while their pay at third-century
BCE Miletus, 30 drachmas per month, was three-quarters that
for *grammatodidaskaloi* (*SEG* 43.381; *SIG*[3] 577). Some no doubt
increased their earnings by moonlighting. At Miletus, *paidotribai* could accompany their charges to crown games with the
permission of their supervisors and after making acceptable arrangements for other boys; but some athletes (like the Ephesian
wrestler Asclepiades) may have put themselves under a freelance

trainer when they started to seek success beyond local festivals.[110] In any case, these trainers' names do not seem likely to enhance a winner's prestige as Menander's and Melesias' did. Was there a new appreciation for their technical contributions? We cannot rule it out; Philostratus testifies to the sophistication of contemporary theories about diet, body types, and training schedules, and a rather earlier papyrus, from the first or second century CE, preserves fragments of a wrestling manual, in the form of a series of instructions from a trainer to an athlete engaged in practice or a match. ("Get next to him. Take his head in your right arm. Mix it up.")[111] However, the specialized approach he reports is not borne out by the behavior of athletes themselves. Instead, their thirst for distinction pushed them towards increased versatility as time went on, so that they could boast of unprecedented sequences and combinations of victories.[112] This is a very modern attitude: great athletes today recognize that individual accomplishments will be surpassed and so strive to be the first to win both the 200-meter and 400-meter races at the Olympics or both the U.S. Amateur and Open at Pebble Beach or to hit forty home runs and steal forty bases in the same season. Even among Greek athletes with less lofty goals, the participants at the Meleagria in provincial Balboura, we meet with *stadion* champions who doubled in wrestling or *pankration*.[113]

Whatever the causes of such results—small fields, the reluctance of ordinary Balbourans to challenge their social superiors, a fix—they are unlikely to include specialized coaching.[114] As it happens, among our very few grave epigrams for *paidotribai* are four for a certain Hermocrates of Hermoupolis Magna in Egypt, who died at thirty-two or thirty-three at the end of the second century CE or the start of the third.[115] Their forty-three lines stress his expertise in wrestling—there are references to Milon and much play with wrestling imagery to express Hermocrates' defeat at the hands of Death—, his strength, his moral qualities, the many ephebes he had crowned in the city's *gymnasia*. But the poems (perhaps unsurprisingly) are much more clearly marked by traditional turns of phrase and generalities than by any new respect for technical know-how.

Let me offer two suggestions, both related to the new environment in which Greek athletics were now set. First, the association with a trainer may have functioned as a signal of social status in itself. This is most clear cut in respect to private trainers—only the well-off could afford one—but is relevant to those attached to public institutions too. The *gymnasium* had always been primarily the haunt of the leisure class, but this reality was intensified in the Hellenistic and Roman periods, when it became the city's main institution of cultural reproduction for élite males.[116] This progression may be exemplified by the development of the ephebate at Athens. Established in the 330s BCE as a compulsory course of military training and service for the city's heavy-armed infantry and cavalry—a group comprising perhaps the top thirty percent of the population—this was reduced from two years to one towards the close of the fourth century. By the third, it was no longer compulsory or mainly military (though it maintained many of its earlier trappings) and had become a kind of finishing school for boys of the most prosperous families, centered around the *gymnasium*. By the second, it took in the élite of other cities as well, and ephebes donated one hundred books to the library. At that point, "agonistic accomplishment, and the badge of *gymnasion* education, were markers of high social status within the eastern, Greek half of the Roman Empire, and sometimes even necessary passports to participation in local politics."[117] This use of trainers as a badge of social distinction makes most sense if there were in fact (or were thought to be) more athletes who could not pay for private coaches and did not benefit from public instruction from trainers in the *gymnasium*: proportions of rich and poor would not have to shift very much to elicit such a response.

My second suggestion on the new willingness to acknowledge the contributions to trainers arises from a number of inscriptions in which athletes advertise victories they have shared with others.[118] These are often associated with other texts presenting athletes as having competed worthily, notably, conspicuously, in a manner worthy of victory, at festivals of the greatest prestige—but not in fact winning.[119] The references to drawn contests, however, have their own implications. Such ties might arise from a number of circumstances—for example, night might fall before the conclusion of a combat event or of the wrestling portion of the pentathlon—and entail different consequences. (Sometimes, both competitors got purses and the right to erect a statue; sometimes, especially in the games that did not offer prizes of value, the wreath was dedicated to the god the festival honored.) But the athletes who had them listed among their achievements were obviously prepared, even eager, to share credit for victory. Not all felt this way: the pancratiast M. Aurelius Asclepiades, victor at all the most prestigious festivals of his time (about 200 CE), member of the council of six important *poleis* and honorary citizen of many others, expresses his disdain for such triumphs in a long inscription celebrating his illustrious career.[120] Yet Asclepiades was unusual in his predilection for over-the-top boasting and implausible claims as much as in his accomplishments. All these inscriptions referring to draws or ties, welcomed or rejected, come from the first few centuries of the current era. They bespeak a new attitude towards victory, one in keeping with sharing credit with coaches and trainers too.

Both suggestions point towards a premium placed on participation in athletics for its own sake. In other words, later Greek athletes put forward a claim to social status based simply on competing in sport.[121] The use of competition in itself as a social marker pervades the subject of the next chapter, on slaves in Greek sport. Sport is generally employed to express and emphasize the gulf between free and slave in the ancient Greek world. But this divide is not always easy to maintain, as slaves were as necessary to athletics as to other aspects of the life of the free citizen, and the status of sport itself could be so high that it blurred distinctions that were of primary importance elsewhere.

Two SLAVES AND ANCIENT
GREEK SPORT

I begin with an inscription, a law regulating the *gymnasium* at Beroea in Macedonia and dating from some time in the first half of the second century before the current era.[1] When it was first discovered about sixty years ago, it was being used as the access ramp to a modern Greek garden.[2] It makes, therefore, a fitting means of approach to my subject in this chapter.

An important section of this law lists those excluded from the *gymnasium* at Beroea (B 26–29):

> No slave is to disrobe in the *gymnasium,* nor any freed slave, nor their sons, nor the *apalaistroi,* nor those convicted of prostituting themselves, nor those engaged in commercial craft, nor drunks, nor madmen.

The inscription then sets out severe penalties for the gymnasiarch who allows a breach of these regulations, along with complex and detailed procedures for accusation, appeal, and the payment of fines.

Such exclusions of undesirables were widespread in the Greek world. Rules prohibiting slaves to exercise in *gymnasia* or *palaestrae*—our concern here—are known from Athens, Crete, Cyzicus, Miletus, Nisyrus (a small island near Cos), Pergamum, Sparta, and Teos.[3] The most famous regulations come from Athens, where they (along with many other laws) are attributed to the early sixth-century lawgiver Solon.[4] The word *xēraloiphein,* "to put oil on dry skin," is used to refer to exercise in reports of the law. This word had apparently become more or less obsolete in the classical period, and so suggests that the customary attribution may be justified this time. Another tradition makes Solon responsible for the money payments granted to Athenian victors at the Olympic and Isthmian Games.[5] In this case, the details are awkwardly anachronistic—the Athenians did not coin money until after Solon's term of office in 594 BCE—but may reflect a similar measure nevertheless, one that encouraged Athenians to distinguish themselves among other Greeks at major panhellenic get-togethers through the same athletic activities that marked them off at home. If this is correct, we have some precious evidence for the role played by athletic sites and activities in constituting and defining citizenship and the citizen body in Greece, an issue to which I will return a little later.

It is noteworthy, I think, that attested instances of the exclusion of slaves from exercise come from the Greek mainland, the islands of the Aegean, and Asia Minor. None is known from the western Greeks. Of course, this may be an accident, a result of the chance survival of our sources, mostly (as from Beroea) laws inscribed on stone. If not, if practices among the colonists of Magna Graecia, Sicily, and beyond really *were* different and slaves *were* welcome to train in their *gymnasia* and *palaestrae*, we may have another trace of the openness to all-comers, the truly democratic spirit, which Stephen Miller has identified as the source for the remarkable athletic success of Croton in particular in the archaic period.[6] Even in the regions of the Greek world where we know of restrictions on slaves, there were exceptions, especially in the Hellenistic and Roman periods. For example, there were private *palaestrae* and even (if we take the curmudgeonly conservative known as the "Old Oligarch" literally) *gymnasia* at Athens, and some slaves, the *khōris oikountes,* lived on their own among the city's other residents.[7]

It is hard to imagine that the Solonic restrictions could be imposed effectively under such circumstances. One attested exception is particularly interesting. From Gytheum in Laconia comes an inscription, dated to 41/2 CE, which provides for slaves to exercise in the *gymnasium* and receive a share of oil on six days in the year "with neither archon nor gymnasiarch preventing" (*IG* 5.1 1208.38 = *SEG* 13.258). Three comments: First, these provisions are among those included in a special donation by a local benefactor, Phaenia Aromatium; they do not represent standard operating procedures. This is further indicated—my second point—by the fact that some opposition or at least neglect is envisaged and taken into account by the donor. Finally, the privilege is a limited one, restricted to only a few days of the year. This seems to be one of those rarest of all exceptions: it proves the rule on the exclusion of slaves.[8]

SLAVE COMPETITORS

If slaves were rarely permitted to exercise in athletic sites, it comes as no surprise that they were almost entirely absent from Greek sporting competitions. Sources, late and somewhat inconsistent as they are, explicitly record their ineligibility at Olympia.[9] An interpretation in Artemidorus' dreambook—a slave who imagines that he competes and wins a crown in games and so will be proclaimed free—indicates that this was the rule in other panhellenic competitions too (Artem. 1.62; cf. 1.58, 59). So the complaint Isocrates puts into the mouth of King Archidamus after the freeing of the Messenian helots is all the more bitter: What Spartan would want to attend Olympia and the other panhellenic celebrations? Once we were honored there more than victorious athletes but now we must see our slaves— the Messenians who long tilled our soil—bringing greater offerings than our own (Isoc. 6.95–96). The Olympic and other festivals once reinforced Spartan superiority and now reflect the citizen status of their ex-slaves.

The only sure instance of their participation comes from Misthra in Pisidia (Asia Minor) in the second century of the current era, where not only the entry but the success of a slave competitor is the subject of a rule: "If a slave succeeds in winning, he must give one-quarter of his prize money to his fellow competitors."[10] This competition, mind you, is otherwise unusual as well: ground wrestling was prohibited in the *pankration* (and so wrestlers were unlikely to win that event as well as their specialty), and an athlete was only permitted a single victory in any day. These provisions bespeak a desire to spread the benefits of victory around, which is consistent with the admission of slaves. Other examples may lurk in the correspondence of Zenon, manager of the estate of King Ptolemy II's chief minister for Egypt in the mid third century BCE.[11] Zenon evinces a lively interest in the education of two boys, Heracleotes and Pyrrhus; Heracleotes is carefully identified as free, and so Pyrrhus is likely a slave. Hierocles, director of a *palaestra* in Alexandria, assures Zenon that Pyrrhus has athletic talent and may (as Zenon wishes) become a winner. "I hope to see you crowned," he adds. Another letter, from the weapons instructor (*hoplomachos*) Paramonus, asks Zenon to buy Sicyonian strigils, six each for men and boys, also likely slaves in training.[12] We can hardly avoid the conclusion that Pyrrhus and the others are being prepared for competitions of some kind: just what, it is impossible to say. Taken literally, Hierocles' turn of phrase would imply that it is the slaves' owner who would be credited with their success, as was the case for the owners of equestrian entries.

Nigel Crowther has suggested another exception, at the Greater Panathenaea at Athens no less.[13] Crowther bases his argument on a passage in the *Eroticus,* another form of exercise—literary this time—ascribed to Demosthenes: "In other competitions, both slaves and foreigners take part, but the *apobatēs* is open only to citizens" ([Dem.] 61.23). He contends that the *apobatēs,* a combination of equestrian and athletic competition in which charioteers dismounted for a time and ran beside their horses, is being contrasted with all other events at the Panathenaea, equestrian and athletic; but I think it more likely that the author is setting the *apobatēs* apart from other equestrian events only.[14] Some of these, like the regular events of the festival's athletic program, were open to all-comers from other Greek cities, and entrants (as we saw in Chapter One) might use others as jockeys or charioteers rather than drive for themselves. Though we have no direct evidence for their status, we should assume that jockeys were generally slaves.[15]

Boy jockeys begin to appear on vases about the traditional date that the horse race entered the Olympic program in 648 BCE and are often shown on Panathenaic prize amphorae.[16] Though nude (and so assimilated to athletes) on these earlier vases, they are usually depicted wearing a chiton and often with negroid features by the Hellenistic period.[17] There is no doubt that Greek boys could ride. In *The Republic,* Socrates recommends that the guardians of his ideal city mount on horseback as young as possible, an age Plato's Athenian Stranger sets at six (Pl. *Resp.* 5.467E, *Leg.* 7.794C); Galen later specifies the age of seven (Gal. *De san. tuenda* 1.8). Writing late in the third century BCE, the Cynic philosopher Teles regards studying under a riding instructor as one of life's painful experiences for a teenage boy (Teles 5). Alexander was still young when he broke Bucephalus (Plut. *Alex.* 6). Ancient writers identified a statue on the Athenian Acropolis as Plato's contemporary Isocrates, riding a horse as a boy, and numerous similar works survive.[18] But horse racing was dangerous—jockeys had neither saddles nor stirrups—and few fathers would want their sons to run the risks.[19] In an early fourth-century BCE inscription, Damonon of Sparta boasts of his many and varied victories in local festivals and makes a point of saying he drove his own chariot (*IG* 5.1 213 = Sweet, *Sport and Recreation,* 145–146). He makes no such claim that either he or his son Enymacratidas, a successful competitor in boys' events, rode their own champion racehorses, and we should therefore conclude that they did not.[20] Artemidorus says that a slave who dreams of riding on horseback through the city will be freed (Artem. 1.56). The telling phrase is "through the city," regarded by Artemidorus as the prerogative of the free; to ride in other contexts is unremarkable.

It is hard to imagine how young boys who needed to earn a wage would become familiar with horses in ancient Greece. Unlike modern North America (say), where the children of ordinary farmers or ranchers may care for and learn to ride horses at an early age, the horse was a luxury animal in ancient Greece, useless for plowing or transport and beyond the means of all but the wealthiest. Most jockeys were surely trained from childhood by masters who had competitive ambitions and the means to gratify them, though of course talented riders might be bought and sold like any skilled slaves. Their lowly status explains their complete absence from texts that, as we saw in Chapter One, cannot quite ignore charioteers and athletic trainers.

The *apobatēs,* however, was one of a set of equestrian events for citizens only, and of these it was the only one to involve a customary athletic activity, running. It is true, therefore, that slaves might take part in other equestrian events and that foreigners might compete in both equestrian and athletic events; true too that the *apobatēs* was the only event involving athletics restricted to citizens. But the statement is so compressed as to be misleading. After all, rhetoric is as important to the author of the *Eroticus* as imparting accurate information. Indeed, the point of the passage, quite explicitly, is that only the best citizens compete in the *apobatēs.* These are citizens as distant and distinct as possible from slaves. This differentiation is all the more crucial in the context of a panegyric to a young citizen of extraordinary charm and beauty; his many suitors may persuade him to indulge in sexual acts that are not only unworthy and demeaning but might imperil his very social and citizen status. At Athens, as at Beroea, those believed to have prostituted themselves faced sanctions.[21]

The gulf between slaves and athletes is an element in an interesting passage of Plutarch's *Life of Aratus* of Sicyon. In the course of his campaign against Aristippus, tyrant of Argos, Aratus held the Nemean festival at Cleonae, on the grounds that this was the ancestral home of the games, and he seized and sold into slavery Achaean athletes who had taken part in the regular celebration at Argos (Plut. *Arat.* 28.3–4). This was an unprecedented breach of the usual rules regarding safe passage to panhellenic games. Plutarch admits as much: to such an extent, he concludes, did Aratus wage war on tyrants. But if there is

any blame here, Plutarch suggests, it falls on the Argives themselves. They took no role in freeing themselves from Aristippus'
rule but looked on at the fighting like referees at Nemea (27.2).
While those who should compete stand aloof, real athletes are
treated as slaves. The implication is the usual one: tyranny turns
the world upside down. Elsewhere, Plutarch plays on the dichotomy between slavery and athletics in a paradox: the Romans,
he says, believe that nothing has been so much to blame for the
enslavement and softness of the Greeks as their *gymnasia* and
palaestrae (Plut. *Mor.* 274D). The dichotomy between slaves and
free men also gives rise to one of the paradoxes characteristic of
Diogenes the Cynic. When the herald at Olympia proclaimed
the famous pancratiast Dioxippus victor in the class of men (*an-
dras*) at Olympia, Diogenes is supposed to have protested. "He
outdid slaves (*andrapoda*)," he said, "I'm the one who surpasses
men" (Diog. Laert. 6.43; cf. 33). Only Diogenes—a man capable
of masturbating in public and asking Alexander the Great to get
out of his sunlight—would go so far as to associate athletes and
slaves and to use a word redolent of slaves' link with livestock to
boot. Or perhaps not only Diogenes but also the sixth-century
BCE philosopher Pythagoras. That sage is said to have compared life to a festival in which some compete, some sell their
goods, but the best attend as spectators. These, of course, represent philosophers—athletes and merchants alike are like slaves
(*andrapodōdeis;* Diog. Laert. 6.8). The usual gulf between athlete
and slave can be bridged for effect in reference to equine competitors too. An epigram by Archias laments the lot of the racehorse Eagle, once a victor in the panhellenic *periodos* and now
fettered to a millstone.[22] Like Heracles', his achievements have
been rewarded with the yoke of slavery.

Athenian sensitivity to the importance of athletic venues in
the establishment of status also resonates through an altercation
that became the subject of a late fifth- or early fourth-century
BCE lawsuit.[23] A violent quarrel broke out in a *palaestra,* in-
flamed (if we read between the lines) when Archippus joked
about Tisis' relationship with his guardian and lover, Pytheas.
Such sexual insinuations impugned Tisis' reputation and might

put his rights as an active citizen at risk. So Tisis lured Archippus to his home, had his servants tie him to a pillar, and whipped him as if he were a slave. By his revenge, Tisis demonstrated which of the two men really had the right to work out in the *palaestra* and which was unfit to exercise that privilege.

One athlete who may be a slave does compete and win on the Athenian stage: Paris, son of the king of Troy. Abandoned early on and raised as a herdsman, he triumphs at his own funeral games in Euripides' tragedy *Alexandros* after his fellow herdsmen have complained about his arrogance towards them. Clearly, these are exceptional circumstances. Furthermore, Paris' social inferiority is only accidental and temporary: he is able to rely on the natural gifts of his birth. And his precise juridical status is left not quite certain, at least in what survives of the play. A series of fragments (fr. 48.1) may belong to a debate on whether or not Paris (also called Alexandros) ought to be allowed to compete.[24] One speaker (perhaps Queen Hecuba, who is of course unaware of his identity) labels him a slave in an attempt, in the end unavailing, to exclude him from competition. Paris is again referred to as a slave elsewhere in the play, when Hecuba and Deiphobus plot to do away with him.[25] Other passages seem concerned with a related but different issue, the moral claims of social superiority, a recurrent Euripidean theme perhaps best known from his *Electra*.[26] It is possible, therefore, that the designation "slave" is not to be taken literally but rather as a means to denigrate Paris because of his humble origins and occupation. (We will find a similar assimilation of slaves and the poor in the Old Oligarch's comment below.)

Against this possibility, we may observe that herdsmen in Greek accounts of royal foundlings are not infrequently slaves— for example, the Median who takes in and raises the future Cyrus the Great (Hdt. 1.110.1);[27] that Paris' double name—a part of his story as early as the *Iliad*—may have come to be considered in the light of the practice of bestowing a new name on slaves as they entered the household; and that Paris may be meant to remind the Athenian audience of another attractive and self-confident young man, raised outside his parents' home

and conspicuously successful in competitions. This was Alcibiades.[28] Though his kinsman Pericles could hardly be confused
with a poor herdsman, free or slave, Alcibiades' spectacular
showing at Olympia in 416 BCE (he entered seven chariots
and finished first, second, and fourth) would have been fresh in
every Athenian's mind when the *Alexandros* was produced the
next spring. So too, the capture of the island of Melos and the
enslavement of its women and children that same winter.[29] It is
to Alcibiades that some ancient sources attribute Athenian policy towards Melos and its terrible consequences; they add that
he bought one of the Melian women on the slave market and
had a son by her (Plut. *Alc.* 16.5–6, [Andoc.] 4.22–23). Echoes of
Alcibiades in *Alexandros* would be more audible if Paris moved
from slave to free (and so reversing and recalling the fate of
many Melians).

In any case, it is clear that thinking of the young herdsman as
a slave helps his enemies fuel hatred for him and his competitive
success and that this hatred is fierce enough to threaten his life.
We find a different take on the incongruity of the slave athlete in a later play, Menander's *Epitrepontes* (lines 320–334). Here
Syrus, a slave charcoal burner, frets about raising a foundling as
he may grow up to feel contempt for his adoptive parents and
to show his true colors: hunting lions, bearing arms, running in
competitions. Syrus then goes on to adduce mythic parallels to
foundlings like Neleus and Pelias, raised by goatherds and later
turned into kings, not to Paris.

OTHER SLAVE SOCIETIES

The virtual exclusion of slaves from Greek sporting competition becomes still more striking if we take a look at some other
slave societies. Take, for example, the slave states of the American South before the Civil War. Here, we are told, slave children often competed in the same sports as their masters: ball
games, jumping contests, footraces.[30] Some scholars stress that
these encouraged their sense of self-worth and identified and

promoted leadership within the slave community. There is some evidence that competition involving physical aggression—wrestling, fisticuffs—was usually avoided on the grounds that it created animosities and rifts within a community that depended on solidarity for its survival; but the prevalence of oral aggression, "playing the dozens" or "talking trash," suggests that this may be an idealized account. It is perhaps more plausible that whatever prohibitions existed were imposed by masters, fearing damage to their human property. Similarly, D. K. Wiggins believes that slaves avoided games in which participants were put "out," eliminated, because real family or social groups were all too likely to be diminished or destroyed by the punishment or arbitrary sale of members. So, for example, slave children played dodgeball, but (says Wiggins) with a significant variation—players who were hit stayed in the game.[31]

What did masters think when slaves and free children played together? Some disapproved. But such games were common nonetheless, especially when free children could find no other playmates or when the slave children were babysitters, and continued until the children were ten or twelve years old. What did the slave children think themselves? Here again play and competition might foster positive feelings of equality with or even superiority to privileged playmates. "We was stronger and knowed how to play," recalled Felix Heywood of Texas in one of the many ex-slave interviews conducted under the Federal Writers Project in the late 1930s. "The white children didn't."[32] When they grew older, slaves shared the general interest in boat and horse races; some rowed in all-slave crews, and others are listed as jockeys in the probate records of the property left by slaveholders at death.[33] They might journey to a neighboring plantation on a Sunday and spend the day competing in such races and other sports. These visits afford the context for a revealing motif that recurs in our accounts of slaves and sport in the American South.[34]

From time to time (so the story goes) a slaveowner would match a particularly strong or courageous slave in a prize fight against another master's champion. The boxing bout would attract high stakes, not least for the fighters themselves: freedom itself figures as a reward from a grateful—and much richer—master. The motif comes into the film *Mandingo,* in which the heavyweight Ken Norton makes a plausible appearance, and is attached to Tom Molineaux, the great Black boxing champion who fought many memorable matches in England in the early nineteenth century and was, according to this account, once a slave. There is, unfortunately, no good evidence for Molineaux' origins: he is variously said to hail from Virginia or Maryland, and the historicity of such stories, or their frequency at least, has been called into question by one of the shrewdest historians of prize fighting, E. J. Gorn. Gorn notes that "except for white rough-and-tumble fighting, boxing was known but not particularly popular in the pre–Civil War South,"[35] and he doubts that many masters would be willing to risk serious harm to something as valuable as a healthy and productive slave. We are not concerned with the reliability of these stories, however, but with the fact that they were told, and told quite often at that.[36]

The image of a Black competing on behalf of his white master still resonates, from Cassius Marcellus Clay dropping his slave name and becoming Muhammad Ali to Curt Flood's unsuccessful argument against the reserve clause in baseball before the Supreme Court in 1972. (The reserve system, he said, was a form of peonage and involuntary servitude in violation of the anti-peonage statutes and the Thirteenth Amendment.)[37] In 2006 National Football League veteran Anthony Prior's *The Slave Side of Sunday* sought to reveal the racism and hierarchy prevalent in a game in which Black players call coaches "boss" and "master" as a matter of course. Such echoes come complete with ironic undertones too: "Cassius" and "Marcellus" were names once borne by the Roman slave-holding élite; A. G. Spalding—calumnied for pitching like a Greek slave in an 1870 loss to the Excelsiors—rose to become president of the National League and a candidate for the U.S. Senate; and, notwithstanding the absence of Blacks from ownership and the front office, Anthony Prior and his colleagues earn a lot more than most.[38]

Given their prominence within the history of American

slavery and its sequels, it is surprising that there are no similar stories from Greek antiquity. Certainly, boxing matches between two champions are set pieces in Greek epic and its later imitators. And such bouts regularly feature combatants who enjoy different social statuses. In Homer's *Iliad* (23.652–699), Euryalus fights Epeius. Euryalus is called "a godlike man, son of lord Mecisteus of the seed of Talaos," himself a champion who defeated all the Thebans in boxing, while Epeius admits that he is a second-rater in battle and soon reveals himself to rank still further down the list in throwing a metal weight—the other Greeks laugh at his effort. He is elsewhere identified as a craftsman, the carpenter who built the Trojan Horse. His motto might be "Make horse, not war." Nevertheless, it is Epeius who wins, another turnabout.

In the *Odyssey,* the antagonists are Odysseus and Irus, a beggar and gofer nicknamed for the female messenger of the gods (18.1–107). To be sure, Odysseus prevails, but this too is a surprise, to Irus if not to us, because the king is disguised as an old vagrant, down on his luck and the subject of abuse. The gulf in social status is significant, then, even if its nature is different than it seems.

Finally, the Hellenistic poet Apollonius of Rhodes recounts an episode from the epic journey of the Argonauts in search of the Golden Fleece (Ap. Rhod. 2.1–97). This time the boxers are both royalty: Amycus, king of the Bebryces, and Pollux or Polydeukes, the son of King Tyndareus of Sparta—or of Zeus—and the patron of Greek boxing. But Amycus, king though he may be, is also a barbarian, a cauliflower-eared giant and the world's biggest bully, who has already killed a number of his neighbors with his fists. Needless perhaps to say, Pollux' Hellenic skill overcomes the rude strength of Amycus, and the barbarian king is laid low forever.

So: we have three Greek stories, three sets of boxers of different social statuses—and no slaves. Why? Once again, some comparative evidence may prove instructive. What may have led masters elsewhere to allow or even encourage slave participation in sport? D. K. Wiggins offers that the motives for American slaveowners were to validate their claims of concern for their slaves' welfare; to provide a safety valve for slaves' physical energy and competitive spirit—and so to enhance their own control over them; and to build communities—a community of slaves who play together, and a community between slave and master, because each engages in and enjoys the same kinds of leisure activities.[39] Wiggins' last motive brings to mind ancient Rome, where emperors such as Otho and Vitellius attended the amphitheater "to please the multitude" and "to win the loyalty of the mob" (Cass. Dio 64.8.2, 65.7.1) and where Julius Caesar and Marcus Aurelius drew criticism for working through chariot races when they ought to have been sharing the excitement of the crowd (Suet. *Aug.* 45.1; SHA *Marc.* 15.1). Or we may think of modern America. Campaigning for vice-president in 1952, Richard Nixon did some grandstanding at Yankee Stadium— and got the Bronx cheer. Nevertheless, all presidents seek to throw out the first ball of the World Series, though few play the game well.[40]

Are the other motives Wiggins suggests relevant to ancient Greece? Probably not. There were relatively few sizeable communities of slaves in ancient Greece. The helots of Messenia are an exception. Archaeological evidence indicates that these state serfs lived in relatively few centers rather than in isolated farmsteads or hamlets. Furthermore, they were not only Greeks but Greeks with a national consciousness, one that included a tradition of victories in the earliest Olympics. This alone might have made their competition in athletics something for their Spartan masters to prevent, unless it was thought to help identify "the strongest and best" of them for the secret service to eliminate (Plut. *Lyc.* 28.3). Among the large concentrations of slaves elsewhere, the mineworkers at Laureion in Attica had little leisure and less physical energy for sport, given their grueling daily grind. In general, Greek masters were keener on keeping slaves isolated and apart than on fostering common interests among them. Greek sport was a means of making and maintaining distinctions, not removing or reducing them. Some readers may remember G. K. Chesterton's story "The Queer Feet." One in the series of Father Brown detective tales, this features an in-genious thief who passes for a waiter when he mingles among the members of an exclusive dining club, and for a guest when he moves through the waiters. When Father Brown reveals his *modus operandi,* a young member of the Twelve True Fishermen protests: "A gentleman never looks like a waiter."[41] In this spirit, Greek sport helped prevent confusion between slaves and free Greeks.

Can we learn more from pondering reasons other masters gave why they, like the Greeks, kept slaves out of sport (or worried that they should)? Neville Hall, writing on the Danish Virgin Islands in the late eighteenth and early nineteenth centuries, notes some nervousness about slaves who rode horses and so rose above their station both literally and metaphorically.[42] The motif is as old as Solomon: "I have seen slaves upon horses, and princes walking as slaves upon the earth" (*Eccles.* 17.7). In his autobiography, the American ex-slave jockey Jacob Stroyer tells of being beaten by a trainer for no good reason, except to teach him his place.[43] Again, I know of nothing similar from Greece. However, the anecdote about Pheidolas' mare mentioned above (Chapter One)—she threw her rider but won an Olympic horse race all the same—has the same effect of cutting jockeys down to size. Aristotle certainly indicates that Greeks were aware of the danger potentially posed by slaves who were physically fit as well as uppity. Cretans (he observes) have conceded to their slaves the same rights they have themselves, except that they are forbidden access to *gymnasia* and the possession of arms (Arist. *Pol.* 1.1264a21).

This collocation is all the more interesting if, as Peter Hunt has shown with some success, Greek warfare depended much more on the direct involvement of slave fighters than our élite citizen sources are willing to admit.[44] Would this practice, awkward enough ideologically, be simply too threatening in fact if slave soldiers and sailors had the experience of participation and, above all, of winning in other areas of competition? (Cylon, whose Olympic wreath spurred him on to attempt to become tyrant of Athens in 632 BCE, might not have been the only athletic victor encouraged to seize political power.) It might, however, be best to admit that ancient Greece stood apart from other slave societies in ways that are relevant to this subject in particular. For one thing, pederasty played an unusually public and prominent role, and one motive for the limits on slaves in *gymnasia* was precisely to prevent their sexual contact with free boys and youths. Similarly, sport itself was more central to Greek society than to most, so that the participation of slaves would carry more meaning. Along these lines, distinguishing the Greeks, I would like to highlight something distinctive of Greek sport if not unique: the practice of competing in the nude.[45]

Like regular festival competition itself, this practice separated the Greeks from their Near Eastern and Mediterranean neighbors, as indeed it was meant to do: only Greeks were permitted to compete at the oldest and most prestigious games, the Olympics. But nudity, ironically, might conceal differences no less than create them. After all, free citizens were not the only males to have bodies. In fact, the most common Greek word for body, *sōma,* came to be used to designate a slave. Now, there was no shortage of ideological means for setting the bodies of slaves and free Greeks apart. Tragedy, for example (to translate Anastasia Serghidou), "places the body of free persons . . . in the realm of endurance, grace, harmony of form, communication and the body of slaves in the realm of physical degradation, poor clothing, fatigue and isolation—in short, in the realm of what is transient."[46] Tragic heroes cover themselves with glory and live on; slaves die anonymous and forgotten, together with their bodies. On coming of age, Athenian boys underwent a *dokimasia,* a scrutiny to determine their eligibility for membership in their father's deme and so for citizenship. There is reason to believe that they underwent this scrutiny naked, that their body itself was the main exhibit to show they were worthy to be citizens.[47] Aristotle divines the intention of nature to make the bodies of free men and slaves different: slaves' bodies, strong for the service they are forced to provide; free bodies, erect and unsuited for servile work (Arist. *Pol.* 1.1254b29–30). Greek artists often depict slaves as grotesque or misshapen, and deformed or dwarfish slaves were status symbols from the Hellenistic period at least. So it was easy enough for a thoughtful Greek to imagine that a slave's body belonged to nature, while an athlete's was trained, shaped, and refined by science and diet, what we might call value-added.[48]

Still, the inconvenient reality, then as now, is that nature sometimes gets it wrong—Aristotle admits as much—and that natural strength and coordination can sometimes compensate for a shortage of instruction and skill, especially in footraces and fights. This is a problem in any society that is hierarchical and competitive. As we will see in Chapter Four, nineteenth-century gentlemen solved it by inventing the idea of the amateur, and so in effect reserving their games, including the modern Olympics, for their own kind. Baseball shut out Blacks for the first half of the twentieth century. Though they now have the chance to prove their equality on the field, those who show themselves superior may still be in for a rough ride. Some may remember the abuse directed at Henry Aaron as he threatened and then broke Babe Ruth's lifetime record for home runs, abuse now aimed at Barry Bonds. (Few of these tormentors, I suspect, knew that Ruth himself attracted taunts for his allegedly Negroid features.) The stakes may have seemed even higher in competitions like the Greeks', where athletes' abilities were on display so nakedly. They took the same way out: exclusion.

But they also followed another unusual practice. The penalty meted out to athletes who committed a foul or who withdrew during the training period at Olympia was a blow from a *rhabdoukhos,* "rod carrier," or *mastigophoros,* "whip bearer" (Arr. *Epict. diss.* 3.15.4, 22.52); even Nero is said to have feared the *agōnothetai,* "supervisors," and *mastigophoroi* at Olympia and to have bought them off (Cass. Dio 62.9.2). Such punishment was regular in competitive contests elsewhere as well. "Homer" (says Heraclitus) "deserves to be expelled from the contests and flogged, and Archilochus likewise" (B 42 DK). In a famous story in Herodotus, Adeimantus reminds Themistocles that runners who commit a false start are whipped. ("Yes," replies Themistocles, "but those who start too late are beaten.")[49]

This beating was a slave's punishment. The fullest expression of this belief occurs in the protreptic for athletes included in the *Rhetoric* ascribed to Dionysius of Halicarnassus (*Rhet.* 7.6). The author, discussing cheats, moves from those who offer bribes to those who take them:

> They are like whores. And whores, it may be, are deceived by their youth, but bribe-takers hand themselves over because of their greed. But they don't get away with it. They are easily observed because of their bodies, both in exercise and from the contests they've been involved in before. In addition, there are the whips and the mistreatment and the indignities their bodies endure, which are the marks of slaves, not of free men, and censure before the spectators instead of praise, applause and crowns. Sometimes the penalty is to be thrown out of stadia and games, but the greatest penalty for those who pride themselves on their freedom is to see themselves incurring the punishment of slaves. If they see that one of their fellow competitors is a slave, they accuse him and exclude him on the grounds that he is unworthy to compete. But though they win the vote of the *athlothetai*, accepting them as free, they cast against themselves the vote that identifies them as slaves.

Whipping, in other words, assimilated the man who proved unworthy to compete to the slaves who were excluded from the games. Furthermore, it did so when he was naked and so unusually exposed and vulnerable, and when the blow might leave a mark that would show his shame to his fellows. So it is, perhaps, that a late sixth-century BCE bronze tablet from Olympia, which sets out regulations for wrestlers, requires the judge to punish infractions by striking "except on the head."[50] For a time at least, a rule-breaker leaves the citizen body and bears a slave's, unlike others who meet and see him naked at the *gymnasium*.

Nigel Crowther concludes a characteristically thorough and perceptive collection of the evidence for the practice (co-authored by Monika Frass) with this remark: "It is not easy to understand why it was considered acceptable under certain circumstances to punish the freeborn in the manner of slaves."[51] One way forward may lead through Page duBois' work on *Torture and Truth*. DuBois notes that, for free Greeks, "Truth is constituted as residing in the body of the slave. . . . The slave, incapable of reasoning, can only provide truth under coercion, can produce only truth under coercion."[52] The slave's body speaks for him. Among the free, however, "silence under torture may be considered as an aristocratic virtue."[53] The Spartan boy provides a paradigm of manliness, remaining mute while the fox gnaws at his inner parts.[54] To be whipped like a slave, then, is not punishment alone. It invites the élite competitor to show whether he really is as unworthy of his status as his transgression suggests—by crying out like a slave. It also affords him an opportunity to recover his status, by staying silent, unlike a slave. In so doing, he reveals a different truth about himself, once again through his body—and this, of course, is one of the things athletic and equestrian competition is about.

SLAVES IN OTHER ROLES

So much for slaves as participants in Greek sport. They might enter into this account in other ways, for example, as functionaries in a festival's various ritual requirements: only freeborn youths (*neaniskoi*) carried containers of wine, milk, olive oil, and unguents in the procession at the Eleutheria at Plataea. Plutarch regards the exclusion of slaves from such a menial task as noteworthy and explains it on the grounds that those who died at the Battle of Plataea in 479 BCE fought for freedom.[55]

More prestigious roles were of course reserved for the élite. So Demosthenes stresses King Philip's arrogance by suggesting that he will send his slaves to preside over the Pythian Games in his absence (Dem. 9.32). As spectators: Aelian mentions a man from Chios who was angry with his slave, and so he threatened him—not with a visit to the treadmill but with a trip to Olympia, where the sun, rain, noise, and stench were proverbial (Ael. *VH* 14.18). The historian Diodorus mentions an annual festival in honor of Iolaus put on by his hometown, Agyrium in central Sicily (Diod. Sic. 4.24.4–6). Involving both athletic and equestrian competition, this festival is attended by the whole community, slave and free alike, though the servants (*oiketas*) meet separately for banquets and sacrifices for Heracles, Iolaus' uncle, and the man he himself served as an assistant.

Slaves might also figure as personal trainers for the rich and famous: Seneca inveighs against body-builders who must put themselves in the hands of slaves of the worst kind, men immersed in oil and wine by turns, but he uses one for his own exercise program.[56] The Latin term Seneca uses, *progymnastes*, is in fact Greek, and perhaps his slave (named Pharius in some manuscripts) was too. Certainly the practice was Greek: the masseur (*aleiptēs*) who administered a treatment for weakness in the arms and legs at the house of Harpalides, perhaps in the first half of the fourth century BCE, was likely a slave member of the household staff.[57] Archimedes' servants (*therapontes*)—so the story goes—used to have to drag him from his diagrams by force when it was time for his rubdown; even then he drew figures on his belly with the strigil.[58]

They might also be watchmen, perhaps analogous to the *palaistrophylakes*, "guards of the palaestra," discussed below: one of the satirical epigrams of Lucillius tells the story of the hoplite-racer Marcus (*Anth. Pal.* 11.85). Slow? He was so slow that he was still on the track at midnight. The public slaves (*dēmosioi*) thought he was a stone statue, and so they closed the stadium.[59] Or prizes: among those won by Homer's heroes at the funeral games for Patroclus is a woman worth four oxen (*Il.* 23.705; cf. 263). Or goods to think with: athletes might be taunted for

their slavish subjection to their trainers or their regimes. I prefer, however, to consider the part played by slaves as workers in
the main Greek athletic sites, the *gymnasium* and *palaestra,* and
on its effects.

Scholars often refer to the "exclusion of slaves from *gymnasia.*" I have done it myself and been rightly rebuked by Larissa
Bonfante. As she says, laws "did not forbid them to enter in
order to do the necessary work" for the *gymnasium*'s upkeep.[60]
Indeed, the very laws that forbade slaves to exercise might be
taken as evidence that they were there all the time—but doing other things.[61] We may invoke another of G. K. Chesterton's Father Brown stories. In "The Invisible Man," a murder
is committed by a man "dressed rather handsomely in red, blue
and gold," under the noses of four witnesses who swear that
no one has entered an apartment. What is more, the victim—a
midget—has disappeared. The killer, it turns out, is the post-
man. "Nobody ever notices postmen, somehow," muses Father
Brown. "Yet they have passions like other men, and even carry
large bags where a small corpse can be stowed quite easily."[62]
No one ever pays attention to the gymnasium's slaves either.
Yet we probably see them all the time, not often dressed in red,
blue and gold, to be sure, but in the many *palaestra* scenes on
archaic and classical Attic vases: small male figures, standing by
or actually lending a hand, helping a boxer or pancratiast wind
on the thongs, for example. Some are surely slaves, either attached to the *palaestra* or the athlete's own. But some may be
free boys too.

It is not always easy to identify slaves on Greek pots; recog-
nizing this, the Beazley Archive—a standard source of images
on Athenian vases—does not use the headings "slave, slaves"
to catalogue depictions. To identify slaves might be a challenge
even for ancient Greeks. At least the Old Oligarch thought so,
alleging that slaves (and foreign residents) were as well dressed
and attractive as the mass of the citizenry ([Xen.] *Ath. pol.* 1.10).
We may discount this gripe on the grounds that the author
likely lumped together all those outside the élite (much as the
Canadian expatriate, financier, and felon Conrad Black referred

to all his employees as "underlings"). Still, there is no doubting the difficulty of reading the iconographic record. Scholars offer a number of criteria to distinguish slaves on Greek vases and other media: foreign names, caricatured features, red or blond hair, short hair and stature, simple or foreign dress (including the lack of a veil for slave women), a position on the margins of the image and outside its emotional field.[63] Useful as these are, they are inevitably far from straightforward to apply in practice: short hair may imply mourning instead of slave status; figures may differ merely for aesthetic reasons (to provide contrast or fill an awkward position on a vase). Some items of barbarian dress became fashionable among the fifth-century BCE élite at Athens: the depiction of slaves on their own tombstones is disconcertingly unlike their representation on others'.[64] It is particularly hard to be sure whether a figure's size is meant to represent slavery or another subordinate status, childhood; after all, the words *pais, paidion,* and their derivatives were commonly used for both slaves and children.[65]

Here are two examples of the problem. On a kylix dated to about 500 BCE, a young man bends over and holds two heavy rocks in his hands.[66] His nude form displays well-developed musculature. Is he a slave doing some heavy lifting to prepare the stadium or *palaestra*? No, a purple fillet in his hair—a token of victory, barely visible in photographs—guarantees that he is an athlete in training. On our second example, an Attic skyphos by the Zephyros Painter (dated about 460–50 BCE), three men work at a sports ground. One draws water; another pours it to damp down the dust; a third uses a hoe to break up and smoothe the ground. We see tufts of hair, thick lips, a hairy belly, a hooked nose, an extra-large penis. As Adrienne Lezzi-Hafter, the publisher of the vase, remarks, these traits "do not belong to the Athenian ideal of beauty."[67] She concludes that the men are slaves, perhaps from the east. Yet athletes often prepared the ground for themselves. A digging tool is a characteristic attribute of the athlete—especially the pentathlete—on Greek vases. Plutarch notes that "we still exercise when we can no longer use mattocks [digging tools used by athletes] or jump-

ing weights or throw the discus or fight in armor," and a Sybarite expresses surprise at seeing athletes at Croton digging up
the *palaestra* ground for themselves.[68] Only a spoiled Sybarite
would say, as this one does, that this is a job for servants (*oiketas*). Furthermore, two of the men on this vase—the smaller
two, as it happens—are infibulated like athletes. If we can be
confident of anything, it is that identification is uncertain. After
all, even long-accepted iconographical conventions in this area
have come under attack.

The *cirrus,* or topknot, has generally been agreed to denote the professional athlete of Roman spectacles. Not long
ago, however, Jean-Paul Thuillier removed his name from the
long list of those who subscribed to this view and argued that
the topknot, like other unusual hair styles, is a marker of age,
not status, meant to help set younger athletes apart from older,
bearded competitors who do not sport it.[69] The sheer mass of
evidence on vases and the difficulty in interpreting it persuade
me to take a different tack towards this set of problems. I will
examine one class of slave that is linked to athletic contexts, the
palaistrophylax.[70] One result of this examination will be to challenge the rigid distinction of slave and free seemingly so carefully delineated by legal provisions and social practices.

PALAISTROPHYLAKES

Let us return to the law on the *gymnasium* at Beroea, with
which we began. Another section of the law sets out the financial responsibilities of the gymnasiarch. One clause deals
with the sale of *gloios,* scrapings of dust, oil, and sweat from the
bodies of athletes, much in demand for therapeutic and magical
purposes.[71]

> The one who contracts out for the revenue of the *gloios*
> is to provide for the services of a *palaistrophylax,* who is
> to be as much under the orders of the gymnasiarch as
> those who belong to the *gymnasium.*

This *palaistrophylax* clearly is a slave. "If one is disobedient or misbehaves, he is to be flogged by the gymnasiarch"; elsewhere in the inscription, the gymnasiarch is mandated to flog slave *paidagōgoi* but only to fine those who are free (B 21–4). Likewise, other *palaistrophylakes* in our sources can only be slaves. The "boy" from the island of Cimolus mentioned in the temple accounts of Delos for 246 BCE, who was purchased "for the *palaestra*," failed to give satisfaction, was sold by public decree, and replaced by another slave purchased in the market (*ID* 290.112–115). His successor, Papus, listed in accounts of 231 BCE and then 7 years later, in 224, must have done a better job (*ID* 316.117, 338Ab.67). Midas, who bears a slave's name and appears in the company of a public slave and, like him—and unlike some free farmers we find in the same accounts for 200 BCE—bears no patronymic (*ID* 372A.99). The *palaistrophylax* who was one of the 30 *sōmata*, "bodies," which the rulers of Bithynia sent to the sanctuary and people of Delphi in the early first century BCE (*FD* 3.4.77). The *palaistrophylax* whom Diogenes the Cynic, mortally ill at Athens, instructed to throw his corpse into the Ilissus—another example of his contempt for convention but delivered with such confidence that his wishes would be carried out that the *palaistrophylax* must be envisaged as a slave (Ael. *VH* 8.14). Even Rhianus, the Hellenistic poet, was once (according to the Byzantine encyclopedia known as *Suda*) guard of the *palaestra* in his native city on Crete and a slave (if he was not really from Ithome in Messenia; *Suda* s.v. *Rhianos*).

We also, however, come across quite a few *palaistrophylakes* who may not be slaves. These are generally later in date than the slaves I have already referred to, none, it seems, earlier than the first century of our era. The most problematic examples are attested in the Peloponnese: assistants *hypēretountas* to the *athlothetai* engaged in the celebration of the Leonidea at Sparta during Trajan's reign (*IG* 5.1 18), those named along with other workers—the dog handler, the provider of oil, the bearer of the palm branch—after catalogues of ephebes from Arcadia about the same time or a little before (*IG* 5.2 47, 48, 53, ?54). The use of the Greek verb *kathistēmi*, "appoint," implies that the Spartan *palaistrophylakes,* like others "appointed" to carry out various functions in rather earlier documents elsewhere, are free citizens.[72] Those from Arcadia are perhaps ephebes with special duties or distinctions, or their younger brothers, though A. H. M. Jones regards them as members of "the staff of public slaves."[73]

There is less doubt about the citizen status of the *palaistrophylakes* known from papyri from Roman Egypt, where they show up in accounts, including payments to minor village officials, and as assistants to important administrative officers like the *stratēgos.*[74] A few may even be persons of substance. In the course of instituting proceedings that will eventually result in his son's admission among those "from the *gymnasium,*" one Psammis says he is a member of that élite class, as was his father's father before him; his father, Dionysus, a *palaistrophylax,* was presumably a member as well (*POxy.* 1266, 98 CE). Two hundred years later, the *palaistrophylax* Aurelius Didymus of the village of Thraso in the Arsinoïte nome was wealthy enough to loan two brothers 3,000 drachmas of silver (*PSakaon* 94, 284 CE). An epigram from Lycia boasts that the *palaistrophylax* Ammonius saw to his own monument himself, an indication of financial resources as well as of foresight (whatever his juridical status; *TAM* 2.470 = *GVI* 258, first century CE).

The ninth edition of the standard Greek lexicon, published in 1940, translated *palaistrophylax* as "superintendent of a wrestling school." The 1996 supplement, responding to comments by Kent Rigsby, offers a correction, "attendant in a wrestling school." This, however, still scants the Egyptian evidence, which locates the term somewhere amidst the realm of the many liturgies imposed on so much of the free population and the jobs they voluntarily undertook for pay.[75] An interesting document from the Hermopolite nome in the third century CE enumerates the participants in a procession: magistrates and their entourage.[76] *Palaistrophylakes* are assigned to various dignitaries: four to the *stratēgos* and to the gymnasiarch, two to the *exēgētēs* and the emperors' chief priest, one each to the *agoranomos* and the chief priests of Hadrian and of Faustina. The *palaistrophylakes* here seem to be the equivalent of Roman lictors, not just bodyguards but representations of the magistrates' power and privileges. If so, the prominence of the gymnasiarch, on equal footing with the *stratēgos,* is remarkable, and the presence of *palaistrophylakes* (rather than some other attendants) may be linked to it. It is better to recognize two disparate cohorts, the slave *palaistrophylakes* and the free citizen officials who share their designation.

Can we clarify the relationship between them? Seventy years ago, Clarence Forbes touched on the *palaestra* at Egyptian Hermopolis, where young men "were assigned a sort of Boy Scout duty, acting as a guard of honor for the *stratēgos* . . . and other officials. . . . They were called *palaistrophylakes,* but manifestly were wholly different from the slaves who bore this title elsewhere."[77] In 1990, Paul Schubert was more cautious on their identity and role—some must be too old for Boy Scouts—but no less certain that the Egyptian *palaistrophylakes* had little to do with their homonymous ancestors in classical Greece.[78] This seems sensible enough. We can all think of examples of words that have changed their meanings or associations. How can an exception prove a rule, as I said it might a few pages ago? Only if "prove" really means "test," as it did when that maxim was devised. "Niggardly" once made the news because of the mistaken belief that it implied an ethnic slur against Blacks. I look forward to the day that "chicanerie" is recognized as a slight on Hispanic Americans—and I bet the Roma people do too. But there may be more to this story than a simple coincidence of terms or chance variation over time. Another Greek word from the athlete's world—*palaistritēs,* with its obvious etymological link to the *palaestra*—covered both slaves and citizens with special distinctions.[79] Let us take a closer look at what *palaistrophylakes* actually did. Two items stand out.

First, free *palaistrophylakes* sometimes retained ties to athletics and athletic venues. This is clearest in the inscriptions from the Peloponnese, where the Spartan Leonidea was a competitive festival, one Arcadian document refers to a gymnasiarch and under-gymnasiarch, and the others too reflect *gymnasium* life.

But, as I have indicated, we cannot be sure of the status of these *palaistrophylakes*. How about our Egyptian examples? *Palaistrophylakes* there often occur alongside guards and soldiers.[80] It is hard to be sure how much their activities revolved around the *palaestra* or *gymnasium;* one fragmentary papyrus that concerns the sale of fish suggests that they may at times have had broader regulatory or supervisory responsibilities. But Sarapiodorus calls himself "*palaistrophylax* of the great *gymnasium*" in a petition on behalf of a boy whose father has died leaving debts (*PRyl.* 121, second century CE).[81]

As for slave *palaistrophylakes,* the most revealing evidence for their duties is a passage in the Hippocratic corpus (*Epid.* 6.8.30). "In Abdera, the *palaistrophylax* wrestled too much with a stronger man and fell on his head. He went away and drank a lot of cold water. On the third day [recounts the author of this section of the sixth book of the *Epidemics*], I went to his house." To no avail: the *palaistrophylax* died two days later. Unfortunately, here too we cannot be sure of his status. The Greek of the oldest manuscripts describes him as "the one who was Cleisthenes'." This could identify him either as Cleisthenes' son (and so presumably a citizen or at least free) or as Cleisthenes' slave, but it would be odd Greek for either. Some more recent manuscripts and the lemma of Galen's commentary read "the one who was called Cleisthenes'"—surely a slave, then—and Galen also knows a reading "the one called Cleisthenes." My assertion that this *palaistrophylax* is a slave is based largely on the date of this work, around the end of the fifth century BCE, long before we hear of free *palaistrophylakes*. If we accept this identification, we have a valuable insight into one role a *palaistrophylax* might play: the sparring partner.

There may be another such glimpse in Demosthenes' *First Philippic,* delivered in 351 (Dem. 4.40–1). Here the young politician criticizes Athens' response to Philip. "You fight him like barbarians box"—not barbarians abroad, probably (for we know of no foreign journeys so early in Demosthenes' career), but those closer to home, perhaps slave sparring partners in the local *gymnasia* and *palaestrae*. Finally, a third instance: Galen, in a lecture delivered at Rome in 177 CE, describes his treatment of a slave who took a blow on the sternum in the *palaestra* (Gal. *De anat. admin.* 7.13). Ancient combat sports were dangerous, boxing above all. Why not use a slave as a partner—he might not be strong enough, skilful enough or brave enough to hurt you—or as a punching bag?[82]

I would use this data on *palaistrophylakes* and other slaves to reach two conclusions. First, we may be confident that in Greece, as in other slave societies, legal and conceptual distinctions between slave and free were sometimes ignored in ordinary life. Excluded from exercise (as in Demosthenes' Athens) or not, slaves might lend a hand—or fist—as required. My second conclusion is more tentative: the participation of slave *palaistrophylakes* in the athletic life of the *gymnasium* prepared the way for, or eased the development of, the use of the term for an office filled by citizens, even citizens connected to the élite and so as socially distant from slaves as possible. Here (as at the end of Chapter One) we may see another instance of the prestige mere association with athletes might bring in the Greek world of later antiquity. A further example, again involving those outside the citizen élite, including slaves, will feature in our next chapter. Greek gladiators' claims to be considered athletes (and so of superior social status) will be weighed and found surprisingly persuasive.

APPENDIX

Evidence for the Palaistrophylax

I. TEXTS

Hippocrates, *Epidemics* 6.8.30	about 400 BCE
Aelian, *Historical Miscellany* 8.14	I/II CE
Suda, s.v. *Rhianos*	X CE (*tēs palaistras phylax*)

2. INSCRIPTIONS

ID 290.112–15	Delos, 246 BCE (*pais eis palaistran*)
ID 316.117	Delos, 231 BCE
ID 338Ab.67	Delos, 224 BCE
ID 372A.99	Delos, 200 BCE
SEG 27.261, 43.381.Bback.98	Beroea, 175–70 BCE
FD 3.4.77	Delphi, ?94 BCE
SEG 8.531 = A. Bernand, *Prose sur pierre*, 41.24	Egypt, 57 BCE (restored)
TAM 2.470 = *GVI* 258	Lycia, I CE
IG 5.2 47.8	Tegea, I CE
IG 5.1 18A.11	Sparta, II CE
IG 5.2 48.28	Arcadia, II CE
IG 5.2 53.6	Arcadia
IG 5.2 54.2.24	Arcadia (restored)
ZPE 7 (1971) 155–56	Rhinocorura (Sinai)

3. PAPYRI

POxy. 1266	98 CE
SB 12495	I CE
POxy. 390	I CE
PStrasb. 847	?150 CE (*parestrophyl . . .*)
	?150 CE (*parestrophy . . .*)
PStrasb. 848	160 CE (*parestroph . . .*)
PStrasb. 791	160 CE (restored)
PBerl. Leihgabe 39.107	161 CE
PSI 1100	II CE
PRyl. 121	II CE
PRyl. 224a	II/III CE
BGU 466	II/III CE
PDiog. 47	?246 CE
SB 9406.309	284 CE
PSakaon 94	III CE
PAmh. 2.124	

Three GREEK GAMES
AND GLADIATORS

Before we make the long journey back to Greek and Roman antiquity, let us linger a while in the more recent past and recall two films of the '80s and '90s. First, *Chariots of Fire,* a British film that won the Oscar for best picture in 1981. Since 1981 may itself count as ancient history for some readers—almost all my students have been born since—I will briefly review the film, which takes its title from a line in William Blake's poem "Jerusalem." It is based on the real-life stories of two members of the British track team at the 1924 Olympic Games in Paris: two sprinters who were once rivals and in the end ran—and won— in different events. Harold Abrahams took the gold medal at 100 meters; Eric Liddell was champion in the 400.[1]

Chariots of Fire contains many elements relevant to Greek sport and social status. For example—to return to a theme of my first chapter—Abrahams uses a professional trainer to gain an advantage over his opponents and incurs criticism as a consequence. It is not quite what a gentleman would do, especially as the trainer, Sam Massabini, is part Arab and so all the more out of place. What is most relevant here, however, is what we may call the ethos of the film. This owes a great deal to the idealized image of ancient Greek athletics and of the Olympics above all that was prevalent at its dramatic date, 1924. It was indeed still in place at the time of the film's release, a few short years before business bought the 1984 Games just down the road from Hollywood, in Los Angeles. (Is it a coincidence, an irony or an omen that Peter Ueberroth, the architect of those games, was born on the day Pierre de Coubertin died?) Abrahams and Liddell train hard and are fiercely competitive. But they do not wish to win for personal motives alone. Each, in his different way, is an idealist, spurred on by a cause greater than himself; each is an outsider, seeking recognition for his people or his principles. Abrahams is a rich man, the son of a financier, seemingly at home in the lush Cambridge colleges in which much of the film is set. But he is also a Jew. Liddell, on the other hand, is the son of a Christian missionary, himself devout and devoted to doing God's work, so much so that he will not run on the Lord's day.

As the plot develops, the rivals enter separate events: Liddell, British champion at 100 and 220 yards the year before, competes at 400 meters because heats for the shorter races are held on Sunday. Both succeed. Their later lives diverged. Abrahams became a power in British amateur athletics and the author of the *Encyclopaedia Britannica* entry on the Olympic Games; Liddell died in China during the Second World War, a missionary like his father. But together their intertwined tales underscore the symbolic power of sport and its ability to diminish difference, all the more so in that the story, rooted though it is in rivalry, ends with both protagonists as winners.

Let us turn to another recent film: *Gladiator,* starring Russell Crowe, the New Zealander who moved to Australia and uses a British accent to play "The Spaniard," a devoted father whose little son speaks Italian.[2] ("*I soldati! I soldati!,*" he cries, when he sees the soldiers sent to kill him and his family.) Crowe is Maximus, once a Roman general and then a slave and a gladiator; he kills the evil emperor Commodus in single combat in the arena before succumbing to his own wounds. *Gladiator* takes place in a very different world than *Chariots of Fire.* The green lawns of Cambridge give way to the dungeons in which gladiators are penned—dark satanic mills if there ever were; the sunlit running track is replaced by the Colosseum, where men are forced to kill for the profit of their owners and the pleasure of the crowd. The film nods in the direction of deeper issues, even inventing a history in which Rome was founded as a republic to imply that there are matters of political principle at stake. Essentially, however, the story is fueled by resentment and revenge, the struggle of two men who in the end kill each other. Their final face-off is as unfair as it is fatal; in *Gladiator,* though winning at all costs is so important, there are no winners.

These two films conform to a conventional contrast between Greek games and Roman gladiatorial spectacles; this contrast has often seemed a convenient way to encapsulate significant distinctions between these two famous cultures of long ago. It is a contrast in which the Romans come off as barbarians, either addicted to the display of others' disfigurement and death or cynically willing to pander to it. To quote the blurb by the publisher (Routledge) for *Spectacles of Death in Ancient Rome,* by Don Kyle, "Rome's legacy is forever stained with the blood of the arena."[3] Central to the contrast, of course, is the assertion or assumption that the Greeks shared our own revulsion at the spectacles of slaughter we imagine when we think of gladiatorial games. So in an entry in Daremberg-Saglio, the great French encyclopedia of classical antiquity, Lafaye wrote: "The characteristic genius of the Greek race inspired in it a distaste for the gladiatorial combats which it never completely surmounted."[4] The year was 1896—not coincidentally, perhaps, the same year as de Coubertin's revival of the ancient Olympic Games. Indeed, de Coubertin himself had played on the contrast in the invitation to the Sorbonne congress of 1894, which led directly to the 1896 games in Athens. He wrote, "Human imperfection tends always to transform the Olympian athlete into a circus gladiator. One must choose between two athletic methods which are not compatible."[5] Twenty-some years later, Jean Hatzfeld offered an echo with an overtone: "We know that purely Greek populations never got the taste for these bloody diversions. But we must note that the rare cities where, in the imperial epoch, troupes of gladiators were established, possessed as well influential and prosperous Italian communities."[6] Similarly, the great German social historian Ludwig Friedländer, whose collection of materials is still worth consulting, argued that in the Greek world, gladiators were popular only among "the mixed half-Asiatic populations of the east."[7]

These views seemed to find support from some Greek texts. For example, Artemidorus, himself a native of the great Asiatic Greek city of Ephesus, discusses a disquieting dream in his manual of divination. A man dreams that he is raised aloft in a kneading-trough full of blood that he drinks. When his mother sees him, she says, "My son, you have disgraced me." What does this portend? The man becomes a gladiator and fights to the finish for many years. Drinking blood signified his cruel and unholy livelihood (Artem. 5.58). Older Greek communities such as Athens tended to convert the orchestras of their theaters for gladiatorial spectacles. Amphitheaters, despite their greater size and superior lines of sight for spectators, were too closely identified with Roman power and the bloodshed that had imposed it; only two cities in old Greece contained them, and both—Corinth and Patrae—were sites of Roman colonies.[8] We might multiply such indications of distaste or hostility towards gladiatorial combat (e.g., Philostr. *VA* 4.22; Lucian, *Demon.* 57; Dio Chrys. 31.121; Plut. *Mor.* 959C), but very few draw the present-day distinction between cultivated Greeks and bestial Romans, with which this chapter began.

Of course, distaste and hostility occur in Roman writers too, products and producers as they are of the same system of rhetorical training and the same moralizing bent.[9] More to the point, as long ago as 1940 Louis Robert collected other evidence for the prevalence and popularity of such spectacles all over the Greek world, some 300 documents from Sicily to Megara to Oenoanda and beyond, from the tradition-steeped communities of old Greece to the oldest and most sophisticated centers of the east. In fact, Robert concluded that far from being hotbeds of enthusiasm, the least Hellenized parts of Asia Minor were also those that yielded the least evidence of gladiators. In a 1971 reissue of his book, Robert characteristically complained that too many had ignored his work, but evidence has continued to appear since (the number of known documents has doubled) and everyone recognizes its significance today.[10] If the place of gladiators in the Greek world took so long to register, the explanation is precisely the stereotype that opposes intellectual and cultured Greeks to raw and savage Romans. In fact (as we shall see), this misrepresents the nature both of gladiatorial spectacles and of competition in the Greek world.

VIOLENT GREEKS

Let us begin with the realities of Greek competition. The so-called heavy events, wrestling, *pankration,* and especially what Homer calls "painful boxing," were often brutal and bloody.[11] There were no rounds or other regular rest periods; barriers forced boxers at least to come into contact; bouts continued until one fighter quit or could no longer go on. Hand coverings may have increased the damage done by a blow; it is perhaps relevant here to note that the *caestus,* the spiked metal gauntlet often thought to characterize a particularly bloody and Roman form of boxing, seems to have been neither spiked nor metal nor Roman at all, but Greek.[12] Injury and even death were not uncommon. For example, an Alexandrian boxer nicknamed Agathos Daimon, "Lucky," won at Nemea and then died in the ring at thirty-five, trying to repeat his triumph at the Olympics (*SEG* 22.354).[13] There can be no question about the popularity of these events among Greeks throughout antiquity.

It is the heavy athletes of the archaic and classical periods, not the runners or pentathletes, who are the subjects of tall tales and the objects of cult worship as heroes, perhaps because of their ability to both inflict pain and endure it.[14] (Odysseus, "the man of constant sorrow," was named for just this mix.) The historian Thucydides dates events by the victories of the heavy athletes Dorieus and Androsthenes (Thuc. 3.8, 5.49.1); the special prestige of the *stadion* champion comes later, after the publication of Hippias' Olympic victor list about 400 BCE. As for later Greeks, prizes in second-century CE Aphrodisias were higher for heavy athletes than for all others.[15] How about equestrian events? Chariots were flimsy; fields, crowded; tactics included leaving the lane and cutting inside on turns; and there was no central barrier to prevent head-on crashes. (This last was an innovation of the Roman circus.) Under such circumstances, it is no surprise that only one team out of 42 survived to finish at the Pythian Games of 462 BCE (Pind. *Pyth.* 5.49–54). The chorus mourns Prince Orestes' imaginary death in a chariot crash in Sophocles' tragedy *Electra*. In real life, reactions might differ. "Many insist that nothing in racing affords such delight as a crash," we read in a literary exercise attributed to Demosthenes, "and they seem to speak the truth."[16] Even the discus had a reputation for danger, though the oddly numerous deaths—of Hyacinthus, Acrisius, Phocus, Crocus, Thermius—in myth can have had little to do with what actually occurred in practice or competition.[17]

In addition, there were distinctively Hellenic blood-sports, wildly popular in the Greek world, inconsequential or child's play at Rome: fighting partridges, quails, and above all cocks.[18] Cock-fighting was in fact virtually emblematic of classical Athens. Cocks were pictured as courting gifts on vases, Right and Wrong Reason appeared on stage costumed as fighting cocks in Aristophanes' comedy *Clouds,* and a certain Conon celebrated the humiliation of a fellow-citizen by crowing over him like a cock.[19] In his *Anacharsis,* the later (and eastern) Greek writer Lucian goes so far as to portray Solon, the legendary lawgiver of Athens in the archaic age, as praising an invented requirement that Athenians of fighting age attend quail and cock fights (Lucian, *Anach.* 37). The reason? They produce an appetite for danger and a wish to be as brave as the birds, a justification much like that some Romans offered for gladiatorial shows. Praising the emperor Trajan, the younger Pliny refers to one of the spectacles he sponsored. This was not lax or undisciplined— that might soften or break the Romans' manly spirit—but rather tended to encourage spectators to face honorable wounds and hold death in contempt, because even among slaves and criminals—the gladiators—the love of praise and desire for victory were apparent.[20]

And speaking of gladiators, most ancient accounts gave credit for their origin to Italian peoples, the Samnites, Oscans or (especially) Etruscans; the omission of the Romans themselves from this list may suggest that blame is being allocated, not credit. But there may be a Greek connection too. John Mouratidis has speculated that Greek colonies in Campania in Southern Italy preserved a Mycenaean tradition of armed combat at funerals. This, he thinks, provided much of the inspiration for the first gladiatorial games in Etruria.[21] Plutarch knows a tradition in which the very site of the Olympics once witnessed a contest of single combat. This (he says) "was carried to the point of murder and the slaughter of the defeated and fallen man" (Plut. *Mor.* 675C).

Perhaps, then, the violence we associate with the gladiators was not so foreign to the Greeks and their games. In the rest of this chapter, I will stress similarities between gladiatorial combat and Greek competition from three points of view: that of the gladiators themselves, that of the members of the élite of the Greek cities of Asia Minor who sponsored gladiatorial spectacles, and our own.

GLADIATORS' CLAIMS

Who were the gladiators of the Greek east? How did they think (and, especially, want others to think) about what they were and did? I begin with a short grave epitaph from Cos, one of the many that furnish our main fund of information on these subjects, and then offer commentary on it.

> His wife and . . . his child, in memory of Zeuxis, nick-named Cinyras. Having won and killed his opponent, he died (Robert, *Gladiateurs,* 191 no. 191).

The first thing to notice here is that this epitaph is in Greek, the language of élite culture in the eastern part of the Roman

Empire. The man it memorializes may also have been a Greek. He certainly wished to pass as one: both his name and his nickname testify to that. We know that many gladiators were indeed Greeks and that Greekness might be a mark of status, at least among Greeks. Plutarch, for example, refers to gladiators "who are not utterly bestial, but Greeks" (Plut. *Mor.* 1099B).

A second point. This memorial was dedicated by the dead man's wife and child. He must therefore have been legally married and a free man—or at least those close to him were eager for him to appear so.[22] Of course, many, probably most, gladiators were slaves, members of gladiatorial troupes. Governors of eastern provinces might buy them *en masse* from contractors and often passed them on to their successors. Individual masters could consign slaves to gladiatorial schools as punishment. But free Greeks too could choose to serve as gladiators. So five fighters identified as free men appear alongside four slaves on a dedication from Aegae in Aeolis, and a woman (on an Egyptian papyrus) laments that her lover has been persuaded by his friends to pursue the career of a *murmillo* (Robert, *Gladiateurs,* 214–215 no. 257; *PRyl.* 1.15). If they did, they must swear to be treated like slaves: to be branded, to be chained, to be killed by an iron weapon (Sen. *Ep.* 37.1; Petr. *Sat.* 117.5). They would also suffer *infamia*: legal limitations, social disgrace, a fate worse than death. (One consolation for losing a son: at least he did not grow up to lose his money and become a gladiator: Sen. *Ep.* 99.13.)

Yet successful gladiators might become famous, as unaccountably desirable as pop stars—gladiator blood was a cure for impotence—and rich. Claudius handed gladiators pieces of gold, and Nero gave one a palace (Suet. *Claud.* 21.5, *Nero* 30.2). Senators were their pals, collected their armor, even emulated them in the arena. (And the emperor Commodus really did fight as a gladiator.)[23] Cities made them citizens: a gladiator who had retired and worked as a referee (*summa rudis*) boasts the citizenship of at least eight communities of northern Greece and Asia Minor and membership in a *collegium* of referees at Rome

(Robert, *Gladiateurs,* 138–139 no. 90). Their images grace mosaics.[24] It might not be a bad choice in a world in which the gulf between rich and poor was great and almost impassable, and an early death was likely in any walk of life.

Now, my third comment on this epitaph. Zeuxis has a nickname: Cinyras. Taking a nickname was a practice of athletes too, in part to foil the curses and charms aimed against them by their rivals (though this strategy did not help "Lucky," the unfortunate Alexandrian boxer). Sometimes gladiators and athletes shared a nickname. Draucus, a name of uncertain etymology connoting speed and agility, was taken by both a *retiarius,* a gladiator who fought with a net and a trident, and a victorious pancratiast from Philadelphia in Egypt.[25] This brings us to the end of the epitaph. Having won and killed his opponent, Zeuxis himself died. Other gravestones include similar signs of the competitiveness of gladiators. Ajax of Thasos boasts, "No adversary killed me; rather, I died on my own" (Robert, *Gladiateurs,* 113–115 no. 55). Others claim their defeats were the result of treachery or a trick or—something else that seems to have brought no discredit—of being overcome by a younger man, a stronger opponent. (It was a younger fellow citizen who put an end to Milon of Croton's long reign as Olympic champion for wrestling in the late sixth century BCE.) This spirit may remind us of Maximus' final fight with Commodus in *Gladiator,* or of Greek athletes' will to win. Philo, a Hellenized Jew living in Alexandria, remarks:

> I know that wrestlers and pancratiasts out of love of
> honor and eagerness for victory often persevere until
> the end of their life. Although their bodies fail, still
> they continue and struggle on with spirit alone,
> which they have accustomed to despise terrors. It is said
> that two athletes in a sacred contest possessed of equal
> strength both suffered and returned the same punish-
> ments. They neither yielded until both died. . . . To die
> for the olive or parsley is a glory to competitors (*Quod
> omnis probus liber sit* 17. 110–113).

Arrichion (already mentioned in Chapter One above) provides an instance. A pancratiast, he was on the brink of conceding when his trainer called out, "What a noble epitaph: not to have given in at Olympia." He persevered, and his rival yielded just before he himself died (Paus. 8.40.1; Philostr. *Gym.* 21, *Imag.* 2.6). As for Zeuxis, he fought to the death, but the victory is said to be worth it.

All this suggests that gladiators in the Greek world sought to represent themselves as athletes.[26] We may adduce other evidence as well. Gladiatorial combats in the eastern Roman Empire are often said to have taken place in the stadium, the venue for athletic competition. This may sometimes be because the Greek word for amphitheater will not fit into the standard meter used for grave epigrams, but it is also confirmed by the archaeological record: stadia were indeed the earliest sites of these spectacles in the Greek east.[27] In addition, though there was a technical term for gladiators in Greek—*monomachoi,* "single fighters"—gladiators were also said to take part in *agōnes,* like athletes, and were referred to as "athletes of Ares" who might, like them, compete (*athlein*) for prizes (*athla*). *Epistatēs* means both a gladiatorial instructor and a trainer of athletes; men are said to enroll themselves (*apographesthai*) as both gladiators and athletes. Furthermore, words from the root *pyg,* more properly used to describe boxers and boxing, are also generally applied to gladiators. So on a stele from Laodicea on the Lycus (Phrygia), Serapias commemorates her husband who fought *pygmaisin* eight times and died at age thirty (*SEG* 47.1742, first/second century CE). Despite the literal translation, "with his fists," the dead man must have been a gladiator. Similarly, Milarus fought in the stadium (*en stadiois*). He calls himself a boxer (*pykteusas*) and links his twelve winning bouts to the labors of Heracles— but his death in the thirteenth (as it seems) marks him too as a gladiator (*SEG* 49.1755, Ilion, second/third century CE).

Cicero certainly saw the similarity between boxers and gladiators, noting that both fought more effectively when their movements were graceful (Cic. *Orat.* 68.228). Gladiators signaled submission by raising a finger—heavy athletes too. Similarly, gladiators (like athletes) generally take care to specify their special training and expertise (as *retiarii, murmillones,* and so on) and also claim to have earned the distinctions of athletes, to be *aleiptos,* "undefeated," *paradoxos,* "exceptional, a champion," and to have gained fame in their endeavors. "Winning six fights, I brought my city honor," claims a Thessalonican, playing on the herald's proclamation for a victorious athlete (Robert, *Gladiateurs,* 79–80 no. 13). Like athletes, gladiators are keen to add luster to their achievements, to trumpet value-added victories. A Phrygian fighter, for example, defeated a *retiarius* despite the blinding morning sun (*SEG* 50.1163, Ephesus, second century CE). They also took a victory lap of their venue after a triumph. And for them too the palm—commonly engraved on gladiators' tombstones—was a symbol of success.[28]

At times, the assimilation of gladiators to athletes is presented pejoratively. Epictetus refers to "these dirty boxers and pancratiasts and those like them, the gladiators" (Arr. *Epict. diss.* 2.18.22). More often, however, the link is a claim for status, one to be compared to the use of athletic terminology by another marginal outgroup: the Christians took it over to glorify their martyrs in particular.[29] The dream-vision of Perpetua, martyred in the amphitheater at Carthage in 203 CE, is of particular interest here, involving as it does a muddle of gladiatorial *munera,* "shows," and Greek *agōnes,* "contests."[30] (In the Roman west, by way of contrast, gladiatorial tombstones tend to emulate those of soldiers and in some respects even of the freedmen who rose to the priesthood of the *seviri augustales.*)[31] It was not just that gladiatorial combat lacked the long history and role in urban life of the great festival competitions of athletes. Gladiators, even those who were free Greeks, can only rarely have sprung from the same exalted social milieu as athletes, who were still at this time drawn in the main from the city's élite. No wonder that gladiators wanted to use the language of athletics or that a gladiatorial *familia* at Sagalassus (Pisidia) might set up an inscription honoring an *agōnothetēs* as if they were athletes who had benefited from his largesse (Robert, *Gladiateurs,* 142 no. 97). It is also significant, however, that these claims need not be resented or rejected. Athletes might accept their association with gladiators, like the champion who sponsored beast hunts and gladiatorial combats, again at Sagalassus (Robert, *Gladiateurs,* 142–143 no. 98). This provides an introduction to our next topic, the ideas of the élite who sponsored and patronized gladiatorial spectacles.

ÉLITE AMBITIONS

In 80 BCE (so says the historian Appian, writing after the lapse of two centuries) there were no competitions at Olympia except the *stadion* race (App. *BC* 1.99). Sulla, who had recently been appointed dictator, summoned the athletes and all the rest of the spectacle to Rome to celebrate all he had accomplished in the Mithridatic and Italian wars. It is not quite clear what this means. We know of one victory at Olympia during that Olympiad, the Argive Epaenetus' in the boys' *stadion.* Because our information comes from the victor list compiled by Julius Africanus, and because it is unlikely that it would include the winner of the boys' race but not of the men's, we may conclude that Appian's account gives an accurate picture at least in regard to the reduction in activities at Olympia. But just what did Sulla do at Rome? One plausible hypothesis is that he invited leading Greek athletes to join in the Ludi victoriae Sullanae, "games for Sulla's victory," inaugurated in the previous year, but there are others too.[32] Nor are his motives unproblematic. Following earlier precedents, the Athenians had instituted a festival, the Sylleia, in his honor in 84 BCE.[33] Perhaps this put the idea in his head; perhaps he was paying the Eleians back for the statue they erected for his arch rival Marius (*IvO* 326); or he may merely have wished (despite Appian's cynicism) to afford the mass of the Roman population a breathing space and a distraction after all the troubles of the civil war.

Amidst all this uncertainty, what matters is that Sulla is described as transplanting Greek competitions to a Roman environment to advertise his success in struggles in both the east and the west of the world the Romans ruled. His staging of Greek contests at Rome had precedents: we hear of those by M. Fulvius Nobilior in 186 BCE, by L. Anicius in 167 BCE, and there must have been others.[34] Nevertheless, they do not look back but forward. Sulla was sensitive to the value of spectacles in shaping his public image as Rome's savior, its granter and guarantor of prosperity and peace.[35] He constructed that image with due care to knit together Italy and the Greek east; for example, he reserved successive but separate days in January, 81 BCE, to mark his victories over Marius and Mithridates with triumphal processions on each. In this way Sulla established a model for future emperors in the use of Greek festival competition to advertise their power and enhance their popularity and prestige in the east and so to present themselves as a force for unity in their far-flung and disparate realm. They too made the Olympics the centerpiece of this strategy. Unlike Sulla, however, they brought their patronage and even their persons to the site of the festival itself.

This is not to say that emperors ignored Sulla's lead in bringing Greek games to Italy.[36] In 2 CE, Augustus established the Sebasta at Naples, a competitive festival on the model of the Olympics (though with an extended program).[37] This, however, was in an area pervaded by Greek culture. ("Sebasta" is Greek for "Augustan.") Though the Ludi pro valetudine (or pro salute) Caesaris, "games for Caesar's (= Octavian's) health," included Greek contests when they were introduced in 30 BCE, it was not until 86 CE that the first Greek-style competitive festival—and the first permanent stadium—were introduced into Rome itself. Domitian's Capitolia, a penteteric festival for Zeus Capitolinus, immediately joined the circuit of major competitions; along with the Actia (discussed below) and Sebasta, all scheduled in the same year, the Capitolia provided a summer tour of the west for the best Greek athletes.[38] As late as 142 CE, Antoninus Pius honored Hadrian with another four-yearly foundation, the Eusebeia at Puteoli.[39] Nevertheless most of the emperors' athletic endeavors were directed towards the east.

Under Roman rule, the old Greek festivals continued to be

held, though the vagaries of warfare and government policy caused even one of the most important, the Isthmia, to become migratory for a time.[40] Robert Weir's important monograph stresses the emperor Domitian's appreciation for the importance of Delphi as a panhellenic site and the influence of the Pythian festival on his Capitoline Games and on more than twenty-five new "Pythian" foundations in the late second and third centuries CE.[41] The Olympics, always the most prestigious festival, survived until 393 CE or even longer (as recent discoveries suggest: see below, Chapter Four).[42] Indeed, they flourished, favored as they were by the patronage of the emperors.[43] Even before he took on the title "Augustus," the Achaean League, which included Elis, erected a colossal gold and silver statue of Octavian in the Temple of the Mother Goddess in the sacred grove, the Altis, depicting Rome's new ruler with the attributes of Zeus, the patron of the sanctuary. He accepted the compliment and the responsibility it implied, seeing to the renovation of the Olympic stadium while his right-hand man, Agrippa, paid for the restoration of Zeus' temple after an earthquake. To compete was as unworthy of Augustus as it had been of Alexander. But chariot victories by Tiberius, his adopted son (? 4 BCE), and Germanicus, his adopted grandson (17 CE) must have seemed consistent with his support for the festival.

Nero went further, forcing the rescheduling of the Olympic festival of 65 to 67 CE so that he could win at all the crown games of the original circuit in one visit to Greece. Our sources are hostile to his ambitions and to the means (bribery, introducing new events, removing statues of previous victors to Rome) by which he gained them, and the Eleians later declared his victories invalid.[44] It may be, however, that (like Sulla and Augustus) he meant his interest to unite his empire as well as to display his own preeminence in it.[45] In this light, Nero (like Augustus, another revolutionary traditionalist) was moving back to the future, proclaiming that Greece was not just a sad relic of bygone glory but a prominent part of the present day. This sentiment certainly seems to have motivated the philhellenic Hadrian. Concentrating though he did on Athens, whose claims as a cultural capital resonated with his own interests, Hadrian still sought links with Olympia, completing the long dormant Temple of Olympian Zeus at Athens, using Phidias' statue of Olympian Zeus on his coins, enlarging the Olympic stadium. Some time later in the second century CE, Herodes Atticus, Greek intellectual and Roman consul, honored such emperors and emulated their works. He and his wife Regilla, priestess of Demeter Chamyne at Olympia, built an aqueduct to bring the festival the first dependable supply of fresh water in its long history. They finished it off with a fountain house decorated with the statues of four generations of two families, the emperor's and their own.

But old Greece, the province of Achaea, was a poorer place in the Roman world, and the center of Greek culture and civilization gradually shifted further to the east. Here too ancient games existed, some in fact founded by the Romans themselves. Sulla (again) was something of a pioneer, establishing the Hecatesia and Romaea in Stratonicea (Caria) in 81 BCE to repay that city for its stand against Mithridates (*OGI* 441). Augustus (as usual) set the standard for his successors with his Actia, an expansion of an existing celebration for Apollo that honored his climactic naval victory over Antony and Cleopatra in 31 BCE.[46] (The first celebration, in 27, was intended to open a new era, reckoned in Actiads on the model of Olympiads.) Those of highest status, the sacred crown games, needed the emperor's approval. Cities usually sought it even for less ambitious undertakings too,[47] and it was usually granted: it was both pleasant and politically astute to give Greek subjects of the Empire what they wanted.

Indeed, the era witnessed a remarkable upsurge in the foundation of festivals; Louis Robert called it a "competitive explosion."[48] One estimate, widely accepted, puts the number of competitive festivals attested during the imperial period as at least 500.[49] Like Sulla too, later leaders used new foundations to reward allies, as Septimius Severus did for those cities that supported him against Pescennius Niger and the Parthians in the late second century CE and early third.[50] An additional motive was that all games, sacred or otherwise, were tied into the

imperial cult and were often conducted under the auspices of
the local priest or regional high priest of the cult.[51] The emperor
also figured in older festivals too, which often took on an epi-
thet such as Sebasteia or Augusteia in his honor. Therefore, in
a work ascribed to Dionysius of Halicarnassus, offering advice
to the orator who is to speak in praise of festivals, the author
urges the orator to include favorable mention of founders, loca-
tions, their frequency, the organizers, the types of crown they
put up as prizes. He should be most careful, however, to end
with praise of the emperor. He is "the real *agōnothetēs* of all contests, since he is in charge of peace, which makes all contests
possible" (Dion. Hal. *Rhet.* 1.7).

Because agonistic festivals remained at the center of civic
life in the Greek east, it is no surprise that the *agōnothetai* and
others who presided over them, the benefactors who supplied
or augmented their prizes, the gymnasiarchs who funded the
day-to-day athletic pursuits of the local élite—that all of these
continued to hold positions of prominence and prestige. Greek
games also allowed individuals and their cities to stake a claim
to be part of the new world the Romans ruled in a way which
afforded access as well to a privileged culture of the past. This
may have seemed especially attractive in the east of the Empire, on the margins of Rome's reach. After all, the cities of the
east were closer to Rome's enemies, to Parthia and Persia, than
to Rome itself. Even their credentials as Greek might not be
above suspicion. Oenoanda in Lycia, for example, was founded
as a colony of nearby Termessus (Pisidia) only in the third century BCE, and it used the local language, distinctive funerary
cult, and regional architecture well into the Roman period. No
wonder, then, that we know of some thirty-odd Oenoandan
festivals featuring Greek games from the eighty years from 150
to 230 CE. No wonder too that some Judaeans chose to take
up Greek athletics—it was a way of fitting into the Romans'
world—or that new festival foundations in the east might bear
names such as the Caesarea (at Corinth and Sparta), the Romaea
(in Lycia), or the Romaea Sebasteia (at Pergamum) as a means
to be Greek and Roman at the same time. The addition of Ro-

maea to the names of existing festivals (such as the Erotideia at Thespiae) had similar motives.

The Greek cities of the eastern empire were not shy about advertising their claims. They were festooned with the trappings of festival competition. Honorific inscriptions, statues, and victory lists in public spaces of every kind and place assured visitors that they had come to the home of real old-fashioned Hellenism;[52] cities piled up prizes and paid appearance fees to big-name athletes so that the visitors would come. If they did not come, then commemorative coins would carry the claims of the cities abroad. Onno van Nijf sums up the situation: "Greek festival culture . . . mobilized the resources of a glorious Greek past enabling urban élites to display their social superiority. . . . At the same time it was clearly focused on Rome and the emperor. . . . Festivals were in many important respects an invented tradition that effectively blurred the boundaries between Greek and Roman."[53]

But there was a downside for individual members of the Greek élite who chose to identify themselves with traditional athletic competition. Roman attitudes towards Greek culture were complex, to Greek athletics not least. One strain was hostile. As Cornelius Nepos puts it, "In almost all of Greece to be proclaimed victor at Olympia was a source of great praise. . . . Among us all such things are classed as disgraceful or base or unable to bring honor" (*Praef.* 5). Romans might deplore the nudity that characterized *gymnasium* life and athletic competition not only because of a feeling that such a display was unseemly for men of high status but because of its associations with homosexuality; for some Romans too this was Greek love.[54] Furthermore, any Greek pleas that athletics led to physical fitness seemed to be belied by their defeat in war and their subjection to the Romans. Finally, whatever the value of athletic exercise and competition for many Greeks, to others they may have appeared to pale beside the advantages of moral, philosophical, and rhetorical training.

In these circumstances, therefore, involvement in agonistic festivals may have looked like a losing strategy for some mem-

bers of the Greek élite. Then why not sponsor gladiatorial spectacles instead? These were clearly acceptable to the Romans,
were unquestionably manly and warlike, and had besides (as I
have just insisted) long been integrated into the Greek world.
(Indeed, the easy availability of stadia gave Greeks who wanted
to pursue this course a positive advantage over those in the
western parts of the Roman world. They might have to construct facilities anew.) That the two kinds of activities were to
be regarded as near equivalents is indicated by very different
pieces of evidence. First, the terms used for staging gladiatorial
combats were simply adopted from the vocabulary of festival
competition. A still more striking sign: in 177 CE, M. Aurelius
approved a Milesian request to turn the Didymeia into sacred
crown games; but he also asserted that other cities should not
feel bound by his acquiescence to spend money on such festivals
(*AE* [1977] 801). In the same year, the emperor and his son Commodus sought to limit expenditures on gladiatorial games in the
provinces.[55] Surely this brace of moderating measures stemmed
from a sense that Greek games and gladiatorial spectacles were
two sides of the same coin (a coin that was spent too freely).
In addition, the emperor played a similar part in both kinds
of activity. He monopolized the capacity to stage gladiatorial
games at Rome itself from very early on just as he reserved the
right to create sacred crown games. Finally, as Alan Cameron
pointed out thirty years ago, the *gymnasium* and the elaborate
institutional infrastructure that supported it disappeared from
the Greek cities of the east about the same time as gladiatorial
games, in the fourth century CE.[56]

Now, ideally a member of the élite in the Greek east would
simply put on spectacles of both types. Here as so often Augustus supplied a model for those who came after him. We have
already noted his festival foundations. In the account of his
achievements that he ordered inscribed on bronze and copied
throughout the Empire, he records: "I gave three gladiatorial
games in my own name and five in that of my sons or grandsons; at these games some 10,000 men took part in combat.
Twice in my own name and a third time in that of my grandson

I presented to the people displays by athletes summoned from all parts" (*Res Gestae* 22). Some soon followed Augustus' lead. A first-century inscription from Ancyra, the modern Ankara, sets out the benefactions of a series of high priests of Augustus and of Rome (Robert, *Gladiateurs,* 135–137 no. 86). In some cases, these men supported both gladiatorial and athletic activity. One, for example, feasted the people, provided oil for those exercising in the *gymnasium* over a period of four months, put on shows and a spectacle with thirty pairs of gladiators, as well as a hunt of bulls and beasts. To be sure, these men were exceptional, the sons of kings. Others may have been unusually generous or ambitious. In a nearly contemporary inscription from Magnesia on the Maeander (Caria), Ti. Claudius Zopas honors his father (Robert, *Gladiateurs,* 168 no. 152). He both gave out oil during a festival for more than the usual number of days and sponsored gladiatorial combats for more days than ever before. Clearly, the older man was an overachiever, perhaps as much in operating in both spheres as in the expense he incurred in each.

However, a newly published series of inscriptions from Thessalonica may indicate that his pattern of activities was not so unusual or at least did not remain so (*SEG* 49.815–818). Invitations to *munera* in the third century CE allow us to trace the career of a local dignitary, Claudius Rufrius Menon, and his involvement with both athletes and gladiators. In the first, dated to 252 CE, Menon appears as *agōnothetēs* of a festival of the Macedonians and announces three days of gladiatorial shows and beast hunts, with eighteen pairs of fighters and eighteen of each kind of local animal. By 259 CE, he has become *agōnothetēs* of a sacred, eiselastic and isolympian festival, the Caesarea Pythia. The next year's invitation provides the benefactor's name in a fuller form: Tib(erius) Claudius Rufrius Menon, styles the festival for which he is *agōnothetēs* as the Caesarea Epinicia Cabiria Pythia, and promises exotic beasts (leopards, hyenas, a lioness). Though there will be only one day of gladiators this time, the public is enticed with the prospect that two pairs will fight to the death. Here it seems that the stature of the Greek festivals that Menon presided over and the elaboration of the spectacles he staged increased in tandem with his own prominence. There seems to be nothing remarkable about Menon otherwise, nor about other *agōnothetai* we hear of who sponsored shows as well (e.g., Robert, *Gladiateurs*, 116–117 no. 59, 144 no. 103, 159–160 no. 133). Still, it may be instructive to consider what factors might influence a patron's choice of benefactions.

We should note at the outset that athletic competitions were part of regularly scheduled festivals, put on by cities at set times; gladiatorial spectacles might be put on by the community but were also open to individual initiative. In the Greek east, they could be mounted when someone wished (though, as we have seen, the emperor controlled this process closer to Rome, and he and others sometimes endeavored to rein in excessive extravagance wherever it occurred). It was therefore rather easier to put on a gladiatorial spectacle than to preside over the athletic competitions at a civic festival. The arbitrary element, and the possibility of its manipulation for personal ends, seems to be behind Plutarch's criticism of leaders who curry favor through banquets or gifts of money, pyrrhic dances, or gladiatorial shows (Plut. *Mor.* 802D; cf. 821F, 823E). But we should not exaggerate the differences here: local notables took it upon themselves to found competitive festivals too from time to time, and anyone who could afford to pay for gladiatorial shows would be a cinch to hold high office in his city and its cults and so play a prominent role at contests of all kinds.

We should also recall that emperors had varying views about the value of spectacles and competitions. Fond as he was of fostering Greek festivals, Hadrian seems to have had little use for athletics themselves. So when C. Julius Demosthenes (one of those local notables) sponsored games at his native Oenoanda, they originally included musical and cultural competitions only; athletics were added under pressure from the local population itself.[57] Nor does Hadrian seem enthusiastic about amphitheater displays (though he put them on and attended them himself: SHA *Had.* 7.12, 9.9, 19.8). In a letter published in 2000, he grants and praises a request from Aphrodisias to require high priests of his cult to donate funds for an aqueduct rather than pay for the usual gladiatorial spectacles (more popular though these may have been).[58] Similarly, Antoninus Pius made a point of commending one Vedius Antoninus, who spent his money on buildings rather than on distributions, shows, and prizes for competitions (*SIG*[3] 880). Sponsoring spectacles, giving out oil, and raising the stakes athletes fought for would do the subject of *these* emperors very little good, at the center of the Empire anyway. Commodus, on the other hand, favored the stadium as well as the amphitheater. His identification with Heracles inspired new festivals to the hero at Tarsus, Tyre, and Nicaea and the renaming of others; he added the name "Commodeia" to the titles of at least sixteen other festivals.[59]

Emperors might even involve themselves in determining the victor in some athletic competitions. M. Aurelius Asclepiades, the great pancratiast, *periodonikēs,* and self-promoter we met above in Chapter One, boasts about 200 CE that he never won "by royal favor."[60] Lest we take this as rhetoric alone— Asclepiades' inscription is not shy about claiming credit—there may be evidence for such imperial interference in the case of Ti. Claudius Rufus of Smyrna.[61] This man fought his way to the finals of the Olympic *pankration* (about 215 CE). When night fell before either competitor had prevailed, the judges apparently awarded him the crown outright nonetheless. Perhaps this was because Rufus (unlike his opponent) had not enjoyed the advantage of a bye. His acquaintance with emperors seems as compelling a motive, however. Nor should we ignore the personal tastes of the élite themselves: these likely figured in no less than the desire to please others. In the last analysis, I suspect that only rarely will we ever be able to determine why members of the élite made the choices they did. As Jason König remarks, "The precise relationship between gladiator and athlete must have been constantly open to debate, and open to a whole range of different representations, carrying with them a variety of different implications for the relationships between Greek and Roman culture more generally."[62] This capacity of these two activities to carry so much meaning, on their own and in conjunction, is perhaps the most significant evidence for their importance.

SPORT OR SPECTACLE?

So far, I have argued that gladiatorial shows were closely enough linked to combat sports at least—to boxing, wrestling, and *pankration*—that gladiators themselves could lay claim to the superior status of athletes. I went on to suggest that sponsoring gladiatorial shows afforded an avenue for the élite in the Greek east to establish and confirm their status, an acceptable complement or alternative to paying for and presiding over traditional festival competition. Now, I move on to my third topic, and the most contentious. I am going to explore the possibility that gladiatorial spectacles have as much right to be considered "sport" as do the events of the standard athletic program of Greek festivals. This requires us to confront both ancient categorizations and our own, in respect to gladiatorial spectacles and to sport itself.

Let us begin with gladiators. There is a tendency, one that films like *Gladiator* do nothing to dispel, to use the term loosely to describe all those who appeared in the arena. This is misleading. A famous letter of Seneca is instructive:[63]

> I happened by chance on a noontime (*meridianum*) spectacle, hoping for entertainment and wit and some relaxation with which people's eyes can rest from human blood. On the contrary: the previous fighting was a source of pity. Now, all trifling aside, it is murder pure and simple. They have nothing to cover themselves; their bodies are completely exposed to blows, every one finds its mark. Why would they need protection, why skill? But many prefer this to ordinary pairs and encores. And why shouldn't they? No helmet, no shield repels the steel. In the morning, people are thrown to

lions and bears—at noon, to the spectators. They order killers to be thrown to those who will kill them in turn and hold back the victor for another slaughter. The only escape for the fighters is death.

The wild-beast fighter (*bestiarius, venator*) shared the day and the amphitheater with gladiators; some eventually got training at the Ludus Matutinus at Rome and so might gain fans and freedom. But they were very different: no one is known to have fought both beasts and men except the emperor Commodus. As for those who fought at noon, these were *noxii,* slaves condemned to die in the arena within a year of their sentence. Once masters could impose this sentence as they wished, selling their slaves to entrepreneurs who stocked amphitheater shows; by the late first century CE, the selling of slaves for this purpose was a prerogative of a public court: as in other areas, the emperors arrogated to themselves and their instruments powers once enjoyed by other élite Romans. In any case, untrained and unprotected, they were destined to die at their first appearance or soon after. It is the true gladiators, those who performed in the afternoon, who took on the distinctive equipment and tactics we recognize from archaeology and art. Advertisements from Pompeii are at some pains to maintain distinctions among these groups (*ILS* 5063, 5063a; cf. Apul. *Met.* 4.13). We should do the same: it is the true gladiators I will deal with here. These (we may conclude from Seneca) had protection, training, and some expectation of leaving the amphitheater alive.

Even among gladiators, however, there are necessary nuances. Most gladiators too were slaves, prisoners of war, or slaves condemned *ad ludum gladiatorium,* "to a gladiatorial school." This was a lighter sentence: according to legislation of the emperor Hadrian, it involved three years as an active fighter, then two more of service to the school. Freedom followed (*Collatio Mosaicarum et Romanarum legum* 11.7). Some fought in groups, as *gregarii,* perhaps as many as half of a spectacle's fighters. But (as we learn from the imperial edict controlling gladiatorial expenses) they were far from valueless. Successful *gregarii* might move on to fight in pairs. Gladiators might reenlist after their five years of service. Such returnees likely made up the majority of the *auctorati*, "paid contractors": daring and desperate young men of the élite (and female thrill seekers) fascinate our sources but likely appear there out of proportion to their actual numbers. Despite their status as free or freed men and women, *auctorati* served under the same terms as other gladiators. I do not think their willing entry into the arena affects our understanding of what they did there. Soldiers are soldiers, whether conscripts or volunteers.

We must now take up the ancient contexts of athletics and gladiatorial spectacles. If the gladiatorial contest was kept distinct from beast hunts and *meridiani,* "noontime spectacles," it was still more out of place in the context of Greek competitive sport. Athletic competitions in the Greek world were components of festivals for the gods. There they were joined by other contests too, for horses and sometimes mules in particular, but even at austere Olympia for heralds and trumpeters as well from 396 BCE.[64] Elsewhere, competitions in *mousikē* were common, in playing musical instruments and singing to them, in reciting poetry, in rhetoric. We hear occasionally of still other competitions: boat races, bull capturing, beauty contests. It is striking, then, that we have so little evidence for gladiatorial combats at such festivals.[65] Certainly they might coexist in other contexts in the western Empire. At Rome itself, C. Scribonius Curio, aiming at election as tribune, enhanced his father's funeral in 53 BCE with two movable wooden theaters, built back to back. He used both to display athletes and then, pivoting them to form an amphitheater, produced a gladiatorial spectacle (Pliny, *NH* 36.24.116–120). Eight years later, Julius Caesar constructed the first stadium at Rome, a temporary structure in the Campus Martius in which he held athletic competitions to mark his triumph. The same sequence of celebrations included gladiators (two eminent Roman citizens among them) fighting in the Forum (Suet. *Jul.* 39; Cass. Dio 43.23–24). Gladiators and athletes were both on display in the Ludi pro valetudine Caesaris. The senator and historian Cassius Dio observed a *gymnikos agōn* at which athletes were compelled to compete and women fought as gladiators (Cass. Dio 76.16.1, 200 CE).

Of gladiators in regularly scheduled Greek festivals, however, there is hardly a trace. The notion that Augustus introduced gladiators into the Panathenaea in 12 BCE rests on a misunderstanding of the text of Cassius Dio.[66] The 240 pairs of *monomachoi* who took part (along with conventional Greek athletes and musicians) in the extraordinary festival for Apollo arranged by King Antiochus IV of Syria at Daphne in 166 BCE were not Roman gladiators but local youths trained in single combat.[67] A dedication from Stratonicea (Caria) may refer to both a gladiatorial spectacle (*[mon]omachia*) and a penteteric festival (*a[gōn]*) for Zeus, Hecate, and Nemesis. The mention of Nemesis, often associated with gladiators, is suggestive, but the text is fragmentary and the relevant readings much supplemented.[68] To celebrate the completion of his city of Caesarea Sebaste in 10/9 BCE, King Herod of Judaea offered a lavish program of musical and athletic *agōnes* as well as horse races and displays of gladiators and wild animals (Joseph. *AJ* 16.136–141, *BJ* 1.415). He meant to inaugurate a penteteric festival in honor of Augustus, and both the emperor and his wife Livia made generous contributions for the occasion. This is of course a new foundation, not a traditional festival. Furthermore, we can not be sure of the relationship between the conventional Greek competitions and the gladiatorial spectacle—were they both meant to be part of future celebrations?—and it is apparent from Josephus' account that Herod's extravagance was unusual and intended to validate his ambitions to rule over a realm more in keeping with his abilities. In any case, philhellene though he was, neither Herod nor his people were Greek. Equally exceptional is another new festival, held at Nicopolis, just outside Alexandria. Here both an amphitheater and a stadium seem to have been involved in a penteteric celebration (in honor of Augustus' defeat of troops of Antony who left the city to meet him) mentioned by Strabo.[69] We know nothing more.[70]

Some traditional boundaries began to be erased in later an-

tiquity. The theater in third-century Aphrodisias, adapted for
gladiatorial spectacles and *venationes*, "wild beast hunts," also
displayed the portrait statues of prominent local boxers.[71] The
circus factions, professional organizations responsible for chariot
racing throughout the Roman Empire, began to extend their
reach to many kinds of shows, such as theatrical exhibitions and
mimes. Associations of athletes worked in concert with guilds of
actors, seeking (and often securing) the same rewards, perhaps
even sharing the same headquarters at times. Mixed entertain-
ments became more popular. Pantomimes entertained in the
intervals between *agōnes* and then (from the second century CE)
became competitors themselves;[72] at Oxyrhynchus in Egypt, six
chariot races shared a sixth-century CE bill with dogs, gazelles,
singing rope dancers, mimes, and a troupe of athletes (*POxy.*
2707). We hear of such hybrid performers as the Green-faction
wrestling dancers from Ephesus.[73] But still, gladiatorial combats
and athletics were kept apart.[74] Once again, Commodus may
have been the only person to compete in both.

We should not, however, be content merely to accept ancient
Greek attitudes here. After all, *we* commonly separate athletics
from equestrian events or treat both apart from contests in *mousikē*, even though all might be part of the same ancient festival
program.[75] Is there a compelling reason for us to group together
Greek games and gladiators? Some have thought so. In a review of recent books on gladiators, Ted Lendon remarks, "The
underlying assumption of most Romance scholarship is that
gladiatorial combat was a sport much like any modern sport."[76]
Lendon is a Canadian raised in Japan who now works in the
United States, and so if anyone knows how the French and Italians think, it ought to be him. Lendon's statement finds support
from Jean-Paul Thuillier, the leading authority on sport among
the peoples of ancient Italy. Thuillier notes that the exclusion
of gladiators from his handbook on Roman sport will surprise
the public at large.[77] His first explanation for his own decision
to leave them out is that their bouts took place at *munera* and
not at *ludi* along with chariot races and athletic contests. He
allows, however, that this is largely a pretext on his part, neces-

sitated by the bloody nature of gladiatorial combat. Because it is uncertain whether the Romans themselves would see a fundamental difference between these various spectacles, Thuillier in the end appeals to our own sense of what is appropriate and to the rigorous standards of the ancient Olympics, which (unlike other festivals) admitted only equestrian and athletic *agōnes*. In doing so, unfortunately, he has forgotten Olympia's trumpeters and heralds. We might also point out (mischievously) that the modern Olympics have not always drawn the lines so clearly: from 1928 to 2000, the medals presented to successful competitors featured a building with a striking resemblance to the Colosseum (as well as a racing chariot more at home in the Circus Maximus).[78]

The German scholar Stefan Müller equates gladiatorial spectacles and Greek athletic *agōnes* on the grounds that they share many of the criteria of a modern sport as defined by Allen Guttmann.[79] Both, according to Müller, are marked by secularization, equality of chances, specialization, rationalization, and bureaucratization; both lack two modern characteristics: quantification and an interest in records.[80] But Müller's argument is suspect. For one thing, Guttmann's categories themselves are not beyond question. Quantification and interest in records are not just evident but prominent in the tombstones and other monuments erected for gladiators, charioteers, and athletes alike. These do not mention the times or distances of individual performances of note, but they certainly enumerate how often competitors won. Athletes tend to specify only victories at major festivals and to lump together lesser triumphs. But they often count these too, and winners who had no successes at panhellenic or regional festivals were happy enough to tally their local triumphs. (The best example is provided by the Spartan father and son Damonon and Enymacratidas discussed in Chapters One and Two; *IG* 5.1 213.) Charioteers' monuments in the Roman circus, despite their lowly social status as slaves or freedmen, are remarkably expansive and detailed. The monument for Diocles, a circus star of the early second century CE, pays particular attention to the ways in which he won, counting times he led from the outset, snatched victory at the end, and came from behind, and displays other quantifiable distinctions as well (*ILS* 5287). For example, Diocles made eight horses winners one hundred times and one, two hundred times.

This variation in patterns of record keeping and record marking, in which charioteers' inscriptions are much the most elaborate, should not be regarded as purely premodern. Take baseball, a sport widely recognized (and ridiculed) for its store of statistics for all situations.[81] Here too concern to keep records and diversity in identifying which ones count are found together. When Sam Rice retired with 2,987 baseball hits in 1934, the career standard of 3,000 had not yet been established. It occasioned more comment when Al Kaline left the game with 399 home runs in 1974, but he had a good reason to leave: he wanted to spend time with his college-bound son.[82] Carlton Fisk's 3,999 total bases and his failure to become the first catcher with 4,000 went unnoticed on his retirement in 1994. This is still not regarded as a milestone fourteen years after. Offensive statistics such as these have developed unevenly. (The American League has kept records on unsuccessful base-stealing attempts since 1928, the National League only from 1950; the definition of a sacrifice fly changed several times before the present version was accepted in 1954.) Defensive statistics for fielders, much harder to determine and evaluate, are still a work in progress.

There is every likelihood that Greek athletes were in fact driven by the desire to set records—not, however, for times or distances but for priority and uniqueness.[83] In fact, athletes' ambition to be the first, say, to win three foot races at Olympia and then to be the only man to do it on the same day encouraged versatility rather than specialization. As I noted above in Chapter One, interest in records of just this kind has heightened within the last few years. The Greeks knew—and we have now rediscovered—that such records last when even the most extraordinary times or distances are surpassed. A more critical weakness of Müller's argument to equate Roman spectacle and Greek sport is logical: two things may be unlike something else (in this case, modern sport) without being of the same type themselves. "Modern sport" and "ancient sport" are not the only categories available.

Another approach to categorizing gladiatorial spectacles involves arriving at a definition of "sport" and then seeing whether it can be made to encompass gladiators. The narrower the definition, of course, the less likely this is. For Gerhard Horsmann, one scholar who has written on this issue at some length, sport must retain its original etymological associations, derived from the late Latin connotations of the verb *deportare*, "to disport oneself." It is a kind of play involving bodily activity. The brutality of their actions and the compulsion under which they act must exclude gladiators (though *auctorati* have something of a case).[84] Such considerations, persuasive as they are, did not prevent Paul Plass from titling his book on "arena sport" *The Game of Death in Ancient Rome.* Nor would they make it easy to treat Greek festival competition as sport. As Horsmann is well aware, "sport," with its overtones of play and implied contrast with what is serious, is a modern invention. My Ottawa high school boasted the English-language motto "Play the game"—not because it was ignorant of classical antiquity (I did five years of Latin there) but because such a slogan is simply not translatable into Greek or Latin. For the Greeks, athletic and equestrian sport was not fun but serious business, essential to establishing and reinforcing hierarchies among individuals and groups of all kinds. The Greek word for contest, *agōn,* is also the ultimate source of an English derivative. It is no accident that it is "agony." And sometimes the Greeks were not just serious about sport but deadly serious. We have already had occasion to mention the boxer Agathos Daimon and pile-ups on the chariot racecourse.

Now let us consider Cimon. Head of a famous Athenian family in the later sixth century BCE, his team of mares won three times at Olympia. He had the tyrant Pisistratus announced as the victor the second time and so won return from exile. His death soon after his third triumph, in 528, is plausibly blamed on Pisistratus' son, Hippias (Hdt. 6.103; Plut. *Cat. Mai.* 5.4; Ael. *VH* 9.32). A young and unproven ruler, he could not countenance such success by a potential rival. Winning at Olympia meant a lot more than just horsing around.

On the other hand, broader definitions may take in too much. Don Kyle—the only ancient historian of this generation to write major books in English on both Greek games and gladiators— leads off a valuable survey of scholarship, in the *Journal of Sport History,* with these words: "Herein 'sport' will generally refer to public, physical activities, especially those with competitive elements, pursued for victory, pleasure or the demonstration of excellence."[85] Under this rubric, Kyle discusses both gladiatorial spectacles and chariot racing (including the Byzantine circus), albeit much more briefly than Greek festival competition. This definition is quoted with approval by Waldo Sweet, author of a sourcebook on sport and recreation in ancient Greece, with the proviso that sport is competitive and recreation is not.[86] Sweet spends more space on "walking and mountaineering," "swimming and boating," "hunting and fishing," and "dining" than on horse racing and chariot racing.[87] This is in line with a definition that stresses physical activity but produces an odd context for what Greeks did at their agonistic festivals. A formulation by H. W. Pleket draws on those of both Kyle and Poliakoff (below) and also emphasizes physical competition and the goal of victory. It would seem to make room for gladiators (though not necessarily for the owners of equestrian entries).[88] In the same year, however, he invoked gladiators' involuntary participation as an argument against Müller.[89]

I am going to spend the rest of this chapter discussing the view of Michael Poliakoff, author of the standard book on Greek combat sports, who rejects the equation of Greek games and gladiatorial contests. His opinions deserve special attention due to the high quality of his work in general, its availability and accessibility (in both English and in German editions), and its influence.[90] To the attempt to equate Greek games and gladiatorial contests, his answer is "No." Poliakoff defines sport and athletics as "activity in which a person physically competes against another in a contest with established regulations and procedures, with the immediate object of succeeding in that contest under criteria for determining victory that are different from those that mark success in everyday life."[91] It should be obvious at once that this definition might apply to gladiatorial combat.

As physical as one could wish, such contests took place under set and recognized conditions.[92] The evening before, combatants dined at a banquet, open to the public—perhaps a form of advertising. The day itself began with a parade through the amphitheater, continued (in the case of mixed spectacles) with beast hunts and the execution of condemned criminals, and ended up with part or all of an afternoon set aside for gladiators. An official examination of weapons and a trumpet blast preceded the fighting, which was supervised by referees. Afterwards, victors—even those who were slaves—were awarded a palm leaf, perhaps a crown as well, and took a triumphant turn around the arena. Some of this—processions, heralds, crowns—recalls athletic festivals. What is as significant is this: as Poliakoff demands, both crowds and combatants understood what to expect *in general;* of course (as in athletics again), *particular* outcomes were unpredictable.[93] Care was taken to avoid collusion—fighters' pairings were determined only shortly before each show—and gladiators themselves were said to have disliked unequal matches, on the grounds that they diminished a victor's glory (Sen. *Dial.* 1.3.4; cf. Quint. *Decl. Mai.* 9.6). Matching was facilitated by ranking gladiators into one of four (or more) *pali,* "ranks."[94]

So far, so good. Poliakoff, however, adds a kicker to his definition of sport: warfare is to be regarded as part of everyday life in antiquity. This proviso leads to an argument against including gladiatorial combat among sports. "A gladiator fighting to kill or disable his opponent and save himself in any manner possible is not participating in a sport but in a form of warfare for spectators." Finally, Poliakoff takes the need of gladiators to put themselves under the control of the givers of the games as another sign that the arena was more purposeful than is consistent with sport's "more arbitrary conventions."

Let us take a closer look at this final section of Poliakoff's definition and its elaboration to exclude gladiators. First, the notion that warfare was part of everyday life in antiquity is far from self-evident. Citizen soldiers were for a long time basically seasonal workers, on campaign in the down times of the agricultural calendar; war was in fact only possible when everyday life came to a stop. To be sure, armies such as those on which Rome relied during the period in which gladiatorial combat was most popular were on duty year round. But they generally served on the frontiers of empire, far away from the city of Rome. Even the Greek East was occasionally threatened rather than under constant siege. Then, in retirement, soldiers often settled in veterans' colonies, out of sight as well as out of mind. Furthermore, the invocation of warfare forces Poliakoff into the rather absurd position of excluding fencing too from the world of sport.[95]

But let us accept Poliakoff's argument here. After all, it really functions as a segue to his most crucial distinction between gladiatorial combat and sport: that gladiators fought in deadly earnest under the direction of and for the entertainment of others. Of course, we might say the same of Greek heavy athletes. Athletes too gave up their usual freedom of action; indeed (as we have seen in Chapter Two), they agreed to submit to the degradation of slaves if they were thought to have infringed the rules of a competition. Yes, but gladiators used weapons and armor and even light-armed *retiarii* wore a loincloth: they were very different from Greek athletes, naked as they were. True. But it is also true that gladiators might make odd soldiers. Some of their equipment—the net and trident of the *retiarius,* the *murmillo*'s fish-crest helmet, the curved scimitar of the Thracian— was out of place in the Roman legions and obsolete most everywhere else. Moreover, one item of gladiatorial equipment that often figures prominently in accounts of the bloodiness of spectacles—the metal *caestus*—has been shown to be a mirage, a form of boxing glove used in later Greek athletics and not metal at all.[96]

I suggest that all this is beside the point. What troubles Poliakoff and prevents him and others from defining gladiatorial combat as "sport" is that combatants died. They did indeed. But so did heavy athletes; and so do boxers and wrestlers today; and football players, many of them high schoolers dehydrated from a summer scrimmage; and the occasional basketball player, like Pistol Pete Maravich, dead in his forties after a pick-up game, or a baseball all-star like Ray Chapman, beaned by Carl Mays' pitch, or hockey's Bill Masterton, who hit his head on the ice in the days before helmets. We may object that those deaths are tragedies, regretted by all. Spectators at gladiatorial games were different: they *wanted* to see deaths. But so, it seems, did some who watched Greek chariot races—or at least they took pleasure from slips and spills that were liable to lead to that result; so perhaps do some fans of what we nonetheless call motor sport today. But (to pursue our objections) that is still not the same. Deaths in the Greek heavy events, and even in modern boxing, are *byproducts* of those sports' dangers, accidents. What puts gladiatorial combat beyond the pale is that deaths were *expected*.

Now, there is no doubt that this was often true. Some gladiatorial bouts were designated *sine missione,* fights to a decision. Nevertheless, such fights were not the only kinds, and even they need not result in death for the loser.[97] A short digression is in order. Soon after the appearance of *Gladiator,* a Canadian newspaper carried the story of a training school for gladiator wannabes run by the Gruppo Storico Romano.[98] Offering three-day or three-month packages of courses in "forms of combat used in fights to the death in ancient Rome," this had been operating for some time in an arena just off the Appian Way; with the success of the film, it was at last fully booked. Clients, both male and female, took Roman names; the manager, a bank clerk, called himself Nero. ("If we were to stand outside cinemas selling ancient Roman weapons, we could become millionaires.") The newspaper ran the story under the headline "We who are about to die . . . take lessons." The reference is to the salute to the emperor gladiators give before they fight to the death in so many Hollywood films, *Gladiator* among them. It is also a salute Maximus, the hero of the film, conspicuously omits—and he is right. The only ancient attestation to the practice comes from a *naumachia,* a naval battle, not from a gladiatorial spectacle at all.[99] Gladiators might hope to survive.

Augustus in fact banned bouts to the death at Rome (Suet. *Aug.* 45.3). After all, he took control of the ancient models for the Gruppo Storico Romano, the gladiatorial schools, and would be concerned to protect his investment in skilled labor. Similarly, officials abroad could hardly hope to take over their predecessors' troupes (as they did) if the turnover was too high.[100] Bouts that were fought "with pointed weapons" or were designated as *apotomos,* "cruel, rigorous," were unusual enough to merit explicit mention on the inscriptions through which benefactors sought credit.[101] They may have required the authorization of the emperor. Others less dangerous must have been the norm, all the more because it was the expense of gladiators that largely led the emperor to reduce costs in 177 CE. Gladiators were normally leased to those who sponsored spectacles, but these sponsors needed to pay the replacement cost for fighters killed or maimed. As Michael Carter comments, this is an early example of the shopkeeper's maxim: "If you break him, then you buy him."[102] Certainly many gladiators died in the course of combat or after losing a bout. (It is interesting here that these were given a ritualized *coup de grâce* away from the arena floor and the eyes of the bloodthirsty crowd, though the precise manner of killing and location are both uncertain.) Many others died later of their wounds. However, no less an expert than Galen was proud of his record as physician to a gladiatorial troupe at Ephesus from 157 to 161 CE.[103] His account of his success in treating wounded fighters must have sounded plausible as well as impressive to his contemporaries:

> Fortunately, though many gladiators died in the
> previous years, under me none of the wounded died, as
> I said, nor did any die from any other wound, and the
> second *archiereus*—after the medical treatment had
> been entrusted to me by the first—likewise entrusted
> the care of the gladiators to me after seven and a

half months. For the first served as *archiereus* around
the autumnal equinox, and the second in high spring.
Again, since all were saved, after him the third and the
fourth and fifth likewise entrusted the medical treatment of the gladiators to me, so that I had plenty of
tests of my training.

It was apparently unusual, moreover, when eleven fights led
to eleven deaths (*ILS* 5062). An inscription from Claudiopolis
(Bithynia) lists gladiators with fifty or sixty fights to their credit;
Pompeian advertisements mention men who survived as many
as thirty bouts, fully half as losers; a Sicilian died at age thirty after twenty-one wins, nine draws—these were clearly not fights
to the death—and four defeats that he survived (*ILS* 5113). Unfortunately, this evidence (and more that could be cited) is too
spotty to permit confidence about casualty rates; Cassius Dio
observes that anyone hoping for an accurate accounting of the
numbers of beasts and gladiators killed during Caesar's spectacle
in 46 BCE would have a hard time getting it—exaggeration being an obstacle even for ancient inquiries (Cass. Dio 43.22.3–4).

Modern estimates (of course) tend to track scholars' over-
all characterization of these spectacles. David Potter, who treats
gladiators along with actors and charioteers in an excellent
overview of Roman "entertainers," suggests that five to ten percent of fighters died in each round of shows.[104] The author of
the standard work on Roman charioteers, Gerhard Horsmann,
thinks gladiators have more to do with warfare than with sport,
and (so) he reckons the death of one combatant in each pair as
the norm.[105] For middle ground, though it is no more solid, we
might have recourse to Georges Ville and his thoughtful and
thorough book on gladiators in the west. He reckons (mainly
on the basis of funerary inscriptions) that twenty percent of
fights resulted in death in the first century CE, about half two
centuries later.[106] (Ville does not speculate on the effects, if any,
of the edict.)

Long-lived gladiators, then—and we hear of one who claimed
to have reached age ninety-nine—would be exceptionally lucky

or exceptionally talented: Ville draws a parallel with air aces of the two world wars, who fought on after their mates died in their first or second duel. Ville's estimate for the earlier period implies that a gladiator might hope to fight from five to ten times before being killed. (A gladiator of average ability would have about six chances in ten of surviving five combats, about one in three of surviving ten.) In fact, some were freed before, after as few as three and seven bouts (*ILS* 5102, 5086). Would others face their tenth fight long before the first three years of their sentence was completed? Would freedom generally intervene? We do not know. Some gladiators fought more than once in the same spectacle; others complain that they fight so infrequently that they lose their edge.[107] Though tombstones occasionally provide both a gladiator's age at death and the number of his bouts, these are of limited use when we can not calculate the length of his career. Still, these are more consistent with a rate of three or four fights a year than with thirteen or fourteen, let alone thirty or forty. In the end, all we can conclude is that the system of incentives would make little sense if there were no hope of achieving them at all. In that case, a sentence *ad ludum* would be virtually as severe as one *ad gladium* or *ad bestias*.

We may well find gladiatorial spectacles reprehensible. I suppose that Romans might be equally horrified at the carnage—an appropriate word, whatever its etymology—on our roads and wonder whether this was some kind of ritualized lottery of death.[108] And I personally object to one very recent way of exploiting human suffering for the entertainment of others: reality TV shows such as *Trauma: Life in the ER* or *Cops*. I am not the only one who sees the similarity. Here is a snippet from a newspaper column, listing ways in which Americans resemble the Romans under Caligula: "They are rich. They grow fat and purge. They have excellent plumbing. They wear clunky sandals and vote in presidents or emperors on the hereditary principle. They watch *Survivor*." But I do not see why such feelings, mine or anyone else's, should substitute for analysis. Many of us find meat unappetizing or deplore the killing of animals to make it or will not eat shellfish because of the laws of *kashrut* or avoid honey in solidarity with the worker bees. Nevertheless, we would all agree (I imagine) that these things are food. Gladiators' claims to be athletes may not have convinced all the Greeks who knew them—issues of context and social status would have carried a lot of weight—but they sound reasonable enough to me.

This chapter has relied upon modern analogies and parallels to illuminate the links between Greek games and gladiatorial spectacles and to judge combatants' claims to be placed in the same category as competitors. The next will return to the relationship between the present and the past. This time, however, appeals to Greek sport to enhance the status of the modern Olympics are found to mystify more than they make clear.

Four   OLIVE-TINTED
SPECTACLES

*Myths in the Histories of the
Ancient and Modern Olympics*

In 1889, A. G. Spalding led a group of professional baseball players on a barnstorming tour of Europe. Himself a former star pitcher, Spalding was also a gifted and imaginative entrepreneur, one of the first players to control his own team, the dominant figure in the sporting goods business in nineteenth-century America, and the originator of a scheme—which found few followers—to give players different-colored hats to indicate their positions. (A contemporary newspaper said it made the team look like a Dutch bed of tulips.) He tried to arrange a game in the Colosseum. Though he offered to pay a $5,000 rental (in the days before $5,000 was chump change for ballplayers) and to donate gate receipts to charity, Roman archaeologists and officials balked, and the game never took place.[1]

Sixty-two years later, Bill Veeck, modern baseball's greatest showman, sought another strategy to associate the game with the world of the amphitheater: Grandstand Managers' Day. Fans of his St. Louis Browns were invited to submit a starting lineup for a game with the equally woeful Philadelphia Athletics. The four thousand entrants were then admitted to a special section of the stands and supplied with large white signs; these bore a large green YES on one side and a red NO on the other. The fans used the signs to determine tactics during the game, deciding (among other things) to play the infield back for a crucial double play and not to start a slow-footed runner from first base on a full count. Playing the fans' lineup and guided by their advice, the Browns won 5–3, ending a four-game losing streak. Like the lucky gladiators who benefited from a Colosseum crowd's support, however, they too had to fight again, and they went on to lose five of their next six games under their usual professional management.[2]

What is going on here? It is true that nineteenth-century ballplayers and their bosses tended to have more exposure to the ancient world than their modern successors (including the Mets' Cleon Jones).[3] Another early titan, Charles Comiskey, was called the Old Roman (because of his patrician profile), and Ernest L. Thayer's 1888 poem "Casey at the Bat" was widely recognized at the time as a parody of "Horatius at the Bridge." Bill Veeck did not need classical models for his promotions: Grandstand Managers' Day took place just five days after the famous pinch-hit appearance by the midget Eddie Gaedel, an event inspired not by dwarf gladiators in the Colosseum but by a New York Giants' mascot. Nevertheless there should be no doubt that the Colosseum (or cinematic representations of it) did lie behind Veeck's experiment in fan power. The parallel with arena etiquette, which encouraged the official who presided over the spectacle to refer a fallen gladiator's fate to the crowd, is too clear. Besides, Veeck had studied Latin in high school—his teacher was named Annie Euripides Goodchild—and the memoir from which I have taken my account refers to a patron of the Colosseum "moaning that he had missed the magic moment when the lion first sank his teeth into martyred flesh because some big slob selling roasted chestnuts had cut off his view."[4]

On each of these separate occasions, then, baseball impresarios were willing to expend considerable effort and expense to link their sport with the gory glory that was Rome, despite there being no real connection whatsoever.[5] This effort is a particularly interesting instance of a widespread phenomenon: the urge to give the practices of the present more legitimacy and to make them more impressive by clothing them in the trappings and authority of the past. It is of course not confined to the world of sport. Invented traditions have been identified in areas as diverse as the whipping of boys at Spartan altars, the dining rituals of Oxbridge colleges, and ceremonies of transition in Africa. But sport does provide a prominent and recurring example, the modern Olympic Games—what I will call (for reasons which will become clear later in the chapter) the International Olympic Committee—IOC—Olympics. Even today, Greek sport is used to establish and enhance status. Every Olympic year—and the games are now biennial—officials, competitors, and commentators vie in paying homage to the original festival and to the supposed survival of its spirit after so many centuries. This homage took a novel and singularly moving form in 2004, when the shotput was staged in the ancient Olympic stadium. Furthermore, the saga of the games has a hero, a man whose gallant and lonely dream to revive the games was finally fulfilled at Athens in 1896. This is the French baron Pierre de Coubertin, who staked a claim to immortality through the Olympics in the manner of the greatest athletes of old. In the case of the Olympic festival, efforts are made to offer specific links with the modern games. De Coubertin's role as their only begetter is too well established to require demonstration. As it happens, however, myths pass for history in both regards.

In this chapter, I will make three arguments above all: first, that our understanding of the ancient Olympics is impeded rather than improved by constant comparisons to the modern games; second, that the usual account of the origins of the modern Olympics and of de Coubertin's position as their prime mover is partial and misleading; and third, that these two facts are interrelated. In doing so, I hope to persuade readers that using the past for the purposes of the present is likely to lead to misrepresentation. What is more important, perhaps, I hope to show that this practice may also limit our ability to shape the future as we wish.

ANCIENT AND MODERN

I will begin with four elements of the IOC Olympics that are sometimes (wrongly) associated with the ancient festival. The first (and easiest to dispose of) is the Olympic motto: "Swifter, higher, stronger." Of course, this is merely a translation of the original, in an ancient language common to all participants or at least to the élites of the European and American nations that once produced the overwhelming majority of them. That original—*citius, altius, fortius*—is not Greek, however, but Latin. Greek athletes, trainers, officials, and others swore an oath to compete fairly, a verbal expression of an Olympic ideal, but we hear of no motto, let alone one in a foreign tongue. Perhaps branding of this sort was unhellenic; at any rate, though states used symbols—Athens' owl, the seal (*phōkē*) of Phocaea—to identify their coins, they did not use mottoes.

And speaking of symbols (our second element): the five interconnected rings are among the world's most recognizable, but have nothing to do with the ancient games. Devised by Pierre de Coubertin in 1913, they were initially meant to stand for the five official IOC festivals held at the time and were later reinterpreted to represent the world's five continents, united in the Olympic movement.[6]

Our third element is the torch relay, most impressive of all sport rituals, combining as it does a dramatic buildup of interest as the torch nears the end of its journey from Olympia to the site of the games and the involvement of thousands of runners; some champions (however briefly: Ben Johnson carried the torch down Toronto's Queen Street on his way to a doping disqualification after the 100 meters at Seoul in 1988); most, ordinary citizens able to take part in this way alone. Nothing expresses so well the modern ideal of participation for those at all levels of ability all over the world or better builds support for the Olympic movement. The modern ideal of participation is appropriate, since the relay is a modern invention, introduced at Berlin in 1936. There were indeed torch races, including relays, at some Greek athletic festivals, and those at night on horseback (as at the festival for Bendis at Athens) must have been spectacular. The ceremonial transfer of the flame from the 2004 games at Athens into Italian hands in December 2005, which took place in the restored Panathenaic stadium amidst skaters and actresses dressed as priestesses, was clearly designed to evoke ancient Greek traditions. In ancient Greece, though the winner of the *stadion* race earned the honor of kindling the great sacrifice to Zeus, which was the signature ceremony of the ancient Olympics, there was no relay there, nor need for a rite of transition when the festival was always held at the same site.[7]

The fourth and final element is the marathon. This is certainly an ancient Greek word; an ancient Greek place (on the coast about 25 miles northeast of Athens); and an ancient Greek battlefield, the scene of a famous victory by the Athenians and Plataeans over a Persian expeditionary force in 490 BCE. Furthermore, it was a Greek who won the first marathon race—but a modern Greek, Spyros (or Spyridon) Louis, at the first IOC Olympics of 1896. (Louis won despite stopping at a taverna for a glass of wine—this was before the days of drug tests.) The marathon was never an ancient Olympic event. The length of the closest thing to it, the *dolichos* ("long race"), is unknown, but it would have been no more than twenty-four lengths of the stadium, about the distance of the 5000 meters today. Actually, far from being an ancient Greek event, the marathon might be regarded as modern English. The race itself was inspired by a poem by Robert Browning, who for the first time—in 1879—combined two unreliable Greek stories about the courier Pheidippides or Philippides (even the name is uncertain) and his run to Athens to announce the victory at Marathon. A French educator, Michel Bréal, admired the poem, recommended the event to de Coubertin, and provided a silver cup for the winner. The distance, precisely 26 miles, 385 yards (42.195 km), first established at the London games of 1908, is owed to the desire of members of the British royal family to see both the start (at Windsor Castle) and the finish (before the royal box at White City stadium).[8] Weary Olympic marathoners should feel fortunate that Bréal did not encourage an event based on the other run attributed to Pheidippides, over the mountains to seek Spartan assistance before the battle. A journey of some 150 miles, this has since given rise to the Spartathlon, inaugurated in 1983.[9]

Quite aside from such misconceptions, it is plausible to think that the ancient Olympics are as different from the modern as they are similar and in significant ways. This is worth stressing. No one has done more than David Young to demystify the nature of Greek athletics—especially in dispelling the myth of amateurism—and the prehistory of the modern games. Throughout this chapter, I am deeply indebted to his three seminal books.[10] Yet even he, acute and clear-eyed critic that he is of unquestioned assumptions in this area, chooses to emphasize the fundamental unity of the ancient and modern games. So poetry—Pindar's ancient epinicians and a modern imitation in praise of the games composed by George Robertson, sixth in the discus in 1896—causes us "to be reminded once again how authentic our own Games are because of genuine influences from ancient Greece."[11] He goes further in his most recent work: "In essence, the two are the same . . . Our Olympics are not so much a revival of the ancient Greek games as a genuine continuation of them."[12] In order to provide a basis for evaluating such claims, I present here twelve important distinctions between the Greek Olympics and our own.

REGULARITY

De Coubertin's Olympics were meant to be held every four years after their inception in 1896. They were indeed repeated in 1900 and 1904. But these festivals did not match the success of the first, and an intercalary Olympics was staged at Athens in 1906 in an attempt to revive the enthusiasm awakened ten years before. This was in fact well attended and featured (among other lasting innovations) an opening parade of teams, but it has never been accepted as an official Olympiad by the IOC. Subsequent Olympics, in 1916, 1940 and 1944, were canceled because of war. More recent competitions have been plagued by the politics of participation. The 1936 People's Olympics in Barcelona, designed as a counter to the Nazi-run games in Berlin and sponsored by the Spanish government, were canceled only because of the outbreak of the civil war. In 1968, the Olympic Project for Human Rights asked Black athletes to boycott the Mexico City games as a protest against racism. (Female athletes preferred to term this a girlcott, a word apparently coined by American runner Lacey O'Neal.) Most refused, on the grounds that they in particular had overcome too much to miss the opportunity to appear on sport's biggest stage; Tommie Smith and John Carlos, gold and bronze medallists at 200 meters, used that spotlight to protest in their own way, by giving their memorable Black Power salutes.[13] But at least one great athlete did heed the call for a boycott, the basketball star Lew Alcindor (later Kareem Abdul-Jabbar). Thirty-two nations, mostly African, refused to come to Montreal in 1976 because of the presence of South Africa. The United States and its allies boycotted the Moscow games of 1980 in response to the Soviet occupation of Afghanistan, a snub returned by the Eastern bloc at Los Angeles four years later. Cuba—one of the world's great sporting nations—and North Korea stayed home in 1988.[14] In none of these games, as a consequence, was the competition world class.

In contrast, the ancient games were held every four years from their beginning for a millennium or more with virtually no break. Admittedly, their traditional foundation date, 776 BCE, is unlikely to be reliable. It was almost certainly fixed by Hippias of Elis, who compiled the first list of Olympic victors about 400 BCE.[15] In the absence of records for the earliest festivals, Hippias probably reckoned back from a significant celebration, perhaps that following the seizure of the Olympic sanctuary from Pisa by Elis (which may be dated to 576 BCE) or that after the final failure of the Persian invasion, a prime opportunity for the expression of panhellenic patriotism and for thanksgiving to Zeus. This was in 476 BCE. Alternatively, Hippias may have dated the first Olympiad by relating the legendary Spartan lawgiver Lycurgus, sometimes said to have been involved in establishing the Olympic truce, to his contemporaries in the Spartan king lists. In any case, even in antiquity Hippias' date drew doubters: Plutarch thought it had no compelling basis (Plut. *Num.* 1.4), and some scholars opted for 884 BCE, explaining that 776 merely marked the Olympiad at which victors were first recorded. Modern archaeologists tend to support a later date. They note, for example, that wells appear in the eastern end of the sanctuary at the end of the eighth century and become more numerous over time, presumably to supply competitors and spectators with water.

Whenever the ancient Olympics began, however, they continued in sequence. There were occasional hiccups. As we have seen, Sulla managed a boycott of his own in 80 BCE when he brought Greece's adult athletes to his Ludi victoriae Sullanae and left only the boys' *stadion* race for Olympia. The *hellanodikai* declared Nero's festival, rescheduled from 65 to 67 CE, an "anolympiad." But over all, the games were remarkably regular before they suffered the fate of other festivals when Theodosius I outlawed pagan worship in 391 and 392 CE—unless they survived until fire destroyed the temple of Zeus and his grandson Theodosius II restated that ban in 426, or even later.[16]

The Greeks could set their calendars by the Olympics. And they did. Timaeus of Tauromenium used Olympiads (along with other means) to date events in his history of Sicily and the western Mediterranean in the late fourth or early third century BCE and the fashion took. So Diodorus of Sicily, writing in the first century BCE, introduces his account of the year 332/1 BCE in this way (Diod. Sic. 17.40.1): "When Niceratus was archon at Athens, the Romans elected as consuls M. Atilius and M. Valerius, and the one hundred twelfth Olympic festival was held, the one in which Grylus of Chalcis won (the *stadion* race)." Such a panhellenic chronology never completely supplanted local systems (especially on documents) but was clearly essential for the many Greeks who (then as now) might not have a complete list of the priestesses of Hera at Argos to hand, all the more when an event of more than regional significance was in question. It was only possible because there were no breaks in the train of festivals. Even Nero's, nullified as it was, kept its place as the two hundred eleventh Olympiad precisely for this purpose.

LOCATION

Held at Athens in 1896 and 1906, the IOC Olympics returned to the Greek capital in 2004. In the meantime, they had traveled to Melbourne and Sydney, Tokyo and Nagano, St. Louis and Stockholm, Cortina and Calgary, to every continent except Africa. Cities compete to host the games, sometimes using bribes and dirty tricks that would put the most drug-dependant athletes to shame. Such competitions were not unknown in antiquity: cities of the eastern Roman Empire sought the status of *neokoros,* a center for the cult of the emperor, with "arguments . . . which are perhaps not so far removed in spirit from the more idealistic elements of modern Olympic bids, with their appeals to historical heritage and tourism potential."[17] But they did not sully the ancient Olympic festival. This always took place at Olympia, an isolated sanctuary at the junction of the Alpheus and Cladeus rivers, about 60 km by road from Elis, the leading city of the region of that name in a fertile part of the northwest Peloponnese, and (according to one of Socrates' interlocuters) a fearsome journey from Athens (Xen. *Mem.* 3.13.5).

PROGRAM

The IOC program is constantly expanding, from the 43 events (the largest number in track and field) in 1896 to the 301 in 2004 at Athens in fields as disparate as synchronized swimming, weightlifting, and archery. One reason for the expansion is the right of host nations to introduce demonstration events, in the hope that these will eventually gain entry as medal sports; so curling, reintroduced after sixty-four years at Calgary in 1988, became part of the official program at Nagano in 1998. As this example indicates, nations generally propose sports in which they have a good chance of winning. This tendency had already led to the creation of a separate quadrennial festival for winter sports, now scheduled to fall at the midpoint of the regular Olympic cycle.[18] Another motive for adding events is gender equality: women too now compete in wrestling, and their program in track and field has gradually grown almost to match men's (though their all-round championship, the heptathlon, comprises seven events rather than ten, and they do not yet race-walk 50 km). Money is a third motive, as the TV networks that provide so much of the income for the games (and their advertisers) push for more telegenic competitions (like beach volleyball) as well as for the most popular to be held at times when they can guarantee the largest and most lucrative audiences.

The ancient festival (see Table 4–1) was much more conservative. New events were added only gradually after 776 BCE (to accept the traditional date), usually one at a time. After the adoption of the *hoplitēs,* the race in armor in 520 BCE, the athletic program remained virtually unchanged (with one exception) for some 900 years. Religious conservatism is often invoked to explain this stability. The fact that what we know about competition in the ancient Greek world invariably comes from the context of cult makes this hypothesis difficult to test. We may note, however, that there were only a few athletic and equestrian events attested elsewhere that could have been added to the Olympic program: there was nothing as widespread as, say, golf is today, which might have been a candidate. The desire to maintain Olympia's distinctiveness must also have mattered here. Practicality too: there were boat races at Isthmia and the Panathenaea, but Olympia was inland, its rivers rarely navigable in the summer (if at all), and its water supply inadequate even for athletes and visitors until the benefactions of Herodes Atticus and his family in the second century CE.

The one area in which the Olympics experienced significant growth in the classical and Hellenistic periods was in the equestrian program. The hunger for Olympic fame must have combined with the political and economic power of the élite who raised and ran horses, a supposition confirmed by the prominence of royal winners in the fourth and third centuries BCE. Nero was merely less fastidious than other monarchs, not more ambitious.

TABLE 4-I. DEVELOPMENT OF THE OLYMPIC PROGRAM

Date	Event
776 BCE	*Stadion*
724	*Diaulos*
720	*Dolichos*
708	Pentathlon
	Wrestling
688	Boxing
680	Four-horse chariot race
648	*Pankration*
	Horse race
632	Boys' *stadion*
	Boys' wrestling
628 (dropped 628)	Boys' pentathlon
616	Boys' boxing
520	Hoplite race
500 (dropped 444)	*Apēnē*
496 (dropped 444)	*Kalpē*
408	Pairs chariot race
396	Trumpeters
	Heralds
384	Chariot race for colts
264	Pairs chariot race for colts
256	Colts' race
200	Boys' *pankration*

PRIZES

One of the IOC's great successes has been its prizes, the gold, silver, and bronze medals awarded to the first three finishers. These have not only contributed a new verb to the English language—"to medal," the usual minimum goal of every Olympic competitor—but have become synonymous with the standing they reward. Winners are now often said to have brought home the gold medal even in contests in which no medals, and sometimes no prizes at all, are on offer. Some Greek festivals also recognized those who finished second or even (though this is less certain) third.[19] Most prestigious among them was the Panathenaea, where in the fourth century BCE those who came in second in athletic events received a fifth of the winner's allotment; equestrian runners-up received as much as seven-twentieths. At the Greek Olympics, however, there was one winner only, his prize a wreath from an olive tree sacred to Zeus, cut in the Altis by a golden sickle in the hands of a boy whose parents were both alive—a sign of good fortune. This too had resonance beyond Olympia: Athenians announced the birth of a boy by a sprig of olive on the door of the house.

GROUPS AND INDIVIDUALS

Both teams and individuals compete in today's Olympics. There are team sports and events (hockey, volleyball, relay races, once tug-of-war) and besides this individuals' results are combined to identify a winning team in (for example) gymnastics and dressage. There was none of this at the Greek festival. There was just one prize, for the winner, and he did not share it. Team competitions were essentially confined to the torch relays, boat races, pyrrhic dances, ball games, and free-for-alls that made up part of the training of young citizens for war and of the program of some local festivals; even in these individual winners might be recognized, as in a torch race on Hellenistic Cos (*SEG* 45.1127).[20] War was the team sport for the Greeks, the clash of massed phalanxes of armed infantry above all.

MEASUREMENT

We have already had occasion to observe that the contemporary concern for measuring individual performances is a relatively recent development. We do hear of some very few individual achievements, by Greek athletes, such as the 55- and 52-foot jumps of Phayllus and Chionis, but these come completely without context. We know nothing about the circumstances surrounding these extraordinary feats, not even at which athletic festival they occurred—another factor that renders them implausible; moreover, no ancient source makes any effort to bring them into relation with each other. Today, of course, every performance is evaluated against earlier standards, with special care to take into account circumstances such as wind velocity and altitude to ensure outcomes are truly commensurable. Just as interesting, I think, is the special attention given the modern Olympic records themselves, even though they may (and often do) fall some way short of a world mark. Is the effect to diminish the distinction of an Olympic champion, even an Olympic record-setter? If so, it is something the Greeks would find hard to understand.

NATIONALISM AND INTERNATIONALISM

Two hundred and two nations took part in the 2004 Olympics, with Kiribati and independent East Timor (Timor Leste) attending for the first time. An official appearance at the Olympics has become a sign of acceptance into the world community on a par with admission to the United Nations, and Kiribati's and Timor's athletes did not shine. But a trap shooter won the first gold medal for the United Arab Emirates, and a weight lifter became the first Thai woman champion (soon followed by another); athletes from Kiribati and Timor will no doubt mount the podium in time. The IOC Olympics are indeed truly international.

Competitors likewise thronged to the ancient festival from all over the Mediterranean basin and beyond, from Marseilles to Mesopotamia, from the Black Sea to the Nile: but all were Greeks. We have already touched on Alexander I's appearance at Olympia (above, Chapter One). His performance in the *stadion* race was praiseworthy in itself (it seems that he ran a dead-heat with the eventual winner), but its real purpose was to establish the credentials of the Macedonian royal family as Greeks rather than wild northern barbarians like their Thracian and Illyrian neighbors. (Only his father Philip's military and political successes permitted Alexander III to turn up his nose at his predecessor's path to acceptance and avoid competitions altogether.) Power had its privileges: Germanicus and Tiberius, potential and real successors of the emperor Augustus, won equestrian victories before Nero's. But another Roman exception to the eligibility of Greeks only may be the result of confusion in our sources. Gaius of Rome is said (by Phlegon, *FGrH* 257 F 12) to have shared the Olympic crown for the *dolichos* in 72 BCE with Hypsicles of Sicyon. A dead-heat seems less probable in a middle-distance race than a sprint, and no Roman citizen would be designated by his *praenomen,* "Gaius," alone. The preferable solution is to imagine that Hypsicles won the race but later became a Roman citizen and took the name Gaius Hypsicles. Auphidius (Aufidius) of Patras, *stadion* champion in 20 BCE, was probably one of the many Romans who had moved to Greece (there was a Roman colony at Patras) and gone native; so also Valerius of Mytilene, winner at the same distance in 45 CE.

The ancient festival, then, was on its face a much more nationalistic enterprise than today's. To some extent, however, this is an illusion. Contemporary competitors must be sponsored by a national Olympic committee,[21] march in an opening procession carrying their national flags, and hear their national anthems (or some approximation) as they receive their medals. Tallies of medals won by each nation may be unofficial but are widely reported nonetheless, and Canada is not the only place where Olympic failures and all too infrequent triumphs are treated as symptoms of the state of the nation.[22] Greeks, for their part, may have entered as individuals—there is no evidence for state support—but cities sent official delegates, *theōroi,* heralds proclaimed the champions' fathers and fatherlands, and winners might find themselves wooed to represent another city in a subsequent festival.[23] The most famous of these free agents was Astylus of Croton. After winning both the *stadion* and *diaulos* races at Olympia in 488 and 484 BCE, Astylus repeated both wins in 480 and even added an unprecedented third victory, in the race in armor. This time, however,—or perhaps the time before—he was proclaimed as a Syracusan, the result of the blandishments and booty of Hieron, soon to become tyrant of Syracuse. In response, the Crotoniates tore down Astylus' statue and turned his home into a prison (Paus. 6.13.1).

CATEGORIES OF COMPETITORS

Though their presence provoked some opposition, not least from de Coubertin himself, women have long vied at the modern Olympics. For the most part, however, they do so apart from men, running and swimming (for example) virtually the same distances but in separate competitions. Mixed teams (in tennis and badminton) are exceptional; only in some sailing and equestrian events is sex irrelevant. De Coubertin envisaged women in a more decorative role than striving and sweating. "Their primary role should, as in the ancient tournaments, be to crown the (male) victors with laurels."[24] In fact, married women were excluded from the ancient Olympic festival, even from crossing the Alpheus—the priestess of Demeter Chamyne alone was excepted—and it is not quite certain that unmarried girls were allowed.[25] And yet (as we saw in Chapter One) both could compete. In antiquity too the equestrian competition was anomalous: as it was owners of an entry who won the wreath and these rarely drove their own chariots or mule carts, let alone rode their own horses, women could compete from afar (as the winners of flat and harness races often do today).

Thus, the modern Olympics group contestants by sex; the Greeks did not. On the other hand, there are no age classes today. Youthful athletes have a clear advantage in some sports. The youngest medalist took part in the first IOC games, a Greek gymnast (Dimitris Loundras) who won bronze in the parallel bars at age ten. Immaturity continues to be an asset in this area. Nadia Comaneci, born in 1961, won her first Olympic gold medal—and the first perfect score of 10 in competition—at Montreal in 1976. She won more in 1980, making nine in all, but retired the next year, already struggling to overcome the changes in her young body. Some precocious stars continue to shine. When Fu Mingxia of China won gold in 10-meter platform diving in 1992, she became, at age fourteen, the youngest Olympic champion ever. "I think" (she said) "a female diver can easily reach the peak of her career before fifteen." Fu went on, however, to double in the 3-meter springboard and the platform events in 1996 and then retired. Her return to world-class competition and her springboard gold medal in 2000 marked her ability and longevity as exceptional. The longest careers, unsurprisingly, occur in sports where suppleness and strength are less essential. A Swedish shooter, Oscar Swahn, won a gold medal in 1912 at age sixty-four and a silver eight years later, at age seventy-two. These were in team events; his son competed alongside him.

In the absence of team events, Greek fathers who appeared together with their sons would have to be rivals (unless the younger man served as a charioteer or driver). Perhaps this was felt to be undesirable. In any case, like the other panhellenic games, the ancient Olympics had age classes early on.[26] That Philostratus could put forward an alternative date (596 BCE) for the introduction of the boys' *stadion* race (Philostr. *Gym.* 13) and that no tale embellishes it (as do the stories about the adoption of nudity for athletes and trainers) suggest that the existence of age classes was taken for granted.

The Olympics differed from the Isthmian and Nemean festivals (and probably from the Pythian too from the Hellenistic period) by dividing athletes into just two classifications, men (*andres*) and boys (*paides*), not three. (The intermediate "beardless youths," *ageneioi*, were lacking.) Boys were seventeen and younger.[27] Because Greek cities had no birth certificates and states used different calendars and varying methods of calculating and affirming majority, a competitor's category had to be determined by officials, influenced as they might be by such criteria as physical development and expert testimony. (It took the intervention of Agesilaus to ensure that the son of Eualces of

Athens was placed in the category of *paides* though he was "biggest of the boys" [Xen. *Hell.* 4.1.40; Plut. *Ages.* 13.3].)[28] They swore to make their judgments as fairly as they could, as they did in allocating horses to the classes of *pōloi,* two- and three-year-old colts, and adult horses when the equestrian program was expanded beginning in 384 BCE.

We do not know whether successful colts went on to repeat as mature horses. Aristotle says that moving into the *andres* category was unusual for victors among the *paides,* because they had a tendency to over-train and burn out, but even the evidence still available—and Aristotle, who compiled lists of Olympic and Pythian victors, had a lot more—does not bear him out.[29] Some might go on to very long careers: Milon of Croton won the boys' wrestling in 540 BCE and then five or even six times as a man, a time at the top of something like twenty-five years, and he was not unique. But none could match the staying power of the owners of horses and mules. Because the owners need not (and generally did not) risk their own bodies, they could enter and win well into old age—another way in which their wealth gave the élite an advantage over poorer contestants, and another in which equestrian events were special. Modern Olympic equestrians, whatever their backgrounds, must compete along with their mounts.

One further divergence merits mention in this connection: as they separate men and women, the IOC Olympics also require wrestlers, boxers, and other fighters, as well as weight-lifters and some rowers, to compete in categories defined by weight. This certainly increases the number of events and of winners—always an important consideration because gold medals, like olive wreaths, do not seem to become less valuable as their availability increases—but is generally justified on the grounds of fair and equal competition. The cultural bias of such arrangements is shown by the lack of divisions by weight (or height or reach or any other corporeal measure) at ancient Olympia. That is one reason boxing, wrestling and *pankration* were known as "the heavy events."

CONTEXT: SECULAR
AND RELIGIOUS

Pierre de Coubertin thought of Olympism as a religion, complete with church, dogma, and cult, and some of his successors on the IOC (Brundage, Samaranch) declared themselves adherents.[30] There is a modern Olympic oath, written by de Coubertin and sworn by an athlete of the host nation on behalf of all since 1920 and (in a modified form) by a judge for all officials since 1972. It highlights the "true spirit of sportsmanship." The Olympic hymn, first adopted officially for Rome in 1960 but a part of the festival since 1896, invokes the "immortal spirit of antiquity/father of the true, beautiful and good." (It was composed by a Greek.) And of course the contemporary games have no shortage of rituals. For all that, the IOC Olympics are secular. Their international spread guarantees this because (whatever the private preferences of IOC members) it would be impossible to find any explicitly religious expressions or acts that would be acceptable to everyone.[31]

The environment of the original games could not be more dissimilar. Like all regular and recurring athletic competitions in ancient Greece, they were a part, however prominent, of a religious festival, in this instance, of one extending over five days from 468 BCE, with a sixth added sometime later.[32] The sanctuary was associated with Zeus in particular and Zeus Olympios, "Olympian Zeus," was the focus of the festival's main ritual, held on the second full moon after the summer solstice. The hecatomb was a sacrifice of one hundred oxen at Zeus' conical altar in the Altis, created from the ashes of earlier offerings and, in the time of Pausanias, about seven meters high and ten meters in diameter (Paus. 5.13.8–11). Other religious observances at the festival included a procession, led by priests of Zeus, around sixty-three of the other altars also located within the Altis, and sacrifices at the shrine of Pelops. Ancient Greek athletes and officials also took an oath (with older family members standing in for *paides*) before an image of Zeus, which Pausanias calls "the one most likely to strike terror into the hearts of sinners"

(Paus. 5.24.9). It held a thunderbolt in each hand. Those unawed by these may have had more reverence for other representations of Zeus at the entrance of the stadium: the Zanes, bronze statues of the god paid for by the hefty fines levied against those caught breaking the rules. Another image of Zeus, the 12-meter high gold and ivory statue by Phidias, looked from his temple towards the stadium to the east. No one at Olympia could ignore the presence of the gods.

FACILITIES

The IOC Olympics provides unmatched stages for athletes—the worldwide television audience in 2004 was estimated at 3.9 billion viewers—and unrivaled windfalls for those who build them. Structures and facilities make up much of the appeal of cities' bids to the IOC and of their justification to citizens. Arenas, stadiums, swimming pools, athletes' villages, the transportation networks needed to link them: all are sold as the games' ongoing legacy. Sometimes they are. The ancient Panathenaic stadium in Athens, rebuilt for Zappas' games of 1870, and the main venue for the IOC games of 1896, was the scene of the archery finals and the end of the marathon in 2004. (Neither, of course, was an event in the Greek Olympics or the Panathenaea.) Calgary's oval has been a magnet for the world's best speedskaters since 1988. Other legacies have been less lucky. Montreal mayor Jean Drapeau told his citizens that the Olympics could no more run a deficit than a man could have a baby. The debt incurred in 1976 was retired in 2006, when little Jean turned thirty, and the vast cavern that remains, one of the most inhospitable places to watch a baseball game outside the planet Neptune, deserves much of the blame for the Expos' departure for Washington.

Olympia was less elaborate. Buildings there certainly were: the most visible were the great temples of Zeus and Hera; the Bouleterion, where athletes swore their oath; the Prytaneion, where victors were feasted. New ones were added as time went by: late archaic treasuries to advertise the prominence of the donor states; the Philippeion, which served the same purpose for Macedon's king; the Echo Stoa; the *palaestra*. Statues of victors—one of their main prerogatives—studded the Altis: Pausanias mentions about two hundred in a selective survey, and more than sixty are known from other sources.[33] But though the stadium was moved and reconstructed, it grew to accommodate only 45,000 or so, and these mostly on earthen embankments. Compare this to the Circus Maximus, where as many as 150,000 Romans could watch chariot races, or the Colosseum, with its carefully demarcated seating areas and entrances, its hydraulic lifts and awnings, its space for 55,000.

Even among Greek festival sites, Olympia was unremarkable in its provisions for visitors; Isthmia, easily accessible on major north-south and east-west routes by both land and sea and an administrative center for Roman Greece, offered much more in the way of comfort (including something like an athletes' village). Epictetus brings out the value of the Olympic experience by enumerating the inconveniences it entails: the heat, the crowds, the noise, the shortage of water and shelter (Arr. *Epict. diss.* 1.6.26–28). Yet it was worth the trouble. A baker boasts on his tombstone that he made the long journey to the Olympic festival from his home in Macedonia twelve times in the third century CE (*SEG* 48.736 [on p. 218]).

COSTUMES

Adidas supplied uniforms for all staff, volunteers, technical officials, and torch runners at the 2004 Olympics. It also made uniforms for about half of all athletes, including superstars such as Australian swimmer Ian Thorpe (the Thorpedo) and American sprinter Maurice Greene. Adidas' uniforms incorporated a number of technological advances. For one, ClimaCool clothing "actively conducts heat and sweat away from the body through a combination of heat- and moisture-dissipating materials. . . . An athlete can actually stay cooler in ClimaCool than they can in bare skin." Costumes made of ClimaCool are customized with the aid of infrared cameras that identify an athlete's crucial heat and sweat zones. (A recent addition to the Olympic oath abjures drugs, but wearing steroids is still legit.) For their part, swimmers such as Thorpe sported the JETCONCEPT body suit, reducing drag and water turbulence enough to improve performance by up to three percent—more than sufficient to make a difference in a race. How do I know all this? Well, Adidas does not exactly keep it a secret: its prominence at the Olympics is treated as an endorsement of its products in itself.

Greek athletes, for their part, were well suited (or unsuited) to evaluate the coolness of bare skin: they competed nude.[34] Homer's heroes compete in loincloths at the Funeral Games of Patroclus, vases show nude athletes by 650 BCE, but no one knows exactly when this practice began or why. To mask social inequality? From admiration of the male body? To distinguish Greeks from barbarians, shocked as they were by public nudity? Nudity is in any case unimaginable at the IOC games, no matter how skinny the beach bikinis or how sleek speedskaters' suits. As a student once remarked, modern athletes wear Nikes, Greeks—Nakes.

OBJECTIVE AND SUBJECTIVE COMPETITIONS

A judges' conspiracy awards a controversial gold medal to a pair of Russian figure skaters (2002). A Romanian official overlooks a gymnast's slip—he is from Romania too (2004). Another judge inadvertently deprives a gymnast of precious points, enough to give him a gold medal; he finishes third (2004). Every IOC Olympics brings its share of scandals. Most involve officials in sports in which judgment determines the winner. Their decisions may be crucial in other sports too, in assigning blame for false starts or awarding points in fencing and boxing. (Two American boxers lost gold medals at Seoul in matches everyone but the judges thought they had won, and only one bout involved bribery.) But most controversies arise in the subjective sports: figure skating, diving, gymnastics.

Judges' decisions were an issue at ancient Olympia too; that is why they swore an oath. The Egyptians supposedly advised an Eleian delegation not to compete in their Olympics if they truly wished to be fair (Hdt. 2.160). About two hundred years later, two *hellanodikai* declared their fellow-citizen Eupolemus (or Eupolis) winner of the *stadion* race for 396 BCE, while one saw Leon of Ambracia come in first. Leon appealed to the Olympic Council and Eupolemus' adherents were fined, but it was his statue Pausanias found in the Altis.[35] After the *hellanodikas* Troilus won two chariot races in 372 BCE, judges were finally barred from competition, though Eleians as a group were still eligible (and often won, especially in boys' events).

So ancient Olympic judges were both corruptible and error-prone, as they are today, and they too had the responsibility for identifying false starts and fouls. But their role was much less prominent simply because ancient Olympic events had clear-cut champions, those who jumped or threw the farthest or finished a race in front. (It is true that we do not know how the Greeks determined the winner of the pentathlon, but they do not seem to have shared our uncertainty.) Even the heavy events were more likely to yield an unquestioned winner because boxers and pancratiasts fought until one conceded or could not continue and wrestlers won on falls, not points. Plutarch tells a revealing story about Thucydides, son of the famous trainer Melesias, and a political opponent of Pericles. Asked by King Archidamus of Sparta which was the better wrestler, Thucydides or Pericles, Thucydides replied, "No one can know. If I throw him, he says it wasn't a fall and persuades the spectators he's won" (Plut. *Mor.* 802C). Pericles' rhetorical ability, it seems, can refute even the most convincing evidence. The contests for trumpeters and heralds, introduced in 396 BCE, may represent an exception to this rule. But it is possible that the Greeks thought loudness something that could be judged objectively; at any rate, the Spartans' assembly always used voice votes, even for electing members of the powerful *gerousia,* "council of elders" (Thuc. 1.87.2; Plut. *Lyc.* 26.3–5).

The ancient Olympics, then, are at least as unlike the IOC brand as they are similar, so much so in fact that a movement arose in Greece in the 1920s to stage "Classical Games" more closely modeled on the ancient festival.[36] In the words of Michael Llewellyn Smith, "The games are an international festival reflecting twentieth- and twenty-first century realities. They have little to do with their origins, despite the adoption of some of the symbolic and historical features of the ancient games."[37] Thai weightlifter, Pawina Thongsuk, could be a poster girl for the differences: a woman (and so unable to appear at Olympia), she would have been ineligible by citizenship as well, won a prize the Greeks did not offer in an event they did not recognize—and in a category, a weight-class, they did not use. And she wore clothes.

It is time to set the ancient Olympics aside for the moment and turn to the origins of the modern games. Here too there is a myth that maintains its hold, a myth that distorts the history of both the distant and the recent past. Once again, it is the demands of the present that brought the myth into being and sustain it. The truth is known to everyone who cares to discover it—thanks in large measure to the researches of David Young. But the truth is an embarrassment to some and of no real use to anyone else, and so it remains unknown to most.

MODERN OLYMPIC ORIGINS

Let us rehearse the usual version of the origins of the modern Olympic festival. At its center is Baron Pierre de Coubertin, the scion of an aristocratic French family. The famous statue of Laocoön was found on an ancestor's land, his father painted classical scenes, and de Coubertin himself was fascinated from his birth in 1863 by the world of the ancient Greeks. As a patriot, he was also shocked and deeply troubled by his country's defeat in the

Franco-Prussian War of 1870 and resolved that such a calamity should not recur. Therefore, he promoted physical fitness among French schoolboys; he was an expert on the training and competitive regime of English private schools and found it plausible that the Battle of Waterloo was won on the playing fields of Eton. He also worked towards cooperation and understanding among the élites whose rivalries, he thought, were so often at the root of war. The revival of the Olympics was the great goal that brought together these strands in de Coubertin's program. His was at first a lonely dream, but his unceasing labors led in the end to glory, the first modern Olympics, in Athens in 1896.

There is much truth in this tale, repeated every two years as the torch makes its way to the site of the next Olympics, but it is not the whole truth. De Coubertin was both a visionary and a man of great energy and commitment, and we would not have the Olympics we do without him. This is not to say, however, that there would be no modern Olympics at all. For de Coubertin had a number of important predecessors in the modern Olympic revival; indeed, researchers reveal new ones all the time.[38] Two were of particular significance, Greek and English movements to found a new Olympic festival that had considerable success. These were movements de Coubertin knew well, once acknowledged, later ignored. They are still less well known than they deserve to be.

The Greek movement for a modern Olympics begins with Panagiotis Soutsos, the brother of the famous Romantic poet Alexandros Soutsos. Himself a poet, Soutsos ran a newspaper in Nauplion, the first capital of newly independent Greece, and in it published a poem called "Dialogues of the Dead" in 1833. This poem made the first reference we know of to a self-conscious revival of the ancient Olympic Games. (The suggestion was put into the mouth of the philosopher Plato, said on doubtful authority to have been a champion wrestler in his youth, but it was his cultural and intellectual authority that counted for Soutsos.) Soutsos followed it up with a detailed formal proposal in his own name, an 1835 memorandum to the Greek government (now located in Athens) in which he envisaged a national celebration, including athletic competitions to rotate among Greek sites on a quadrennial basis. It was to begin on 25 March, the date of the outbreak of the Greek war of independence. Many of us have been moved to write to our governments: few can have had so gratifying a reception as Soutsos. Not only was his letter delivered—a lot to ask in many parts of the world these days—but it was read, its message hit home, its proposals accepted, by the interior minister of the time. Unfortunately, the young Greek king's senior advisor was less keen (the idea was another's, after all), and other priorities intervened. The ambitious quadrennial festival was shelved, though 25 March did become a national holiday.

The story does not end there. Evangelis Zappas, a rich Greek living in Romania, knew both Soutsos and his idea—Soutsos had continued to put it forward for twenty years—and had the resources to get governments back on track.[39] He financed an Olympic festival that was held at Athens in 1859, four years before Pierre de Coubertin was born. It was not an unqualified success. Influential politicians feared that Greece would seem both un-Christian and out-of-step among the leading nations of Europe if it revived an old-fashioned and pagan festival and insisted that much of the time be given over to competitions in agriculture and technology. Attendance and provisions for spectators were poor; the favorite in the long-distance race collapsed and died. But make no mistake: this was the first modern Olympics, put on, fittingly enough, by Greeks in Greece.

Zappas himself died not long after, in 1865. His will, however, left a fortune for future celebrations of the modern Olympics, and a second festival took place in 1870. This went better: Zappas' money paid for the purchase, excavation, and refurbishment of the ancient Panathenaic stadium, and crowds reached thirty thousand, an extraordinary number for an athletic competition at the time. Competitors wore light-colored tunics meant to recall the nude athletes of old. Winners received cash; olive crowns; and medals of gold, silver, and bronze. Though further Olympics were funded by Zappas' money, in 1875 and

1888, they were sorry affairs, poorly planned and run. The 1888 festival in fact dispensed with athletic competitions altogether as the proponents of modernism—and opponents of sport—prevailed; the canceled competitions were held only some months later, in 1889, and restricted to students. Fortunately, another movement to revive the Olympic Games had long been active in far-away England.

William Penny Brookes was a doctor in the Shropshire village of Much Wenlock, a vicinity best known from its cameo in Housman's poem *Wenlock Edge*.[40] Devoted to the welfare of his neighbors, mostly farmers and laborers, he formed the Much Wenlock Agricultural Reading Class and then, convinced that physical fitness was as important as intellectual endeavor, organized what he called the Wenlock Olympian Class (later, the Wenlock Olympian Society). This held its first annual Olympic Meeting in 1850, with nine events (a mix of ancient and modern including cricket, soccer, and track and field) for three age classes, and generous cash prizes. A parade of the athletes and officials preceded competition.

Brookes' games caught on immediately and gradually expanded to accommodate events for all-comers from other parts of England as well as for local villagers, and contests in tilting at the ring from horseback, arithmetic (for boys), and knitting (for girls). Soon, they outgrew Much Wenlock. Brookes staged countywide Shropshire Olympian Games alongside his village festival in 1860 and joined with other English enthusiasts (organizers of Olympics at Liverpool among them) to form a national Olympic association to hold games at the Crystal Palace in London in 1866. Among the contests were wrestling, boxing, swimming, fencing and gymnastics, as well as the first attested steeplechase for track and field athletes. A second national Olympics was held in Birmingham in 1867, but the 1868 games, scheduled for Manchester, were sabotaged by a boycott of élite athletes organized by the fledgling Amateur Athletic Club. (In this regard too modern Olympic history goes back further than is usually known.)

Brookes' later attempts to hold national Olympics likewise came to little or nothing. But his village games survived and are still held today. The Greeks and Dr. Brookes knew and supported each other's work. Brookes sent £10—a considerable sum—for the winner of an event at the 1859 Zappas Olympics, and Paulos Giannopoulos, the vice-president of the organizing committee for the 1875 festival, observed in his official report that "Dr. Brookes in Wenlock, England has founded Olympic games."[41] Pierre de Coubertin knew them too. In an article he published in his new journal, *La revue athlétique,* in 1890 he recounted a visit he made to a special edition of Brookes' Much Wenlock games produced in his honor earlier that year. He notes the Zappas Olympics of 1859 and states, "If the Olympic games which modern Greece could not bring back to life are revived today, the credit is due not to a Greek but to Dr. Brookes."[42] De Coubertin planted a tree during his visit with Dr. Brookes, and it thrives to this day. Brookes' memory has fared less well.

Two questions inevitably arise. Why were the earlier and quite successful modern Olympics virtually unknown before the last twenty years and still largely ignored today? And why did de Coubertin's revival take hold when the others dwindled and disappeared? The first question is easy to answer. Zappas died some thirty years before the first IOC games in 1896. His Olympics, held in a distant corner of the world only recently reclaimed for Europe and by a people regularly slighted in favor of their classical forebears, attracted little attention, much of it dismissive. As for Dr. Brookes, though he lived into old age, he too died before de Coubertin's debut, in 1895. Alone in the spotlight, the baron naturally stressed his own accomplishments (which were admirable enough) and gradually wrote his predecessors out of the story. No one missed them. The IOC was content to take sole credit, all the more when (as we shall see) Zappas and Brookes had some ideas it found unpalatable. And its standard version—our standard version—has everything it needs to hold the stage for a contemporary audience: an impossible dream, a single-minded hero of aristocratic descent who makes it work on his own. It's like "Man of La Mancha," except this time the windmills get whipped.

I have some personal experience of the tenacity of de Coubertin's tale. Shortly before the 2004 summer games, I was interviewed on the ancient Olympics by a reporter for CBC Radio. I answered his questions and then tried to change the subject. "Listen," I said, "the real story isn't about the ancient games, it's about the modern ones. The 1896 Olympics weren't the first, you know." I thought he might be keen for a scoop, but I was wrong. "Oh, well," he said, in a world-weary way, "nothing turns out to be the way people think it is when you look into it." That's as far as his interest went. Because of laziness? Cheap cynicism? Sure, but there is more to it than that. The world already has a satisfying story about the origins of the modern Olympics and no one feels the need for another. Without some present purpose, there is no point in reinterpreting the past, except for historians. And even these, I suppose, could be thought to have three powerful modern motives: breakfast, lunch, and dinner.

The second question is more complicated: Why did de Coubertin's revival succeed when the others faded and were forgotten? It has two interconnected answers. First, the Greek and English Olympics were just that: national competitions. This was certainly true to the spirit of the originals, as was the participation of Greeks at Zappas' festivals, from Turkey and Albania as well as Greece itself. But it necessarily limited their influence and appeal. De Coubertin's Olympics were conceived as international from the beginning and attracted a bevy of the world's rich and famous as patrons. Consider the honorary sponsors of the 1894 Paris conference that led directly to the first IOC Olympics: they included the Prince of Wales, the Crown Prince of Sweden and Norway, the King of the Belgians, the Crown Prince of Greece, a Russian Grand Duke. Similarly, though at a somewhat less exalted level, the first IOC made room for a Russian general, an English lord, one count from Belgium and another from Italy (soon replaced by a duke). Their prestige and power, and their willingness to lend them to a common enterprise, were essential to de Coubertin's success. But they were not sufficient. After all, the idea of an international Olympic festival was not new: Brookes had made just such a proposal no later than 1880, in a letter to the Greek chargé d'affaires in London, John Gennadius. (He intended Athens as the site.) This fell flat, however. Why was de Coubertin able to put his plan into effect?

Here we must trace the second answer to this question. The Greeks and Dr. Brookes encouraged competitors from all sectors of society, rich and poor alike. Zappas may have lived in Romania, but he was born in Greece and fought in the Greek war of independence: wealthy or not, he was a patriot and a nationalist above all else. And one of Brookes' chief aims was to improve the physical well-being of the ordinary Englishmen he lived among. Both movements directly and indirectly encouraged athletes outside the élite. Greek and English competitors received subsidies for travel to their games; the Greeks got room, board, and uniforms to boot. Just as vital were the cash prizes both Olympics offered, large enough to compensate athletes for the time they needed to train, travel, and compete and to provide some incentive for them to do so.

For de Coubertin as for his successors, this was anathema. A competition that allowed, let alone invited, participants from among the poor must also have some winners outside the élite. (In fact, most of the victors in the 1859 and 1870 Athens games were laborers and other employees.) What, then, of the claim that wealth and social status were the rewards of merit, that privilege was the external sign of superiority? The young Alexander hinted at a similar concern when he explained his unwillingness to compete at Olympia despite his speed. "It's not a fair contest," Plutarch imagines him as saying (Plut. *Mor.* 331B). "If I win, I defeat private citizens; if I lose, it will be as a king." Such an outcome was to be avoided at all costs—and it was, by the restriction of the IOC Olympics to amateurs. There were no money prizes, only medals, symbolic tokens of no value for exchange. (In fact, the 1896 games awarded silver medals for first place—gold was too much like money.)

More than this, only those who had not competed for money or other prizes of value in the past were eligible. Fields henceforth were dominated by those with the leisure and resources to compete with little or no need to calculate the cost. For example, almost all the U.S. contingent at the 1896 games had attended Ivy League colleges or MIT; the father of a Princetonian among them, a banker, paid the way for his son and three schoolmates. The individual tragedies and farces this caused are notorious. Jim Thorpe, the Native American who was later voted the athlete of the half-century, lost his gold medals for pentathlon and decathlon at the 1912 Olympics because he had played semi-pro baseball; as a result, Avery Brundage moved up from sixth to fifth in the pentathlon.[43] When Brundage himself presided over the IOC fifty years afterwards, its policies forced hockey fans to watch Canadian college kids instead of the best players in the world. Absurd though it was, however, de Coubertin's insistence on amateurism gained his games the crucial cachet they required.

Let us pause here to note a number of ironies. The so-called first modern Olympics came very close to catastrophe. De Coubertin himself was distracted, devoting much of his time to his wedding and to a book on French history he seems to have undertaken as a favor to his bride. (Her father was an authority on the subject.) He did very little to organize the games, which is one reason there were in the end so few foreign athletes. The prime minister of the day was one of the many prominent Greeks who thought athletic competition hurt his country's reputation rather than enhanced it. The main credit for rescuing the games must go to the royal family and especially to Crown Prince Constantine, no figurehead but a tireless organizer who was not shy about using his position and personal influence to overcome the inertia and opposition of the government.

But he was not alone. The Greek trade unions also took the cause of the Olympics as their own. Self-interest helped spur them on: the Olympics might bring new visitors to Greece, the beginnings of a tourist industry, and any building boom would put money in workers' pockets. They were also proud to remind the world of a time when Greece led the way and had no reason to be disdainful of the strength, sweat, and physical sacrifice this had involved. Greek workers swelled the ranks of a demonstration against the government's economic policies; the balky prime minister resigned; another party, more supportive of the Olympic project, won the ensuing election; the games opened as planned, saved (in part) by the activities of the kind of men de Coubertin was at such pains to exclude. A century later, a government eager to complete facilities for the 2004 games at Athens put pressure on workers to get the job done on time. Thirteen laborers died during the final push. "We have paid for the Olympic games in blood," said Andreas Zazopoulos, head of the construction workers' union. Another irony.

A third irony is more closely connected to the theme of this chapter. De Coubertin did not justify his restriction of the IOC Olympics to amateurs by referring to its convenience for the élite or by expatiating (as some contemporary advocates did) upon the higher tone it imparted to the proceedings. He did not have to. He merely pointed to the ancient Greeks. It was common knowledge in de Coubertin's time that Greek athletics, at least at its peak in the archaic and classical periods, was the pursuit of amateurs. Classical scholars thought so too. But they were wrong. Yes, the Olympics and other crown games of the panhellenic circuit offered only wreaths, and later festivals that sought to share their status emulated them. But homecoming heroes did not go unrewarded. For example, Athens gave them cash grants—the equivalent of a year's wages for an ordinary citizen to Olympic champions—and a lifetime of free meals as well as less tangible marks of esteem. At other festivals, there were prizes of value in themselves. It was not just the distinctive amphoras that victors took away from the Panathenaea but the oil inside them; this could be sold for significant sums, again roughly equal to a year's pay (and more for equestrian winners). Nothing prevented these victors from moving on to Olympia and the other crown games, and they usually did. Amateurism was an invention of the mid-nineteenth century, devised precisely for the purpose to which de Coubertin put it: to preserve high-status competition (and its benefits) for the élite. This modern ideology was then read back into the ancient evidence or, all too often, allowed to substitute for it. In this area too we can see the history of the past used to shape the present, to the detriment of both.

AN OLYMPIC TRUCE?

I conclude with another attempt to make the past do the present's work: the Olympic truce campaign being conducted by the government of Greece.[44] De Coubertin believed that his Olympics could foster understanding among the élite and so peace between their nations. As he put it in an 1892 speech, "Let us export rowers, runners and fencers; there is the free trade of the future, and on the day when it is introduced within the walls of old Europe the cause of peace will have received a new and mighty stay."[45] This has now become a cornerstone of the modern Olympic movement. The second fundamental principle of the Olympic Charter states, "The goal of Olympism is to place sport at the service of the harmonious development of man, with a view to promoting a peaceful society concerned with the preservation of human dignity."[46] The ancient Olympic truce—dated to the ninth century BCE on the official IOC website—has now been drafted into the service of this ideal. This truce figures in books about Greek history as well. An excellent and up-to-date textbook prepared by a panel of distinguished experts and published by the Oxford University Press states, "During the Olympic games . . . a sacred truce banning war throughout the Greek world was declared for the month in which the games were held."[47]

Nevertheless, this too is a myth. Some Greeks wished otherwise. Thus Eusebius, writing in the fourth century CE, says that the truce was established so that there would be no wars among the Greeks (*Chron.* 1.192 Schoene; cf. Phlegon, *FGrH* 257 F 1.2–3). Moreover, these Greeks lived long after the Greek world came under the *pax Romana*—their Roman rulers were now the arbiters of disputes among Greek cities—and were besides misled by earlier Greek proponents of panhellenism who had chosen the Olympic festival as a stage for promoting the unity of the Greek élite as a prerequisite for internal security or external expansion.[48] The truce did forbid attacks on Eleian territory—not that this prevented Eleian troops from invading the sanctuary during the pentathlon at the festival of 364 BCE. (They hoped, vainly, to drive out the Arcadians, who had seized the sanctuary some time before and were presiding over the games in their place [Xen. *Hell.* 7.4.28–32].) Otherwise, the truce guaranteed only safe passage for those traveling to the games, something that would have been unnecessary if all hostilities were suspended.[49] Of course, once they reached Olympia, travelers would find the sanctuary bristling with weapons dedicated by Greeks to celebrate victories in wars against other Greeks and overlooked by the statue of Victory by the famous sculptor Paeonius, commissioned by Messenians to mark their role in the capture of a Spartan garrison on Sphacteria in 424 BCE.

All the same, it is the ancient Olympic truce that the government of Greece has made the cornerstone of the appeal for a cessation of war during the two weeks or so of the modern games. To this end, the Greeks have appointed a special ambassador and founded the International Olympic Truce Centre at Athens. This campaign has met with impressive support. The IOC has set up an International Olympic Truce Foundation in Lausanne; the call for an Olympic truce has been endorsed by the U.N. General Assembly; Secretary-General Kofi Annan called on all groups engaged in armed conflict to respect the truce during the Turin winter games of February 2006; prominent—and progressive—historians of ancient Greece, such as Paul Cartledge of Cambridge, have signed on.[50]

Now, I do not see how anyone could object to something that might stop or slow down wars or other armed conflicts for however short a time or save even one human life. The Olympic truce campaign must therefore be judged a good thing. But is it the best thing possible? I am not sure, and consequently, I do not count myself among its adherents. For one thing, it is never wise to formulate public policy on the basis of misunderstandings and myths. The invasion of Iraq is an all too contemporary warning of where lies and misrepresentations may take us. If something is worth doing, it should be pursued on its own merits, not because of what the Greeks did—much less because of what they did not do. But my reservations would still hold if the ancient Olympic truce was as extensive as the modern Greek campaign presents it.

Following the path of the ancients can limit us as much as lead us on. Effective as it has been in garnering sympathy, the truce movement has yet to make any discernible difference in armed conflicts. As Michael Llewellyn Smith remarks, "It is a pleasing concept which would not survive the harsh realities of modern interstate relations."[51] Llewellyn Smith's skepticism is grounded in experience: he is a former British ambassador to Poland and Greece. Perhaps a fairer criticism is that it is an open question whether the campaigners' admirable efforts are directed at the most meaningful goal. It is not difficult to imagine other appeals that might enlist the Olympic movement in the interest of peace. Perhaps (for instance) the IOC should refuse to recognize delegations from countries that have engaged in an illegal or aggressive war since the last festival. This would disqualify a number of important sporting nations—the United States, the United Kingdom, Australia, Italy, others in the coalition of the willing to invade and occupy Iraq—from the next Olympics. Think how well Canadians would shine then; even I might win an Olympic medal.

Lest this suggestion seem outlandish, I point out that it merely follows existing precedents. Germany and several of its allies (Austria, Bulgaria, Hungary, Turkey) were not invited to the 1920 games in Antwerp on the grounds that they had been instigators of the First World War; Antwerp was in fact chosen over the prewar favorite, Budapest, as a tribute to the gallant Belgians who were the first victims of German aggression.[52] The ban on Germany extended to the 1924 games as well. Without recognized national Olympic committees, Germany and Japan were excluded from the 1948 games in a London still rebuilding from the Blitz.[53] Those concerned with ancient precedents may recall Lichas' flouting of the ban on Spartan participation in the Olympic festival of 420 BCE (mentioned above in Chapter One). A response to a Spartan incursion into Eleian territory during the truce, this ban is generally thought to have lasted a generation.

Or maybe (I do not want to seem too self-interested) there should be other criteria. The members of the Organization of American States, Canada included, shirked their obligation to the democratically elected president of Haiti, Jean-Bertrand Aristide, when he appealed for help against a gang of thugs, torturers, and terrorists in 2004. The IOC could stigmatize and sanction those who are quietly complicit in aggression as well as active warmongers. In both strategies, there is the advantage of being able to bring pressure to bear on an identified body—the IOC—with known members (some of whom also know quite a bit about thuggery and torture). It might turn out that only Greeks were still eligible to compete, just as in ancient times. Who knows? Reflection and debate might well lead us to the conclusion that the Olympic truce movement is indeed the best way to use the games to promote world peace; but that is a decision we should not reach without allowing for alternatives, both ancient and those the Greeks never dreamed of.

CONCLUSION

L̲et us linger in the present for a few more pages and consider a peculiarly modern manner in which sport intersects with social status.

One of the odder aspects of North American sport is the exploitation of native peoples, otherwise likely to be dispossessed and marginalized, for the names of professional and college clubs: the Cleveland Indians, Washington Redskins, Chicago Black Hawks, Florida Seminoles, North Dakota Fighting Sioux, and other members of a uniquely flourishing tribe. The appearance of predators (Lions, Tigers, Screaming Eagles), weather warnings (Storm, Heat, Blizzard), and similar appellations (Fury, Wild) in their midst indicates that it is the supposed savagery and fierceness of native North Americans that is being invoked. (The Tennessee Vols are meant to recall volunteers in the Mexican War of 1846, not furry little rodents snatched away by owls.)

Long accepted when not ignored, this particular kind of claim for status has recently caused considerable controversy. Responding to the protests of native groups, the National Collegiate Athletic Association banned teams' use of American Indian nicknames and mascots during its post-season tournaments on the grounds that they are "hostile and abusive." Such concerns had already changed the St. John's Redmen into the Red Storm, the Marquette Warriors into the Golden Eagles; the Columbus Blue Jackets of the National Hockey League, for their part, insisted that players were not trading on the reputation of a famous Shawnee leader but recalling the blue uniforms of Union soldiers in the Civil War or asserting a likeness to a variety of wasp. A different approach to the problem inspired an intramural basketball team at the University of Northern Colorado in 2002. Styling themselves "the fighting Whites," players—many Native American—recruited a mascot, a Caucasian with a suit, tie, and briefcase, and competed under the slogan "everythang's gonna be all white."

No one has intervened on behalf of totemic vanquished warriors of antiquity: the University of Southern California's Trojans, Michigan State's Spartans, let alone the geographically challenged Spartans of Solon, Iowa. Nor do I wish to claim that this contemporary phenomenon of identification maps directly onto ancient sport history. After all, team sport itself played a very minor role in Greek competition. But the use of sport to attain and enhance social status—and the conflicts and tensions such claims may entail—runs throughout our evidence from antiquity. This strategy for success brings past and present together as much as ties to Trojans or Spartans and makes up the theme for this book.

For example, the modern Olympic movement has from its inception sought validation through its connections with the original games. However misleading in detail, this aim is in keeping with the traditions of the ancients themselves. Two thousand years earlier, gladiators in the eastern Roman Empire represented themselves as Greek athletes; furthermore, they fought in spectacles run by the same regional and local élites who also used their roles in Greek agonistic festivals to display their prominence. In so doing, they followed the paths of their still earlier predecessors, the archaic, classical, and Hellenistic Greeks who gained prestige through athletic success. The richest and most powerful—kings, queens, despots among them—used these advantages to improve their odds and extend their competitive careers through horse, mule, and chariot racing.

But these strategies, endemic and long-lived though they might be, could be contested or counterproductive. Some emperors were more tolerant of gladiatorial extravaganzas than others—these were therefore not always a reliable road to imperial favor. However eminent they might be, athletes who broke the rules risked a beating, a sanction that otherwise marked men as slaves; their status was thus challenged and diminished even if for only a short time. Those who succeeded might be thought to owe their standing to the help of coaches and trainers. Equestrian victors, indebted as they visibly were to the skill and courage of jockeys, drivers, and charioteers, might find themselves figured as unmanly: women too could buy or hire helpers. Yet women in turn might find their claims to status undercut by allegations that they were mere means to pass messages between men or by insinuations that they had rivaled men, only to remain unfulfilled as wives and mothers.

Then as now, such contradictions sometimes lie hidden. ("Matthew sensed there were unresolved football issues somewhere beneath the surface, as there so often are with upholsterers.")[1] It is one of the historian's main challenges to reveal them. And just as dissonance and debate, conflict and contradiction in the historical record can be especially telling, so too skepticism about our kinship and continuity with antiquity may result in a better understanding of the way they were and the way we are.

So inconsistencies in the application of the amateur ideal, and objections to its effects, helped students of the ancient world recognize that the Greek attitude allegedly underpinning it was a modern invention. Today's Olympic truce movement may yet encourage a more accurate perception of its ancient model, the *ekecheiria*. (This was just a safe passage for those traveling to the panhellenic festivals.) Conversely, the popularity of gladiatorial spectacles in the Greek east calls into question our standard stereotypes of the Greeks and Romans—cultured and crude—and the gladiators' ambitions to be seen as athletes invite us to examine our very definition of sport. It is this productive interplay between the present and the past that makes the study of ancient sport so rewarding.

NOTES

PREFACE

1. Mitchel, "Lykourgan Athens: 338–322."

CHAPTER ONE

1. Toews, *A Complicated Kindness,* 39.

2. See Kennedy, *A Course of Their Own;* McDaniel, *Uneven Lies.*

3. Quoted in Stuller, "Holding the bag," 68.

4. For the physical demands of auto racing, and the recent efforts of drivers to meet them more successfully, see Severson, "At 190 m.p.h., who needs a spare tire?"

5. Here, as often, actions speak louder than words: South African swimmer Natalie Dutoit made the 800-meter open final at the 2002 Commonwealth Games after winning the 50-meter race for athletes with disabilities. Oscar Pistorius, a South African sprinter with two prosthetic legs, is a candidate for the national 1,600-meter relay team. If he runs at Beijing, he will find it difficult to outdo the American gymnast George Eyser, who won a gold and several other medals at the 1904 Olympics on a wooden leg. Top-flight athletes in baseball have included pitchers Mordecai "Three-Fingered" Brown and Jim Abbott (who was missing most of his right forearm), one-armed outfielder Pete Gray, and Dummy Hoy. The first deaf major-leaguer, Hoy is said to have changed the game forever when he played at Oshkosh in the late 1880s. Unable to hear the umpire's call on each pitch, he asked a coach to signal balls and strikes, and the practice soon caught on.

6. Chambers, "Conflicting Rulings Keep Cart Issue in Courts," *New York Times,* April 10, 2000.

7. See the U. S. Golf Association, *The Rules of Golf,* retrieved November 6, 2007, from http://www.usga.org/rules.

8. Vial, "À propos des concours de l'Orient méditerranéen à l'époque hellénistique," 372.

9. For the place of horses in Greek life, see now Griffith, "Horsepower and donkeywork."

10. We know less about equestrian victors at local festivals. However, the overseer of the charioteers of Melon, one of the Thebans who overthrew their pro-Spartan oligarchy in the early fourth century BCE, is said to have owned the best mount in the city and to have won the horse race at the Heracleia: Plut. *Mor.* 587D.

11. See now Papakonstantinou, "Alcibiades in Olympia," and below, Chapter Two.

12. Isoc. 16.46; Diod. Sic. 13.74.3; quotation, Isoc. 16.33.

13. Paus. 6.9.4–5; Nicholson, *Aristocracy and Athletics,* 221 n. 72. For a survey, see Di Vita, "Olimpia e la Grecità siceliota."

14. For Hieron's equestrian victories and their dates, see Schade, "Die Oden von Pindar und Bakchylides auf Hieron."

15. Panathenaea: *IG* 2^2 2311 = S. G. Miller, *Arete* no. 120.

16. The scale of the celebration may have resulted from the sixty-year period during which Agrigentum had no Olympic victors to welcome; see Di Vita, "Olimpia e la Grecità siceliota," 70.

17. See Golden, *Sport and Society,* 43–45; on Hippias and Olympic victor lists in general, see now the important study by Christesen, *Olympic Victor Lists and Ancient Greek History.* Christesen stresses the impact of Elis' late-fifth century conflict with Sparta on the make-up of Hippias' list.

18. For older victors, see Golden, *Sport and Society,* 117–123. Among younger ones, the son of Ptolemy V was no older than 4 when he won a Panathenaic chariot race in 182 BCE, if Tracy and Habicht are correct in restoring his name at *IG* 2^2 2314.56 (Tracy and Habicht, "New and old Panathenaic victor lists," 221). As we will see below, the Ptolemies were aggressive in using family members, including minors, to make propaganda in competitive festivals. On this occasion, the young Ptolemy's victory would announce the arrival of a long-awaited heir; Bennett, "Arsinoe and Berenice at the Olympics," 93.

19. Diog. Laert. 8.53; Bell, "The marble youths from Grammichele and Agrigento," 224–226.

20. See now Dillon, "Did parthenoi attend the Olympic Games?"

21. See now Kyle, "'The only woman in all Greece'"; Hodkinson, "Female property ownership and empowerment in classical and Hellenistic Sparta," 111–113; and cf. Kyle, "Fabulous females and ancient Olympia" and *Sport and Spectacle*, 188–196.

22. Memorials: Paus. 6.1.6, 12.5; epigram: *Anth. Pal.* 13.16 = *IG* 5.1 1564a (*IvO* 160) = S. G. Miller, *Arete* no. 151b.

23. *Andragathias*, Xen. *Ages.* 9.6; cf. Plut. *Ages.* 20.1.

24. Kyle, "'The only woman in all Greece'," 191; cf. Kyle, *Sport and Spectacle*, 196.

25. See here, above all, Nicholson, *Aristocracy and Athletics*, 25–116, to which I am deeply indebted.

26. For their age and social status, see Chapter Two below.

27. We may note, as parallels, that the *aulos* players who accompanied dramatic performances are ignored in official Athenian victory inscriptions—they were low-status technicians, often foreigners, hired for a wage—and that Pindar and Bacchylides say nothing about the *theōroi* who assisted competitors in various ways; Wilson, "The musicians among the actors," 46–54; Rutherford, "Theoria and the Olympic Games," 173.

28. Paus. 6.13.9, cf. *Anth. Pal.* 6.135; Ebert, *Griechische Epigramme*, 46–48.

29. Future historians may hesitate to believe that U.S. Secretary of Commerce Malcolm Baldrige was killed in a rodeo accident at sixty-four, but it happened in 1987 nonetheless.

30. *IG* 5.1 213 = Sweet, *Sport and Recreation*, 145–146.

31. Crashes: see Crowther, "Reflections on Greek equestrian events." Difficult: note the praise of Theognetus of Aegina, boys' wrestling champion at Olympia, as a "dexterous charioteer of wrestling" ([Simon.] *Anth. Pal.* 16.2; Ebert, *Griechische Epigramme*, 58–59).

32. In a much later poem, Polynices' failure to hold on to the reins of his chariot prefigures his inability to retain control of Thebes; Nagel, "Polynices the charioteer."

33. Thuc. 5.49–50.4; Xen. *Hell.* 3.2.21–22; Paus. 6.2.2; Roy, "Thucydides 5.49.1–50.4"; Hornblower, "Thucydides, Xenophon and Lichas"; Hornblower, *Thucydides and Pindar*, 273–286.

34. See W. Hansen, "The winning of Hippodameia"; Davidson, "Olympia and the chariot race of Pelops."

35. For the iconography of this pediment and its implications, see Barringer, "The temple of Zeus at Olympia, heroes, and athletes."

Barringer refutes arguments that the pedimental sculptures could be intended to recall Myrtilus' treachery (though later Greeks may have interpreted them in this way).

36. Hansen, "The winning of Hippodameia," 26.

37. Theopompus *FGrH* 115 F 350 = Schol. A Hom. *Il.* 1.38.

38. Schol. bT Hom. *Il.* 1.38.

39. See Kertész, "New aspects in the connections between Macedonia and the ancient Olympic Games"; Scanlon, *Olympia and Macedonia;* Adams, "Other people's games."

40. Hdt. 5.22; Roos, "Alexander I in Olympia"; Kertész, "When did Alexander I visit Olympia?" Alexander was not listed among Olympic victors and we are nowhere told how this impasse was resolved. Might the story merely reflect the divided opinion about Alexander's eligibility?

41. Diod. Sic. 17.16.3–4; Mari, "Le Olimpie macedoni di Dion tra Archelao e l'età romana."

42. Romano, "Philip of Macedon, Alexander the Great and the ancient Olympic Games"; Kertész, "Studies on ancient sport history," 47–52.

43. Slowikowski, "Alexander the Great and sport history."

44. They also commissioned royal portraits showing themselves in the nude, an emulation of victory statues meant to establish their athletic vigor; see Hallett, *The Roman Nude,* 57–58. This kind of pretence did not impress Plutarch, whose essay on diagnosing flattery notes that every king who can wrestle is called "a Heracles": Plut. *Mor.* 56F. For a further link between athleticism, sovereignty and divinity, see Munn, *The Mother of the Gods, Athens, and the Tyranny of Asia,* 22–23.

45. Diog. Laert. 4.30; Ebert, *Griechische Epigramme,* 176–181; Tracy and Habicht, "New and old Panathenaic victor lists"; Kertész, "Studies on ancient sport history," 52–58. A Panathenaic prize amphora dated to about 310 BCE, found at Cassandrea (Potidaea) in the north Aegean, seems to commemorate a victory in the four-horse chariot race. If, as is usually the case, it was dedicated by the victor, it too may be evidence of equestrian competition among the highest levels of Macedonian society; Barringer, "Panathenaic Games and Panathenaic amphorae under Macedonian rule," 245.

46. *SIG*³ 314, cf. Paus. 6.15.10; Vollgraff, "Inscriptions de Béotie," 365–375.

47. Paus. 6.17.3; Tracy and Habicht, "New and old Panathenaic victor lists."

48. Criscuolo, "Agoni e politica," 319–320; Kosmetatou, "Bilistiche and the quasi-institutional status of Ptolemaic royal mistress."

49. Asclepiades or Posidippus, *Anth. Pal.* 5.202; Cameron, "Two mistresses of Ptolemy Philadelphus," 295–304.

50. Despite the doubts of Matthews, "Sex and the single racehorse."

51. Posidippus, AB 78.7–8 (see below, n. 54); for the date, see C. Bennett, "Arsinoe and Berenice at the Olympics," 93–94.

52. A Ptolemy and a whore recur in a competitive context in an epigram by Dioscorides, which upbraids their son for winning a torch race at Alexandria (*Anth. Pal.* 11.363). This has no obvious connection to our poem.

53. Callim. *Suppl. Hell.* 254–269, fr. 384, 384a Pf.; Golden, *Sport and Society,* 86–88; Hunter, "Poems for a princess."

54. G. Bastianini and C. Gallazzi (with C. Austin), eds., *Posidippo di Pella.* I cite the text by C. Austin and G. Bastianini, eds., *Posidippi Pellaei quae Supersunt Omnia* (= AB); the volume includes Italian and English translations. There is also an excellent English translation by Nisetich, "The poems of Posidippus."

55. For the identification of Berenice of Syria, the daughter of Ptolemy II and wife of Antiochus II of Syria, see Thompson, "Posidippus, poet of the Ptolemies," 274–279, and cf. Criscuolo, "Agoni e politica," 328–330, and Bennett, "Arsinoe and Berenice," 92–93.

56. See Fantuzzi, "The structure of the *Hippika*," 213–215.

57. AB 77, cf. 85.2; A. Szastyńska-Siemion, "*Dapana* und *ponos* bei Pindar."

58. Something similar may lie behind the mutilated text of AB 71.2. Despite Nisetich, Austin-Bastianini, and others, I doubt that Hippostratus won both the *stadion* race and the horse race at the same Pythian festival (though this is certainly not impossible and we know too few winners at these games to exclude Hippostratus). Rather, his horse Aethon too is spoken of as if an athlete, winning a Pythian *stadion* race. In this way, Hippostratus can claim the double triumph boasted by the text, as both he and his horse are proclaimed as victors. So too Callicrates' tracehorse is proclaimed at Delphi at AB 74.11 and cf. *Anth. Pal.* 9.20. See Kosmetatou, "Constructing legitimacy," 228.

59. AB 73, 75, 87; Bettarini, "Posidippo e l'epigramma epinicio," 13–14.

60. Contrast the care with which Posidippus details the charioteer's eye and fingertips in AB 67.3–4, which is not a victory epigram.

61. See Bernardini in Bernardini and Bravi, "Note di lettura al nuovo Posidippo," 156–158; Bingen, "La victoire pythique de Callicratès de Samos"; Bing, "Posidippus and the admiral," 246–255.

62. See Fantuzzi, "Posidippus and the ideology of kingship," 395–399; Fantuzzi, "Posidippus at court," 253–262; Bettarini, "Posidippo e l'epigramma epinicio," 21–22.

63. Or, following the text Austin and Bastianini now prefer, "And I do not magnify my father's glory"; Austin and Bastianini, "Addenda et corrigenda ad editionem minorem."

64. *OGI* 1.56. For the Ptolemies' focus on the family, see Kosmetatou, "Constructing legitimacy."

65. AB 82.5–6; Casanova, "Tra vecchio e nuovo Posidippo," 137–138.

66. See Willcock, *Pindar,* 69–72.

67. Young, *The Olympic Myth of Greek Amateur Athletics,* 107–176. The excellent extended discussion by Pritchard, "Athletics, education and participation," permits me to restrict my own comments here. I touch on some issues in *Sport and Society,* 141–157, and "Demosthenes and the social historian," 171–172. See also Kyle, *Sport and Spectacle,* 205–216.

68. Arist. *Rh.* 1.1365a20, 1367b18; B. Biliński, "Un pescivendolo olimpionico."

69. See Crowther, "Athlete and state," 34–37.

70. See Pleket, "Zur Soziologie," 191 n. 140.

71. *IEph.* 1415, 2005; Robert, "Sur des inscriptions d'Éphèse," 14–32; Brunet, "Olympic hopefuls from Ephesos," 227–230; Slater and Summa, "Crowns and Magnesia," 297–298.

72. See the studies of Pleket: "Games, prizes, athletes and ideology"; "The participants in the ancient Olympic Games: Social background and mentality," 148–149; "Zur Soziologie," 207–208.

73. See Nicholson, *Aristocracy and Athletics,* 119–215. For a different take on this material, cf. Burnett, *Pindar's Songs,* 51–53.

74. I use "coach, trainer" interchangeably to translate the Greek words *paidotribēs* (literally, "boy-rubber, masseur"), *aleiptēs* ("anointer, oiler"), *gymnastēs* ("athletic trainer"), *epistatēs* ("overseer"). Aristotle distinguishes between *paidotribēs* and *gymnastēs* (Arist. *Pol.* 4.1288b10–22), but his grounds are unclear, and the use of these four terms in other authors depends on nuances peculiar to them or no longer apparent. See Pritchard, "Athletics, education and participation," 33–42; König, *Athletics and Literature,* 305–306; and for a possible

distinction between *epistatēs* as a publicly-paid local official and *aleiptēs* as a freelance trainer, Brunet, "Olympic hopefuls from Ephesos," 225–226.

75. Leyshon, review of Fried, 151.

76. See Nicholson, *Aristocracy and Athletics,* 157–160; Hubbard, "Sex in the gym," 1–2; Hubbard, "Pindar's *Tenth Olympian* and athlete-trainer pederasty," 138–140.

77. See Burnett, *Pindar's Songs,* 203–219.

78. Trainers named Hegesias and Epilycus are identified (like their athletes) and wreathed (unlike them) on a *psyktēr* by Phintias that depicts pentathletes (Boston, Museum of Fine Arts 01.8019, *ARV*^{2} 24, 11, 520–515 BCE). Was it one of them who commissioned the vase?

79. For this and other examples from inscriptions, see Robert, *Études anatoliennes,* 138–146; Robert, "Un citoyen de Téos," 520–529.

80. *SIG*^{3} 1066; Moretti, *Iscrizioni,* 160–162. The two men may be brothers.

81. König, *Athletics and Literature,* 301–344, is now fundamental for our understanding of this remarkable work and the place of trainers within it.

82. On Galen's ideas on exercise and training, delineated most fully and forcefully in *Protrepticus,* "Exhortation for Medicine," see especially König, *Athletics and Literature,* 254–300, and cf. Schmidt, "Das Bild des Berufsathleten"; Boudon, "Réflexions galéniques sur la médecine du sport chez Hippocrate"; Nieto Ibáñez, "Galen's treatise." For the debate, cf. van Nijf, "Athletics, *andreia* and the *askēsis*-culture in the Roman east," 280–283.

83. In practice, doctors and trainers may have been less antagonistic. A memorial for an eighteen-year-old youth who died in Lydia in the imperial period includes among his friends both a doctor and a trainer (Robert, "Un citoyen de Téos," 525–527). The combination of skills in both areas, perhaps signaled by the noun *iatraleiptēs,* is said to have been as old as Herodicus of Selymbria in the fifth century BCE (Plut. *Mor.* 554C).

84. For Epictetus' use of athletic imagery, see Arr. *Epict. diss.* 1.18.21–23, 24.1–2, 2.5.15–17, 17.29–31, 18.22–27, 20.9–10, 25.1–5, 4.4.11–12; Long, *Epictetus,* 120–125, 196.

85. *SEG* 50.546; Robert, "Un citoyen de Téos"; *FD* 3.1 200, 220.

86. Pleket, "Mass sport and local infrastructure," 151; cf. Pleket, "The infrastructure of sport," 628–629.

87. Cf. Pleket, "The participants in the ancient Olympic Games," 148 and "Zur Soziologie," 185–194. Pleket argues that lower- and middle-class athletes began to become more common as early as 400 BCE; cf. "Einige Betrachtungen zum Thema," 83.

88. *IEph.* 1605; Brunet, "Olympic hopefuls from Ephesos," 221–224.

89. For this and other similar careers, see Pleket, "Mass sport and local infrastructure," 158–160.

90. See A. S. Hall and Milner, "Education and athletics at Oenoanda," 15, 38–40; van Nijf, "Local heroes," 322–323; and "Athletics, *andreia* and the *askêsis*-culture," 268–269.

91. See Shipley, *A History of Samos,* 213–216.

92. See van Nijf, "Local heroes," 326.

93. Pleket, "Zur Soziologie," 200–201.

94. Langenfeld, "Artemidors Traumbuch als sporthistorische Quelle," 12–13. The athletes, hunters and farmers envisaged by one of Plutarch's friends as attending a symposium represent different temperaments but the same social class: Plut. *Mor.* 618F.

95. *IG* 7 530; Moretti, *Iscrizioni,* 99–103; Crowther, "The role of heralds and trumpeters," 149.

96. Cf. Crowther's second thoughts at *Athletika,* 245.

97. *IG* 5.1 669; West, "M. Oulpios Domestikos and the athletic synod at Ephesus," 85; *P London* 1158, 1178; Pleket, "Zur Soziologie," 201–202.

98. It is worth noting that "the dummy's" older brother bears the same nickname—it may represent an Egyptian word and not a Greek insult at all—and that both are *apo gymnasiou,* usually a designation of the Greek élite; see Poliakoff, "Guilds of performers and athletes," 296–297.

99. Heavy events: Dickie, *"Palaistritēs/*'palaestrita'," 146–151.

100. Gleason, *Making Men,* 159.

101. Stratonicus of Alexandria, crowned for both wrestling and *pankration* at Olympia in 68 BCE, is sometimes said to be another on the strength of an addition in the Armenian translation of Euseb. *Chron.* on *Ol.* 178. This transmits Eusebius' information that Sosibius won four crowns at the Nemean festival on the same day, competing as both boy and *ageneios,* and then continues: "entering the gymnic competition, not having a horse. But that also happened to be ascribed to the influence of his friends or the kings. Therefore, the events that transpired were not considered to be valued as well." Commentators

have explained that Stratonicus' supporters intervened to bring him victory in the horserace. But it is more likely that the reference to his horse is meant to confirm that his four victories were in athletic events only and that any assistance he received involved his entry into two age classes; cf. the story of Agesilaus and the son of Eualces: Xen. *Hell.* 4.1.40.

102. See Pleket, "Zur Soziologie," 198–200.

103. Van Nijf, *"Aristos Hellenōn,"* 281; Milner, "Victors in the Meleagria and the Balbouran elite."

104. Roueché, *Performers and Partisans at Aphrodisias,* 191, 210; Newby, *Greek Athletics in the Roman World,* 253–254; A. S. Hall and Milner, "Education and athletics at Oenoanda," 28; van Nijf, "Athletics and *paideia,"* 215–221.

105. See Pleket, "The infrastructure of sport," 637–640; van Nijf, "Athletics, *andreia* and the *askêsis-*culture," 278, and "Athletics and *paideia,"* 220.

106. See Weir, *Roman Delphi and Its Pythian Games,* 131–133.

107. Van Nijf, "Athletics, *andreia* and the *askêsis-*culture," 284, cf. König, *Athletics and Literature,* 15–17 and Spivey's phrase "Second Agonistic" ("Kings and colossi").

108. See van Nijf, "Athletics and *paideia,"* 209–212; König, *Athletics and Literature,* 305–315.

109. *P London* 1178; Pleket, "Zur Soziologie," 203–204.

110. *IEph.* 1112; Brunet, "Olympic hopefuls from Ephesos," 224–227.

111. *POxy.* 466; Poliakoff, *Studies in the Terminology of the Greek Combat Sports,* 161–172.

112. See Young, "First with the most."

113. See Milner, "Victors in the Meleagria and the Balbouran elite," 60–61.

114. For the possibility that some results, especially those in which élite and apparently less distinguished athletes were named joint victors, were fixed, see van Nijf, "Local heroes," 326–327. I say more about joint victors below. For a nice parallel of Australian Aborigines humoring a Spanish priest's vanity by allowing him to win a series of athletic contests, see Chatwin, *The Songlines,* 50.

115. *SEG* 20.661–664; E. Bernand, *Inscriptions métriques de l'Égypte gréco-romaine,* 115–127; Legras, *Néotês,* 68–72.

116. See, e.g., Kah and Scholz, eds., *Das hellenistische Gymnasion* and König, *Athletics and Literature,* 47–63.

117. König, *Athletics and Literature*, 59.

118. See Crowther, "Resolving an impasse."

119. See Robert, "Études d'épigraphie grecques," 27–29, and *Hellenica* 11–12, 355–358. For a late second-century CE example, a boy wrestler from Cilicia (who is careful to note that he sometimes won too), see Borgia, "Rapports entre villes en Cilicie."

120. *IG* 14 1102, cf. 1104; Moretti, *Iscrizioni*, 228–235; Poliakoff, *Combat Sports in the Ancient World*, 125–127.

121. An *agonothetēs* is said to have feasted both winners and losers in an early second century BCE inscription from Gerasa (in modern Jordan) (*SEG* 7.825; Robert, "Inscriptions grecques de Phénicie et d'Arabie," 735–738). The decree in his honor was set up by a group of *technitai* connected to the theater, and the *agonothetēs'* generosity may reflect the customs of dramatic competitions (though athletes were certainly involved in these contests).

CHAPTER TWO

1. *SEG* 27.261, 43.381 = S. G. Miller, *Arete* no. 185; Gauthier and Hatzopoulos, *La loi gymnasiarchique de Beroia*.

2. Gauthier and Hatzopoulos, *La loi gymnasiarchique*, 12.

3. For the evidence, see Crowther, "Slaves and Greek athletics," 38 n. 10.

4. Aeschin. 1.138–139; Plut. *Sol.* 1.3, *Mor.* 152D, 751B; Schol. Pl. *Phdr.* 231E; Kyle, "Solon and athletics"; Mactoux, "Lois de Solon," 338–354.

5. Plut. *Sol.* 23.3; Diog. Laert. 1.55; Weiler, "Einige Bemerkungen zu Solons Olympionikengesetz"; Kyle, "Solon and athletics."

6. S. G. Miller, "Naked democracy."

7. [Xen.] *Ath. pol.* 2.10; Lapini, "Note testuali sulla" Ἀθηναίων πολιτεία della pseudo-Senofonte."

8. Slaves elsewhere might share in free distributions of meat from a sacrifice or of oil provided by a generous gymnasiarch. See, e.g., *IPriene* 123, first century BCE (meat); *IPriene* 113, 80–75 BCE (oil); Forbes, "The education," 354–355.

9. Philostr. *Gym.* 25, Jo. Chrys. *Mom. in Ac. princ.*, Migne, *PG* 51:76. 5–10, *hom. in Heb.*, Migne, *PG* 63:133.9–12. For Dion. Hal. *Rhet.* 7.6, see below.

10. Gardiner, "Regulations for a local sports meeting." The translation of *synagōnistai* by "fellow competitors" in this text is not quite certain; see Aneziri, "Les synagonistes du théâtre grec aux époques hellénistiques et romaine," 57 n. 28.

11. *P. Cairo Zeno* 59060 (= A. S. Hunt and Edgar, *Select Papyri* 1 no. 88), 59061, 59098. See Forbes, "The education," 355–357; Legras, *Néotês*, 25–27 (where, however, Pyrrhus is said to be free). The quotation below is from *P. Cairo Zeno* 59060.

12. *P. Cairo Zeno* 59488. Cf. *P. Cairo Zeno* 59296; *PSI* 4.364.

13. Crowther, "Slaves and Greek athletics," 37; but see now his second thoughts at Crowther, *Athletika*, 279.

14. Cf. Golden, *Sport and Society*, 3.

15. See S. G. Miller, *Ancient Greek Athletics*, 78. For a contrary opinion, see Nicholson, *Aristocracy and Athletics*, 96.

16. See Maul-Mandelartz, *Griechische Reiterdarstellungen in agonistischem Zusammenhang*, 105–116, 210–211.

17. See, e.g., the bronze jockey, about ten years old, on horseback, dating from the second half of the second century BCE, found off Cape Artemisium in 1928: Rühfel, *Das Kind in der griechischen Kunst*, 280–286; Hemingway, *The Horse and Jockey from Artemision*, 111–113.

18. Plut. *Mor.* 839C, with the correction of the manuscripts' *kerētisai, kerētizōn* to *kelētisai, kelētizōn;* Chamoux, "Celetizontes pueri."

19. For an illustration of a young and naked jockey being dragged along after falling from his mount during a race, see the Apulian volute krater by the Sisyphus Painter, about 420 BCE, Munich, Antikensammlungen 3266; Rühfel, *Kinderleben im klassischen Athen*, 59 no. 33. For the death of a horse-trainer thrown by a mare, see *Anth. Pal.* 7.332. Xenophon advises the young man (*neos*) against breaking in a horse himself: Xen. *Eq.* 2.1.

20. For possible citizen boy jockeys, see Paus. 6.2.8 (Olympia, early fourth century BCE) with the cogent objections of Nicholson, *Aristocracy and Athletics*, 243 n. 74, and *IG* 12.9 952 (Heracleia at Chalcis, 120–100 BCE), with the arguments of Knoepfler, "Contributions à l'épigraphie de Chalcis 2," 182–184.

21. Aeschin. 1.29–32; Dover, *Greek Homosexuality*, 19–39.

22. *Anth. Pal.* 9.19, cf. 20, 21; Juv. 8.57–67.

23. Lys. fr. 75 Thalheim = 17.2 Gernet-Bizos = Dion. Hal. *Dem.* 11.

24. I cite the play according to Martin Cropp's text and numeration of the fragments in Collard, Cropp, and Gibert, eds., *Euripides: Selected Fragmentary Plays 2.*

25. Fr. 62b 24, 31, 41, 62c 5, 62d 35, 43, 62a 10 (supplement); cf. 61a (which may also be read as attributing slaves' victories to their master, here Priam).

26. Fr. 54, 57, 59, 61b. See Lens Tuero, "Una dimensión ideológica del *Alejandro* de Eurípides."

27. Cyrus was as high-handed as a ten-year-old as Paris was about ten years older and likewise incurred resentment; Hdt. 1.114. Paris' work as a cowherd is mentioned in a number of Euripides' other plays, but nothing definite is said about his juridical status: Eur. *Andr.* 280, *Hec.* 646, *IA* 180, 574, 1291. He is raised by a free *oiketēs*, "servant," in the king's employ in Apollod. 3.12.5.

28. For other unexpected appearances of Alcibiades on the Athenian stage, see Vickers, *Pericles on Stage.*

29. It is generally thought that Euripides' *Trojan Women,* presented at the same festival as *Alexandros,* gained much of its dramatic power from its reflection of this contemporary catastrophe of war.

30. See, e.g., King, *Stolen Childhood,* 43–55; Wiggins, *Glory Bound,* 3–20.

31. Wiggins, *Glory Bound,* 10–11.

32. Quoted by Wiggins, *Glory Bound,* 15.

33. D. K. Wiggins, "Sport and popular pastimes," 66–67; Fogel, Galantine, and Manning, eds., *Without Consent or Contract,* 76.

34. See Gorn, *The Manly Art,* 34–35; Sammons, *Beyond the Ring,* 31; Sugden, *Boxing and Society,* 21–22.

35. Gorn, *The Manly Art,* 35.

36. For an example, see Dorson, *American Negro Folktales,* 132–135.

37. See Jacobs and Winter, "Antitrust principles and collective bargaining by athletes"; Patterson, *Slavery and Social Death,* 25–26.

38. Levine, *A. G. Spalding and the Rise of Baseball,* 151 n. 30.

39. Wiggins, "Good times on the old plantation," 272–273.

40. The first George Bush was on the Yale baseball team, but as a president, he was strictly bush league.

41. Chesterton, *Father Brown,* 73.

42. N. Hall, "Slaves' use of their 'free' time." Note here the care some Attic vase-painters took to contrast youths of the leisure class, the ideal type of rider, with grooms and stable hands (likely slaves); see Padgett, "The stable hands of Dionysos," 68–70.

43. Stroyer, *My Life in the South*, 19–25.

44. P. Hunt, *Slaves, Warfare and Ideology*.

45. Cf. Golden, *Sport and Society*, 65–69.

46. Serghidou, "Corps héroïque et expérience du moi servile dans la tragédie," 392: "une 'culture somatique', qui place le corps des personnages libres . . . dans le domaine de l'endurance, de la grâce, de l'harmonie de contours et de la fonction communicative, et le corps des personnages serviles, dans le domaine de la déchéance physique, de la pénurie vestimentaire, de la fatigue et de l'isolement, en un mot, de l'inconsistance corporelle." It is worth noting, however, that Hippocratic medical writings—somewhat more practically—make little or nothing of physical differences between slaves and the free; McKeown, "Seeing things."

47. See Robertson, "The scrutiny of new citizens at Athens."

48. See Weiler, "Physiognomische Überlegungen zu *mens sana in corpore sano.*"

49. Hdt. 8.59; cf. Plut. *Them.* 11, *Mor.* 185B.

50. See Siewert, "The Olympic rules."

51. Crowther and Frass, "Flogging as a punishment in the ancient games," 76.

52. DuBois, *Torture and Truth*, 68.

53. DuBois, *Torture and Truth*, 26.

54. See Hammond, "A famous exemplum of Spartan toughness."

55. Plut. *Arist.* 21.4; for the ideology of the Eleutheria, see van Nijf, "*Aristos Hellenôn*," 273–277.

56. Sen. *Ep.* 15.3, 83.4. For the authority of a bought trainer, a *paidotribēs*, cf. Arr. *Epict. diss.* 4.1.117; for his moral failings, Synes. *Ep.* 32.

57. Hippoc. *Epid.* 7.9. The *aleiptēs* from Tralles who was a member of the household of Arruntianus Demonicus and set up a first- or second-century CE memorial for his life-partner may have been a freed slave; Sayar, *Die Inschriften von Anazarbos und Umgebung* 1, 129 no. 219.

58. Plut. *Marc.* 17.6, *Mor.* 786C, 1094BC.

59. Slaves made an unusual appearance at the Capitoline Games, founded by the emperor Domitian on the model of a Greek competitive festival in 86 CE: in the proclamation "Sardinians for sale, each more worthless than the other" (Plut. *Mor.* 277C, Festus p. 428 Lindsay). Ancient explanations, diverse, ill-informed, and implausible, make no obvious connection between this piece of Saturnian verse and sport. The Capitoline Games were also anomalous in including

freed slaves among their cultural competitions. Like the Sardinians, this provided Roman coloring for the Greek-style celebration; so too the cultural program included Latin poetry and oratory, and chariot races were staged in the Circus Maximus rather than a Greek hippodrome with entries from the *factiones,* "teams," familiar from Roman spectacles. See Caldelli, *L'Agon Capitolinus,* 165–166; Rieger, "Die Capitolia des Kaisers Domitian."

60. Bonfante, "Nudity as a costume in classical art," 556.

61. The Canadian politician Elsie Wayne played on a similar imprecision during her term as mayor of Saint John, New Brunswick. Her office entitled her to an invitation to the annual St. Patrick's Day dinner in 1984, but the local St. Patrick's Society did not admit women. Mayor Wayne therefore attended as one of the waitresses— they (like the female piano player) had long been present but unaccounted for at the society's gatherings. Hersey, *Elsie!—An Authorized Biography of Elsie Wayne,* 173–176.

62. Chesterton, *Father Brown,* 93–94.

63. The standard discussion is still Himmelmann, *Archäologisches zum Problem der griechischen Sklaverei.* See since, e.g., Oakley, "Some 'other' members of the Athenian household"; Llewellyn-Jones, *Aphrodite's Tortoise,* 140–142; Schumacher, *Sklaverei in der Antike,* 71–90.

64. M. C. Miller, *Athens and Persia in the Fifth-Century BC,* 160–161; Kosmopoulou, "'Working women',' 304–306.

65. See Le Dinahet, "L'image de l'enfance à l'époque hellénistique," 91; S. Lewis, *The Athenian Woman,* 28–35; Golden, "*Pais,* 'child' and 'slave'."

66. Würzburg, Martin von Wagner Museum, L 476 = Sinn, ed., *Sport in der Antike,* 124–127 no. 41 (ill. 84).

67. Lezzi-Hafter in Bloesch, ed., *Greek Vases from the Hirschmann Collection,* 80. The vase, Inv. Gr 18, no. 39 in the publication of the collection, is now at the Archaeological Institute of the University of Zürich and partly illustrated in S. G. Miller, *Ancient Greek Athletics,* 118 no. 205.

68. Attribute: see, e.g., S. G. Miller, *Ancient Greek Athletics,* 19 no. 19, 66 no. 121, 153 no. 237; Plut. *Mor.* 793B; Sybarite: Ath. 12.518D. Note too the use of *paprorysso,* "dig along, alongside," in competitive contexts: Arr. *Epict. diss.* 3.15.4 = Epict. *Ench.* 29.2; Diog. Laert. 6.27.

69. Thuillier, "Le *cirrus* et la barbe." So the *cirrus* worn by a plump child (identified as a slave) who passes an athlete jumping weights and

a discus on a sarcophagus from Aphrodisias is meant to emphasize his youth; Chaisemartin, "Agonistic images on Aphrodisian sarcophagi," 244–245.

70. See Rigsby, "Notes sur la Crète hellénistique," 350–355. I list all the sources known to me in the appendix to this chapter.

71. B 97–99; Kennell, "'Most necessary for the bodies of men'," 128–133. The great baseball star Ty Cobb's barbers are said to have sold his hair clippings to fans; Stump, *Cobb*, 216.

72. Cf. *IG* 2² 1011.21, Athens, 107/6 BCE; *AthMitt* 32 [1907] p. 273 no. 10, Pergamum, ? first century BCE.

73. A. H. M. Jones, *The Greek City from Alexander to Justinian*, 221.

74. *POxy.* 390, first century CE; *PRyl.* 224a, *PStrasb.* 791, 847, 848, *PBerl. Leihgabe* 39, all second century CE; *BGU* 466, *SB* 12495, second or third century CE; *SB* 9406, third century CE.

75. *Palaistrophylakes* do not appear among the liturgies listed in N. Lewis, *The Compulsory Services of Roman Egypt* (though other similar figures do, e.g., *agoraphylakes, halōnophylakes, pediophylakes*). The most comprehensive investigation of guards, watchmen and their sources of support in Greco-Roman Egypt admits the function of *palaistrophylakes* is unclear but situates them within the Gauverwaltung, "district administration"; Homoth-Kuhs, *Phylakes und Phylakon-Steuer im griechisch-römischen Ägypten*, 98 n. 250.

76. *PAmh.* 2.124; Alston, *The City in Roman and Byzantine Egypt*, 191.

77. Forbes, *Greek Physical Education*, 251, on *PAmh.* 2.124.

78. Schubert, *Les archives de Marcus Lucretius Diogenes et textes apparentés*, 229.

79. See Dickie, "'*Palaistritēs*'/'*palaestrita*'," with the addition of *SEG* 44.501; and, for further discussion of the meaning of the word, Pleket, "The infrastructure of sport," 637–638.

80. *PRyl.* 224a, *PDiog.* 47, *PBerl. Leighabe* 39, *SB* 9406.

81. Our earliest Egyptian evidence, an inscription dated to 57 BCE, mentions oil and a running track among other appurtenances of athletic sites, but the presence of a *palaistrophylax* is due to an ambitious restoration; *SEG* 8.531; A. Bernand, *La prose sur pierre dans l'Égypte hellénistique et romaine*, no. 41.24.

82. A young man, *neaniskos*, appears as a wrestler's sparring partner at Arr. *Epict. diss.* 1.24.1–2, but nothing is said of his social status.

CHAPTER THREE

1. For what follows, see Blaydes and Bordinat, "Blake's 'Jerusalem' and popular culture"; Solomon, "Villainless quest."

2. See the studies in Winkler, ed., *Gladiator;* Cyrino, *Big Screen Rome*, 207–256.

3. The book itself is a sober and sensible account, focusing on the disposal of the bodies of gladiators, other fighters, and beasts in particular.

4. Lafaye, "Gladiator," 1565: "Le génie propre de la race grecque lui inspira pour les combats de gladiateurs une répugnance qu'elle ne surmonta jamais complètement."

5. Coubertin, *Olympism*, 301.

6. Hatzfeld, *Les trafiquants italiens dans l'Orient hellénique*, 336: "On sait que les populations purement grecques n'ont jamais pris goût à ces divertissements sanglants; mais il faut noter que les rares villes où, à l'époque impériale, des φαμιλίαι μονομάχων paraissent être établies . . . possédaient également des communautés italiennes influentes et prospères." For this and similar judgments, see Robert, *Gladiateurs*, 13–15.

7. Friedländer, *Roman Life and Manners under the Early Empire*, 2.85.

8. Welch, "Negotiating Roman spectacle architecture in the Greek world"; König, "Favorinus' Corinthian oration in its Corinthian context," 146–151.

9. Wiedemann, *Emperors and Gladiators*, 128–164.

10. Robert's own subsequent studies, published in the volumes of his *Hellenica*, remain fundamental: 3 (1946) 112–150, 151–162, 5 (1948) 77–99, 7 (1949) 126–151, 8 (1950) 39–72. More recent works include Rizakis, "*Munera gladiatoria* à Patras"; Papastolou, "Monuments de combats de gladiateurs à Patras"; Coleman, "Ptolemy Philadelphus and the Roman Amphitheatre"; Kayser, "La gladiature en Égypte"; Ritti and Yilmaz, "Gladiatori e *venationes* a Hierapolis di Frigia"; Nigdelis and Stephani, "*Nea epitymbia mnēmeia monomachōn apo tē Beroia*"; Bouley, *Jeux romains dans les provinces balkano-danubiennes;* Daszewski, "Les gladiateurs à Chypre"; Rumscheid and Rumscheid, "Gladiatoren in Mysala."

11. For the rules and routines of the heavy events, see Poliakoff, *Combat Sports;* S. G. Miller, *Ancient Greek Athletics*, 46–60; *Il.* 23.653.

12. Lee, "The later Greek boxing glove and the Roman caestus."

13. For other examples, see Brophy, "Deaths in the pan-Hellenic games"; Brophy and Brophy, "Deaths in the pan-Hellenic games II"; Scanlon, *Eros and Greek Athletics*, 299–322. The epigrams of Lucillius (who wrote in the time of Nero) make sport of the injuries suffered by incompetent boxers (*Anth. Pal.* 11.75–81, 258, cf. 12.123; Robert, "Les épigrammes satiriques de Lucillius sur les athlètes").

14. See Fontenrose, "The hero as athlete"; Bohringer, "Cultes d'athlètes en Grèce classique"; Kurke, "The economy of kudos." We may compare the modern heavyweight boxing champions. There is a story found in no less an authority than Martin Luther King, Jr.— that the last words of a Black man about to be executed in the U.S. South were "Save me, Joe Louis" (M. L. King, Jr., *Why We Can't Wait*, 119). Muhammad Ali and Mike Tyson, in their different ways, are as numinous.

15. *CIG* 2758; Roueché, *Performers and Partisans at Aphrodisias*, 51–53.

16. [Dem.] 61.29; Crowther, "Reflections on Greek equestrian events."

17. For collections and discussions of these stories, see Moreau, "Le discobule meurtrier"; Scanlon, "Death and the discus in Greek and Hindu myth."

18. Morgan, "Three non-Roman blood sports."

19. Courting gifts: Koch-Harnack, *Knabenliebe und Tiergeschenke*. *Clouds:* Csapo, "Deep ambivalence." Conon: Dem. 54.9.

20. Pliny, *Pan.* 33.1; cf. Cic. *Tusc.* 2.17.41, *Phil.* 3.14.35, *Mil.* 34.92, Sen. *Ep.* 70.20–22 (*bestiarii*); Enenkel, "The propagation of *fortitudo*."

21. Mouratidis, "On the origin of the gladiatorial games." Note here that both the arena's oval shape and its wooden bleachers for spectators may be anticipated in classical and Hellenistic Corinth and that the Italian amphitheatre may originate in Campania, an area rich in Greek culture. See Bomgardner, *The Story of the Roman Amphitheatre*, 37–39, with the skeptical comments by Welch, "Recent work on amphitheatre architecture and arena spectacles," 496.

22. In the passage mentioned above, Plutarch describes Greek gladiators at the meal before combat busy with entrusting *ta gynaia* to their friends' care and freeing their slaves (Plut. *Mor.* 1099B). *Ta gynaia* is generally not a complimentary term—"their little women"— but these gladiators, slave owners themselves, are likely free and may be making provisions for their legal wives.

23. Kyle, *Spectacles*, 225–228.

24. Many are shown in Weeber, *Panem et Circenses,* 4–39.

25. Carter, "A *doctor secutorum* and the *retiarius* Draukos from Corinth."

26. It is ironic that modern athletes (and their fans) now seek to enhance their status by claiming to be gladiators. This strategy goes back at least as far as the 1880s, when baseball's Pete Browning—the original Louisville slugger—was known as "The Gladiator." Among more recent examples: the girlfriend of tennis player Guillermo Canas, suspended for testing positive for a banned substance, supported his appeal by saying, "He's like a gladiator, so he's fighting for sure" (*The Globe and Mail* [1 September 2005] R6). A book on women in American combat sports—written by a former professional athlete—is entitled *Female Gladiators: Gender, Law and Combat Sports in America* (by S. K. Fields, Urbana-Champaign, IL, 2005). CTV television broadcasts of Canadian Football League games in 2005 featured a segment in which commentator Glen Sutor picked "Glen's Gladiators," hardworking and effective linemen. NFL tackle Esera Tuaolo revealed his sexuality only in retirement, explaining, "The NFL is a super macho culture. It's a place for gladiators and gladiators aren't supposed to be gay" (Zirin, *What's My Name, Fool?,* 211–212).

27. Welch, "Greek stadia and Roman spectacles."

28. Suet. *Calig.* 32.2; Carter, "Palms for the gladiators."

29. Merkelbach, "Der griechische Wortschatz und die Christen," 108–136; Winter, "Die Stellung der frühen Christen zur Agonistik," 18–19. Acrobats and other performers also modeled themselves on athletes in their epigraphic accounts of their careers.

30. See Robert, "Une vision de Perpétue, martyre à Carthage en 203"; Carter, "Palms for the gladiators," 655–658.

31. Hope, "Negotiating identity and status" and "Fighting for identity."

32. Matthews, "Sulla and the games of the 175th Olympiad (80 BC)"; Caldelli, *L'Agon Capitolinus,* 16–17.

33. *Hesperia* 17 (1948) 44 no. 35. For other Republican examples of Greek games in honor of Roman leaders—the earliest at Syracuse in 210 BCE—see Erkelenz, "Cicero, *pro Flacco* 55–59," 44 n. 9.

34. Crowther, "Greek games in Republican Rome"; Thuillier, *Le sport dans la Rome antique,* 47–48; Schulze, "Roman games and Greek origins in Dionysius of Halicarnassus."

35. Sumi, "Spectacles and Sulla's public image."

36. For accounts of Greek athletics in the Roman west, see now König, *Athletics and Literature*, 205–235; Newby, *Greek Athletics*, 22–44. For sites connected to Greek athletics at Rome itself, see Lee, "Venues for Greek athletics in Rome"; Rausa, "I luoghi dell'agonismo nella Roma imperiale."

37. For Augustus and sport, see Fortuin, *Der Sport im augusteischen Rom*, 51–72. Sebasta: Caldelli, *L'Agon Capitolinus*, 28–37; Maróti, "Zur Regelung der Sportwettkämpfe der *Sebasta* in Neapel."

38. Caldelli, *L'Agon Capitolinus;* Rieger, "Die Capitolia des Kaisers Domitian." For the relationship of such Roman festivals to the older panhellenic games, see Stirpe, "Concomitanze di feste greche e romane."

39. Caldelli, *L'Agon Capitolinus*, 43–45.

40. Kajava, "When did the Isthmian Games return to the Isthmus?"

41. Weir, *Roman Delphi and Its Pythian Games*, 140–211.

42. For the special status of the Olympic festival in the early Greek world, see now Nielsen, *Olympia and the Classical Hellenic City-State Culture.*

43. Scanlon, *Eros and Greek Athletics*, 40–63; van Nijf, "The Roman Olympics."

44. Suet. *Nero* 22–25, Cass. Dio 63.9.3–21.1; Kennell, "*Nerōn periodonikēs.*"

45. Alcock, "Nero at play?"; cf. Champlin, *Nero*, 53–83.

46. Lämmer, "Die Aktische Spiele von Nikopolis"; Gurwal, *Actium and Augustus*, 65–85; Klose, "Zur Entstehung der Preiskronen."

47. For the emperors' involvement in Greek festivals, see, e.g., Mitchell, *Anatolia*, 217–225; Santi Amantini, "Olimpiade e imperatori romani"; Herz, "Herrscherverehrung und lokale Festkulture im Osten des römischen Reiches (Kaiser/Agone)"; Wallner, *Soldatenkaiser und Sport;* Klose, "Festivals and games"; Hupfloher, "Kaiserkult in einem überregionalen Heiligtum." Many of these new foundations incorporated the designation "*Olympia,*"—"Olympic"—in their name. (See Farrington, "Olympic victors"—with the addition of the Olympia at Bostra [Arabia], *SEG* 47 (1997) 2247; Leschhorn, "Die Verbreitung," 46–57.) This was another means for emperors to associate themselves with the ancient Olympics. For participation by Romans and other Italians outside the élite, see Errington, "Aspects of Roman acculturation in the East under the Republic"; for Roman participants in

panhellenic competitions, see Mann, "Griechischer Sport und römische Identität," 134–136; for the Olympics, see below, Chapter Four.

48. "Explosion agonistique": Robert, "Discours d'ouverture," 38.

49. Leschhorn, "Der Verbreitung," 31; cf. Leschhorn, "Griechische Agone," 399.

50. Leschhorn, "Griechische Agone," 414–415.

51. Carter, "*Archiereis* and asiarchs."

52. The effect must have been like that described in L. S. Cunningham's memoir of a childhood in New York: "I lead a baseball-dominated life. Not only does the stadium emit strange lights and sounds . . . but the entire neighborhood is designed around the sport. Bronze statuettes of baseball heroes pose at the intersections like signposts. . . . Every day, I walk through an outdoor baseball hall of fame" (*Sleeping Arrangements*, 24).

53. Van Nijf, "Athletics, festivals and Greek identity in the Roman East," 197; cf. van Nijf, "Local heroes," 334.

54. Crowther, "Nudity and morality"; Williams, *Roman Homosexuality*, 63–72; Mann, "Griechischer Sport und römische Identität." On nudity in Roman culture more generally, see Hallett, *The Roman Nude*, 61–101.

55. SHA *Marc.* 9.4, 27.6; Carter, "Gladiatorial ranking."

56. Cameron, *Circus Factions*, 214–217.

57. C. P. Jones, "A new Lycian dossier," 486–488.

58. Reynolds, "New letters from Hadrian to Aphrodisias," 16–19.

59. Miranda, "Testimonianze sui Kommodeia."

60. *IG* 14 1102; Moretti, *Iscrizioni agonistiche greche*, 226–235 no. 79; Poliakoff, *Combat Sports*, 125–127.

61. *IvO* 54 = *SIG*³ 1073; Poliakoff, *Combat Sports*, 127–128; Crowther, "Resolving an impasse," 135–137.

62. König, *Athletic Training*, 25.

63. Sen. *Ep.* 7.3–5; Wistrand, *Entertainment and Violence in Ancient Rome*, 16–20; Edwards, "The suffering body"; Cagniart, "The philosopher and the gladiator."

64. Crowther, "The role of heralds and trumpeters."

65. Despite Ville, *La gladiature en Occident des origines à la mort de Domitien*, 214–215.

66. Cass. Dio 54.28.3; Habicht, "Was Augustus a visitor at the Panathenaia?"

67. Polyb. 30.25.1–26.1 = Ath. 5.194C–195F; Carter, "The Roman spectacles of Antiochus Epiphanes at Daphne, 166 BC."

68. Hornum, *Nemesis, the Roman State, and the Games;* Robert, *Gladiateurs,* 172 no. 167.

69. Strabo 17.1.10 (795); Kayser, "La gladiature en Égypte," 467–468.

70. It is possible that the (fictional) gladiatorial spectacle mounted by Demochares in Apuleius' *Metamorphoses* is envisaged as part of the Eleutheria at Plataea in the mid-second century CE, but nothing in the text renders it likely; Apul. *Met.* 4.13; van Nijf, *"Aristos Hellenôn,"* 287.

71. Newby, *Greek Athletics,* 257.

72. Robert, "Pantomimen im griechischen Orient," 118–122.

73. *IEph.* 6.2949; Slater, "Orchestopala."

74. We should note that cock fights were not held at Greek competitive festivals either, despite their combination of two elements of *agōnes,* emotional energy and preparation for war (Dumont, "Les combats de coq furent-ils un sport?").

75. Our neglect of *mousikē* has Greek precedent. "Most men" (says Pausanias) "take no account of the competitors in the musical contests, and I think that they are not worth much trouble" (Paus. 10.9.2). For interesting and insightful accounts of the links and parallels between drama and athletics, and arguments for studying them together, see Larmour, *Stage and Stadium;* Scanlon, *Eros and Greek Athletics,* 277–292.

76. Lendon, "Gladiators," 400.

77. Thuillier, *Sport,* 12: "le grand public." Both gladiatorial spectacles and *venationes* had found a place in Weiler, *Der Sport bei den Völkern der Alten Welt,* 253–261.

78. See Hopkins and Beard, *The Colosseum,* vii–ix.

79. Guttmann, *A Whole New Ball Game,* 5–6.

80. Müller, *Das Volk der Athleten,* 227–229.

81. See Schwarz, *The Numbers Game.*

82. James, *The New Bill James Historical Baseball Abstract,* 796–797.

83. Young, "First with the most."

84. Horsmann, "Sklavendienst, Strafvollzug oder Sport?," 236–241.

85. Kyle, "Directions in ancient sport history," 7 n. 1; cf. Kyle, "Games, prizes and athletes in Greek sport," 105; Kyle, *Sport and Spectacle in the Ancient World,* 18–22, 270 ("however distasteful it might be, we can consider gladiatorial shows a Roman spectator sport"), 298, 340–341. The chapter on Roman gladiators is one of the two longest in Nigel Crowther's exceptionally wide-ranging *Sport in An-*

cient Times (103–123, with Crowther's justification at 119–120). Among subscribers to Kyle's definition we might include the organizers of the Battle of the Hockey Enforcers, staged in Prince George, British Columbia in April 2005. While Minneapolis backed out of a similar series of fights between tough guys on skates, newspapers in other big cities sneered ("Bozo night in Canada: A Prince George cultural event" read a cartoon in the Vancouver *Sun*) and police checked to see if the battle contravened the Criminal Code, a crowd of 2,000 paid up to $200 to see hockey live up to its derisive nickname, "ice boxing."

86. Sweet, *Sport and Recreation in Ancient Greece,* ix.

87. Similarly, Wallner's *Soldatenkaiser und Sport* treats baths, swimming and hunting as well as gladiatorial spectacles and Greek competitions (including those of trumpeters and heralds; 14–18). He notes that *Nikephoros,* since 1988 the journal of record for ancient sport, also casts its net widely and defines its subject as "sports—in the widest sense of the word."

88. Pleket, "Mass sport and local infrastructure," 151.

89. Pleket, "Sport and ideology in the Graeco-Roman world," 319; cf. Pleket, "The infrastructure of sport," 629.

90. See, e.g., its use by Caldelli, *L'Agon Capitolinus,* 3–4; Pleket, "Mass sport and local infrastructure," 151.

91. Poliakoff, *Combat Sports,* 7.

92. What follows is necessarily schematic; for the likelihood of variation and novelty, see Hopkins and Beard, *The Colosseum,* 70–73.

93. As Carter puts it, "Rules, standards of combat and perhaps even an unwritten 'code of conduct' governed the contests" ("Gladiatorial combat: The rules of engagement," 112).

94. Carter, "Gladiatorial ranking," 7–16.

95. Cf. Thuillier, *Sport,* 13.

96. Lee, "The later Greek boxing glove and the 'Roman' caestus."

97. See G. Ville, *La gladiature en Occident des origines à la mort de Domitien,* 403–424; Coleman, "*Missio* at Halicarnassus."

98. B. Johnston, *The National Post* (21 July, 2000) A3. See also F. Lidz, "Sudden death," *Sports Illustrated* 94.8 (23 February 2001) 66 and, for the Gruppo itself the account retrieved 12 November 2007 from http://www.gsr-roma.com/.

99. Suet. *Claud.* 21.6; Garello, "Sport or showbiz?" Asterix and Obelix also get it right: see Hopkins and Beard, *The Colosseum,* 59.

100. Carter, "*Archiereis* and asiarchs," 43–44.

101. Robert, *Gladiateurs*, 258–261; Carter, "Gladiatorial combat with 'sharp' weapons."

102. Carter, "Gladiatorial ranking," 102.

103. Galen, *Comp. Med.* 3.2 = 13.599–600 Kühn; Scarborough, "Galen and the gladiators"; for the dates, see Nutton, "The chronology of Galen's early career," 161–165.

104. Potter, *Gladiators: Sports and Entertainment in the Roman World;* cf. Potter, review of Wiedemann, *Emperors*, 231: "Gladiatorial combats seem to have ended in the death of one of the combatants about one in ten times."

105. Horsmann, "Sklavendienst, Strafvollzug oder Sport?," 240.

106. Ville, *La gladiature en Occident des origines à la mort de Domitien,* 318–325. Hopkins and Beard reckon one gladiator in six died in every show, some 8000 every year (*The Colosseum,* 86–94).

107. Robert, *Gladiateurs*, 294 n. 4.

108. Cf. Merkelbach, "Der griechische Wortschatz und die Christen," 134. I wonder too what they would make of the "hooligan industry," the T-shirts, pins and other paraphernalia with the insignia of the more infamous of England's soccer thugs, to say nothing of the TV documentaries and books about—and often by—them; see Foer, *How Soccer Explains the World,* 98–103.

CHAPTER FOUR

1. See Levine, *A. G. Spalding and the Rise of Baseball,* 105.

2. In July 2006, fans of the Schaumburg Flyers in the Northern League began to use the team's website to decide players' positions and batting order. After winning the pennant in the season's first half, the team swiftly descended into the cellar, perhaps because fans and players of opposing teams voted too. The present practice of allowing baseball fans to keep balls hit into the stands (and of throwing them balls at the end of the inning) is a more lasting example of spectator influence on the game. It resulted after an 11-year-old boy refused to return a ball hit into the bleachers at Philadelphia's Baker Bowl in 1923, and he won a subsequent court case.

3. Though there are exceptions: Houston Astros pitcher Brad Lidge, who spent three years at Notre Dame, describes himself as an admirer of Herodotus ("Smart Astros," *SI.com,* 30 May 2006).

4. Veeck with Linn, *Veeck as in Wreck,* 342. For Ms. Goodchild, see p. 28; for Grandstand Managers' Day, pp. 219–221.

5. The most recent discussion of the gesture by which the Colosseum crowd condemned a fighter to death—*verso pollice,* "by turning the thumb"—argues that the gesture resembled an umpire's out call. I suspect that this is a coincidence. See Corbeill, *Nature Embodied,* 41–66.

6. See Young, "The riddle of the rings."

7. It is therefore a glaring anachronism when Pericles is made to say that patriotism is like the Olympic torch, as constant and quietly burning, in the excellent production "Thucydides: The Peloponnesian Wars and Plato: Alcibiades I" (Films for the Humanities and Sciences, Princeton, 1993).

8. For the name of the runner, the ancient traditions, and the origins of the modern race and its early runnings, see Siewert, "Die Namen der antiken Marathonläufer"; Kertész, "Schlacht und 'Lauf' bei Marathon—Legende und Wirklichkeit"; Martin and Gynn, *The Olympic Marathon.*

9. See Lennartz-Lohrengel and Lennartz, "Von Pheidippides zum Spartathlon."

10. Young, *The Olympic Myth of Greek Amateur Athletics, The Modern Olympics,* and *A Brief History.*

11. Young, *The Modern Olympics,* 158. Robertson, thought to be the last surviving competitor of the 1896 games when he died at age 94, was less generous to contemporary Greeks, recording the opinion that Louis had been helped by a lift from a Greek cavalry horse.

12. Young, *A Brief History,* 138–140.

13. It is less well known that the two men were barefoot to symbolize poverty and wore bead necklaces to represent lynching; that the white silver medalist, Peter Norman of Australia, put on an Olympic Project for Human Rights patch in solidarity; and that George Foreman waved the American flag after winning the gold medal for boxing with no protest from the IOC.

14. China's human rights record, its occupation of Tibet, and its unwillingness to condemn the Sudanese government's actions in Darfur have all motivated calls to boycott the 2008 Olympics in Beijing.

15. See now the full discussion by Christesen, *Olympic Victor Lists and Ancient Greek History.*

16. See the skeptical review of the evidence in Weiler, "Theodosius I. und die Olympischen Spiele."

17. J. König, *JRS* 95 (2005) 255, reviewing B. Burrell, *Neokoroi.*

18. The desire for victory provides at least a partial explanation for decisions to drop sports, such as lacrosse or, more recently, baseball, that influential IOC members think unlikely to produce triumphs for their compatriots. An ancient parallel: The Nikephoria at Pergamum was like the Olympics in respect to its athletic and equestrian program, but it modeled its cultural competitions on the Pythian Games. It is possible that each type of competition was quadrennial and that (like the modern Olympics) the Nikephoria took a different form every two years; Musti, "Un bilancio sulla questione dei *Nikephoria* di Pergamo" and "*Isopythios, isolympios* e dintorni."

19. See Crowther, "Second-place and lower finishes in Greek athletics—*pentathlon.*"

20. See Crowther, "Team sports in ancient Greece." The torch race: Gauthier, "Du nouveau sur les courses aux flambeaux d'après deux inscriptions de Kos."

21. Although exceptions are occasionally made for political reasons, as for individual Timorese who took part before their country secured its independence.

22. Australia, for example, devoted considerable resources towards ensuring a creditable showing at the Sydney games in 2000.

23. See Crowther, "Athlete and state."

24. Quoted in Simri, "The development of female participation in the modern Olympic Games," 189.

25. See Dillon, "Did parthenoi attend the Olympic Games?"

26. See Golden, *Sport and Society*, 104–116; Petermandl, "Überlegungen zur Funktion der Altersklassen bei den griechischen Agonen."

27. See Crowther, "The age-category of boys at Olympia" and "The Sebastan Games in Naples (*IvO* 56)."

28. Anyone who remembers the sprinter Stella Walsh—revealed to have male genitals almost forty years after winning the Olympic 100-meter sprint for women in 1932—or the more recent scandal over a forged birth certificate at baseball's Little World Series will sympathize with their predicament.

29. See Crowther, "Boy victors at Olympia."

30. See Crowther, "The state of the modern Olympics," 445–446.

31. After all, some Canadians stopped singing our national anthem when God was injected into "O Canada!" in 1980, and many others find it hard to justify his presence there in the middle of a Winnipeg winter.

32. See Lee, *The Program and Schedule of the Ancient Olympic Games.*

33. See Herrmann, "Die Siegerstatuen von Olympia."

34. See Shapiro, "Modest athletes and liberated women," 321–329; S. G. Miller, "Naked democracy"; Christesen, "On the meaning of *gymnazō*"; Thuillier, "La nudité athlétique, le pagne et les Étrusques"; Scanlon, "The dispersion of pederasty and the athletic revolution in sixth-century BC Greece."

35. Paus. 6.3.7, 8.45.4; Crowther, "'Sed quis custodiet ipsos custodes?'"

36. See Kitroeff, *Wrestling with the Ancients,* 92–97.

37. Llewellyn Smith, *Olympics in Athens 1896,* 8–9. A full account of the modern Greek engagement with the ancient festival and its modern version is available in Kitroeff's *Wrestling with the Ancients.* Kitroeff speaks of "the invented tradition" of continuity between the modern games and the ancient ones (3, 237) and argues that many of the classical trappings of the IOC games were designed to counter Greek demands to become their permanent hosts, on the grounds that only they could maintain their traditions. The brief account in Biddiss, "The invention of modern Olympic tradition," 130–133, also foregrounds differences. See also Spivey, *The Ancient Olympics,* xv–xix; Crowther, "The state of the modern Olympics"; Kyle, *Sport and Spectacle,* 94–101.

38. See Rühl, "The Olympian Games at Athens in the year 1877"; Rühl and Keuser, "Olympic Games in 19th century England with special consideration of the Liverpool Olympics"; Hirsch, "Olympic Games on the Drehberg in Anhalt-Dessau in the age of Goethe"; Weiler, "The predecessors of the Olympic movement, and Pierre de Coubertin."

39. See now Young, "Evangelis Zappas: Olympian sponsor of modern Olympic Games."

40. Though (by a nice coincidence) *A Shropshire Lad* (which includes the poem *Wenlock Edge*) was published in 1896, there is no evidence that Housman (a native of neighboring Worcestershire) ever met Brookes or attended his games at Much Wenlock; see Stallings, "'The time you won your town the race'."

41. Young, *The Modern Olympics,* 52.

42. Coubertin, "Les Jeux Olympiques à Much Wenlock," 705, as translated by Young, *The Modern Olympics,* 81.

43. Brundage is said to have been very proud of his final placing. A more intentionally comic figure, Archie Jones in Zadie Smith's novel

White Teeth, likewise treasured his tie with a Swedish gynecologist for thirteenth in track cycling at the 1948 Olympics, an achievement unfortunately lost to history through the sloppiness of a secretary; Z. Smith, *White Teeth,* 15–16.

44. See Kitroeff, *Wrestling with the Ancients,* 196–197, 220–222.

45. Coubertin, *Olympism,* 297.

46. See, e.g., Gerling, "The idea of peace as Coubertin's vision for the modern Olympic movement."

47. Pomeroy et al., *Ancient Greece,* 128.

48. For example, Lys. 33.1–2, Isoc. 4.43; Raubitschek, "The Panhellenic ideal and the Olympic Games"; Bollansée, "Aristotle and Hermippos."

49. See Lämmer, "Der sogenannte Olympische Friede in der griechischen Antike." Crowther demonstrates contrasts between the spirit of the modern and ancient games in this area in "The ancient Olympics and their ideals."

50. See Buckley, "Stopping the bullets."

51. Llewellyn Smith, *Olympics in Athens,* 246.

52. See Senn, *Power, Politics, and the Olympic Games,* 36–37; Lennartz, "The exclusion of the Central Empires from the Olympic Games in 1920."

53. See Buschmann and Lennartz, "Germany and the 1948 Olympic Games in London."

CONCLUSION

1. A. M. Smith, *44 Scotland Street,* 31.

WORKS CITED

Adams, W. L. (2003). "Other people's games: The Olympics, Macedonia and Greek athletics," *Journal of Sport History* 30: 205–217.

Alcock, S. E. (1994). "Nero at play? The emperor's Grecian Odyssey," in J. Elsner and J. Masters, eds., *Reflections of Nero: Culture, History and Representation* (Chapel Hill, NC) 98–111.

Alston, R. (2002). *The City in Roman and Byzantine Egypt* (London).

Aneziri, S. (1997). "Les synagonistes du théâtre grec aux époques hellénistique et romaine: Une question de terminologie et de fonction," in B. LeGuen, ed., *De la scène aux gradins. Théâtre et représentations dramatiques après Alexandre le Grand* (Aix and Perpignan) 53–71 (*Pallas* 47).

Austin, C., and G. Bastianini, eds. (2002a). *Posidippi Pellaei quae Supersunt Omnia* (Milan).

———. (2002b). "Addenda et corrigenda ad editionem minorem *Posidippi Pellaei quae Supersunt Omnia*," in G. Bastianini and A. Casanova, eds., *Il papiro di Posidippo un anno dopo. Atti del Convegno internazionale di studi, Firenze 13–14 giugno 2002* (Florence) 161.

Barringer, J. M. (2003). "Panathenaic Games and Panathenaic amphorae under Macedonian rule," in O. Palagia and S. V. Tracy, eds., *The Macedonians in Athens 322–229 B.C. Proceedings of an International Conference held at the University of Athens. May 24–26, 2001* (Oxford) 243–256.

———. (2005). "The temple of Zeus at Olympia, heroes, and athletes," *Hesperia* 74: 211–241.

Bastianini, G., and C. Gallazzi, with C. Austin, eds. (2001). *Posidippi di Pella: Epigrammi (P. Mil. Vogl. VIII 309)* (Milan).

Bell, M., III (2005). "The marble youths from Grammichele and Agrigento," in R. Gigli, ed., *Megalai Nésoi: Studi dedicati a Gio-*

vanni Rizza per il su ottantesimo compleanno 2 (Catania) 213–226.

Bennett, C. (2005). "Arsinoe and Berenice at the Olympics," *Zeitschrift für Papyrologie und Epigrafik* 154: 91–96.

Bernand, A. (1992). *La prose sur pierre dans l'Égypte hellénistique et romaine* (Paris).

Bernand, E. (1969). *Inscriptions métriques de l'Égypte gréco-romaine: Recherches sur la poésie épigrammatique des Grecs en Égypte* (*Annales littéraires de l'Université de Besançon* 98: Paris).

Bernardini, P., and L. Bravi (2002). "Note di lettura al nuovo Posidippo," *Quaderni Urbinati di Cultura Classica* 70: 147–163.

Bettarini, L. (2005). "Posidippo e l'epigramma epinicio: Aspetti linguistici," in M. Di Marco et al., eds., *Posidippo e gli altri: Il poeta, il genere, il contesto culturale e letterario. Atti dell'incontro di studio, Roma, 14–15 maggio 2004* (Pisa) 9–22.

Biddiss, M. (1999). "The invention of modern Olympic tradition," in M. Biddiss and M. Wyke, eds., *The Uses and Abuses of Antiquity* (Bern) 125–143.

Biliński, B. (1990). "Un pescivendolo olimpionico (Aristoteles Rhet. 1.7 1365a—Ps. Simonides fr. 110 D.)," *Nikephoros* 3: 157–175.

Bing, P. (2003). "Posidippus and the admiral: Kallikrates of Samos in the Milan epigrams," *Greek, Roman and Byzantine Studies* 43: 243–266.

Bingen, J. (2002). "La victoire pythique de Callicratès de Samos," *Chronique d'Égypte* 77: 185–190.

Blaydes, S. B., and P. Bordinat (1983). "Blake's 'Jerusalem' and popular culture: 'The Loneliness of the Long-distance Runner' and 'Chariots of Fire'," *Literature Film Quarterly* 11: 211–214.

Bloesch, H., ed. (1982). *Greek Vases from the Hirschmann Collection* (Zurich).

Bohringer, F. (1979). "Cultes d'athlètes en Grèce classique: Propos politiques, discours mythiques," *Revue des études anciennes* 81: 5–18.

Bollansée, J. (1999). "Aristotle and Hermippos of Smyrna on the foundation of the Olympic Games and the institution of the sacred truce," *Mnemosyne* 52: 562–567.

Bomgardner, D. L. (2000). *The Story of the Roman Amphitheatre* (London).

Bonfante, L. (1989). "Nudity as a costume in classical art," *American Journal of Archaeology* 93: 543–570.

Borgia, E. (2001). "Rapports entre villes en Cilicie: Une nouvelle inscription d'Elaiussa-Sébasté," in E. Jean, A. M. Dincol, and S. Durugönül, eds., *La Cilicie: Espaces et pouvoirs locaux (2ᵉ millénaire av. J.-C.—4ᵉ siècle ap. J.-C.). Actes de la table ronde internationale d'Istanbul, 2–5 novembre 1999* (Istanbul) 349–362.

Boudon, V. (2002). "Réflexions galéniques sur la médecine du sport chez Hippocrate: La notion d'*euexia*," in A. Thivel and A. Zucker, eds., *Le normal et le pathologique dans la Collection hippocratique: Actes du Xᵉᵐᵉ colloque internationale hippocratique (Nice, 6–9 octobre 1999)* (Nice) 711–729.

Bouley, E. (2001). *Jeux romains dans les provinces balkano-danubiennes du IIᵉ siècle avant J.-C. à la fin du IIIᵉ siècle après J.-C.* (Paris).

Brophy, R. H., III (1978). "Deaths in the pan-Hellenic games: Arrachion and Creugas," *American Journal of Philology* 99: 363–390.

Brophy, R., and M. O. Brophy. (1985). "Deaths in the pan-Hellenic games II: All combative sports," *American Journal of Philology* 106: 171–198.

Brunet, S. (2003). "Olympic hopefuls from Ephesos," *Journal of Sport History* 30: 219–235.

Buckley, W. (2004). "Stopping bullets when running and jumping starts," *The Observer* (28 March 2004), "Sport," p. 13.

Burnett, A. P. (2005). *Pindar's Songs for Young Athletes of Aigina* (Oxford).

Buschmann, J., and K. Lennartz (1998). "Germany and the 1948 Olympic Games in London," *Journal of Olympic History* 6.3: 22–28.

Cagniart, P. (2000). "The philosopher and the gladiator," *Classical World* 93: 607–618.

Caldelli, M. L. (1993). *L'Agon Capitolinus: Storia e protagonisti dall'istituzione domizianea al IV secolo* (Rome).

Cameron, A. (1976). *Circus Factions: Blues and Greens at Rome and Byzantium* (Oxford).

———. (1990). "Two mistresses of Ptolemy Philadelphus," *Greek, Roman and Byzantine Studies* 31: 287–311.

Carter, M. (1999). "A *doctor secutorum* and the *retiarius* Draukos from Corinth," *Zeitschrift für Papyrologie und Epigrafik* 126: 262–268.

———. (2001). "The Roman spectacles of Antiochus Epiphanes at Daphne, 166 BC," *Nikephoros* 14: 45–62.

———. (2003). "Gladiatorial ranking and the *SC de Pretiis Gladiatorum Minuendis* (*CIL* II 6278 = *ILS* 5163)," *Phoenix* 57: 83–114.

————. (2004). *"Archiereis* and asiarchs: A gladiatorial perspective," *Greek, Roman and Byzantine Studies* 44: 41–68.

————. (2006a). "Gladiatorial combat with 'sharp' weapons (*tois oxesi sidērois*)," *Zeitschrift für Papyrologie und Epigrafik* 155: 161–175.

————. (2006b). "Palms for the gladiators: Martial, *Spect.* 31 (27[29])," *Latomus* 65: 650–658.

————. (2007). "Gladiatorial combat: The rules of engagement," *Classical Journal* 102: 97–114.

Casanova, A. (2002). "Tra vecchio e nuovo Posidippo," in G. Bastianini and A. Casanova, eds., *Il papiro di Posidippo un anno dopo. Atti del Convegno internazionale di studi, Firenze 13–14 giugno 2002* (Florence) 129–142.

Chaisemartin, N. de (1993). "Agonistic images on Aphrodisian sarcophagi," in C. Roueché, ed., *Performers and Partisans at Aphrodisias in the Roman and Late Roman Periods* (*Journal of Roman Studies* Monograph 6: London) 239–248.

Chamoux, F. (1987). "Celetizontes pueri," in J. Servias, T. Hackens, and B. Serrais-Soyez, eds., *Stemmata: Mélanges de philologie, d'histoire et d'archéologie grecques offerts à Jules Labarbe* (Liège) 443–450.

Champlin, E. (2003). *Nero* (Cambridge, MA).

Chatwin, B. (1987). *The Songlines* (Harmondsworth).

Chesterton, G. K. (1955). *Father Brown: Selected Stories* (London).

Christesen, P. (2002). "On the meaning of *gymnazō*," *Nikephoros* 15: 7–37.

————. (2007). *Olympic Victor Lists and Ancient Greek History* (Cambridge).

Coleman, K. M. (1996). "Ptolemy Philadelphus and the Roman Amphitheatre," in W. J. Slater, ed., *Roman Theater and Society* (Ann Arbor, MI) 49–68.

————. (2000). *"Missio* at Halicarnassus," *Harvard Studies in Classical Philology* 100: 487–500.

Collard, C., M. J. Cropp, and J. Gibert, eds. (2004). *Euripides: Selected Fragmentary Plays 2* (Oxford).

Corbeill, A. (2004). *Nature Embodied: Gesture in Ancient Rome* (Princeton, NJ).

Coubertin, P. de (1890). "Les Jeux Olympiques à Much Wenlock: Une page de l'histoire de l'athlétisme," *La revue athlétique* 1: 705–713.

————. (2000). *Olympism: Selected Writings* (edited by N. Müller). (Lausanne).

Criscuolo, L. (2003). "Agoni e politica alla corte di Alessandria: Riflessioni su alcuni epigrammi di Posidippo," *Chiron* 33: 311–333.

Crowther, N. B. (1980–1981). "Nudity and morality: Athletics in ancient Italy," *Classical Journal* 76: 119–123 (= Crowther, *Athletika*, 375–379).

———. (1983). "Greek games in Republican Rome," *Antiquité classique* 52: 268–273 (= Crowther, *Athletika*, 381–385).

———. (1988). "The age-category of boys at Olympia," *Phoenix* 42: 304–308 (= Crowther, *Athletika*, 87–92).

———. (1989a). "The Sebastan Games in Naples (*IvO* 56)," *Zeitschrift für Papyrologie und Epigrafik* 79: 100–102 (= Crowther, *Athletika*, 93–96).

———. (1989b). "Boy victors at Olympia," *Antiquité classique* 58: 206–210 (= Crowther, *Athletika*, 109–113).

———. (1992a). "Second-place and lower finishes in Greek athletics (including the *pentathlon*)," *Zeitschrift für Papyrologie und Epigrafik* 90: 97–102 (= Crowther, *Athletika*, 323–329).

———. (1992b). "Slaves and Greek athletics," *Quaderni Urbinati di Cultura Classica* 40: 35–42 (= Crowther, *Athletika*, 247–253).

———. (1994a). "Reflections on Greek equestrian events: Violence and spectator attitudes," *Nikephoros* 7: 121–133 (= Crowther, *Athletika*, 228–240).

———. (1994b). "The role of heralds and trumpeters at Greek athletic festivals," *Nikephoros* 7: 135–155 (= Crowther, *Athletika*, 183–202).

———. (1995). "Team sports in ancient Greece: Some observations," *International Journal of the History of Sport* 12: 127–136 (= Crowther, *Athletika*, 351–360).

———. (1996). "Athlete and state: Qualifying for the Olympic Games in ancient Greece," *Journal of Sport History* 23: 34–43 (= Crowther, *Athletika*, 23–33).

———. (1997). "'Sed quis custodiet ipsos custodes?' The impartiality of the Olympic judges and the case of Leon of Ambracia," *Nikephoros* 10: 149–160 (= Crowther, *Athletika*, 71–81).

———. (2000). "Resolving an impasse: Draws, dead heats and similar decisions in Greek athletics," *Nikephoros* 13: 125–140 (= Crowther, *Athletika*, 297–311).

———. (2004a). *Athletika. Studies on the Olympic Games and Greek Athletics* (*Nikephoros* Beiheft 11: Hildesheim).

———. (2004b). "The state of the modern Olympics: *Citius, altius, fortius?*" *European Review* 12: 445–460.

————. (2007a). "The ancient Olympics and their ideals," in G. P. Schaus and S. R. Wenn, eds., *Onward to the Olympics: Historical Perspectives on the Olympic Games* (Waterloo, ON) 69–80 (= Crowther, *Athletika*, 11–22).

————. (2007b). *Sport in Ancient Times* (Westport, CT).

Crowther, N. B., and M. Frass (1998). "Flogging as a punishment in the ancient games," *Nikephoros* 11: 51–82 (= Crowther, *Athletika*, 141–168).

Csapo, E. (1993). "Deep ambivalence: notes on a Greek cockfight," *Phoenix* 47: 1–28, 115–124.

Cunningham, L. S. (2005 [1989]). *Sleeping Arrangements* (London).

Cyrino, M. S. (2005). *Big Screen Rome* (Malden, MA).

Daremberg, C., and E. Saglio, eds. (1877–1919). *Dictionnaire des antiquités grecques et romaines d'après les textes et les monuments* (Paris).

Daszewski, W. A. (2001). "Les gladiateurs à Chypre: Remarques à propos d'une figurine de Nea Paphos," in E. Papuci-Wladyka and I. Sliva, eds., *Studia Archeologica: Liber Amicorum Ianussio A. Astrowski ab Amicis et Discipulis Oblatus* (Cracow) 75–85.

Davidson, J. (2003). "Olympia and the chariot-race of Pelops," in D. J. Phillips and D. Pritchard, eds., *Sport and Festival in the Ancient Greek World* (Swansea) 101–122.

Di Vita, A. (2005). "Olimpia e la Grecità siceliota," *Sicilia Antiqua* 2: 63–73.

Dickie, M. W. (1993). "'*Palaistritēs'/'palaestrita*': Callisthenics in the Greek and Roman gymnasium," *Nikephoros* 6: 105–151.

Dillon, M. P. J. (2000). "Did parthenoi attend the Olympic Games? Girls and women competing, spectating, and carrying out cult roles at Greek religious festivals," *Hermes* 128: 457–480.

Dorson, R. M. (1967). *American Negro Folktales* (Greenwich, CT).

Dover, K. J. (1978). *Greek Homosexuality* (Cambridge, MA).

duBois, P. (1991). *Torture and Truth* (London).

Dumont, J. (1988). "Les combats de coq furent-ils un sport?" *Pallas* 34: 33–44.

Ebert, J. (1972). *Griechische Epigramme auf Sieger an gymnischen und hippischen Agonen* (Abhandlungen der sächsischen Akademie der Wissenschaften zu Leipzig, Philologisch-historische Klasse 63.2: Berlin).

Ebert, J., and P. Siewert (1997). "Eine archaische Bronzeurkunde aus Olympia mit Vorschriften für Ringkämpfer und Kampfrichter," in J. Ebert, *Agonismata: Kleine Schriften zur Literatur, Geschichte und Kultur der Antike* (ed. M. Hillgruber et al.) (Stuttgart) 200–236.

Edwards, C. (1999). "The suffering body: Philosophy and pain in Seneca's *Letters*," in J. I. Porter, ed., *Constructions of the Classical Body* (Ann Arbor, MI) 252–268.

Enenkel, K. A. E. (2005). "The propagation of *fortitudo*: Gladiatorial combats from ca. 85 BC to the times of Trajan and their reflection in Roman literature," in K. A. E. Enenkel and I. L. Pfeijffer, eds., *The Manipulative Mode: Political Propaganda in Antiquity: A Collection of Case Studies* (Leiden) 275–294.

Erkelenz, D. (1999). "Cicero, *pro Flacco* 55–59: Zur Finanzierung von Statthalterfesten in der Frühphase des Koinon von Asia," *Chiron* 29: 43–57.

Errington, R. M. (1988). "Aspects of Roman acculturation in the East under the Republic," in P. Kneissl and V. Losemann, eds., *Alte Geschichte und Wissenschaftsgeschichte. Festschrift für Karl Christ zum 65. Geburtstag* (Darmstadt) 140–157.

Fantuzzi, M. (2004a). "The structure of the *Hippika* in P. Mil. Vogl. VIII 309," in B. Acosta-Hughes, E. Kosmetatou, and M. Baumbach, eds., *Labored in Papyrus Leaves: Perspectives on an Epigram Collection Attributed to Posidippus (P. Mil. Vogl. VIII 309)* (Washington, DC) 213–224.

———. (2004b). "Posidippus and the ideology of kingship," in M. Fantuzzi and R. Hunter, *Tradition and Innovation in Hellenistic Poetry* (Cambridge) 377–403.

———. (2005). "Posidippus at court: The contribution of the *Hippika* of P. Mil. Vogl. VIII 309 to the ideology of Ptolemaic kingship," in K. Gutzwiller, ed., *The New Posidippus: A Hellenistic Poetry Book* (Oxford) 249–268.

Farrington, A. (1997). "Olympics victors and the popularity of the Olympic Games in the Imperial period," *Tyche* 12: 15–46.

Foer, F. (2004). *How Soccer Explains the World* (New York).

Fogel, R. W., R. A. Galantine, and R. L. Manning, eds. (1992). *Without Consent or Contract: The Rise and Fall of American Slavery. Evidence and Methods* (New York).

Fontenrose, J. (1968). "The hero as athlete," *California Studies in Classical Antiquity* 1: 73–104.

Forbes, C. A. (1929). *Greek Physical Education* (New York).

————. (1955). "The education and training of slaves in antiquity," *Transactions of the American Philological Association* 86: 321–360.

Fortuin, R. W. (1996). *Der Sport im augusteischen Rom: Philologische und sporthistorische Untersuchungen* (Stuttgart).

Fried, R. K. (1991). *Corner Men: Great Boxing Trainers* (New York).

Friedländer, L. (1908). *Roman Life and Manners under the Early Empire* (7th edition, tr. J. H. Freese and L. A. Magnus: London).

Gardiner, E. N. (1929). "Regulations for a local sports meeting," *Classical Review* 43: 210–212.

Garello, F. (2004). "Sport or showbiz? The *naumachiae* in the Flavian amphitheatre," in S. Bell and G. Davies, eds., *Games and Festivals in Classical Antiquity. Proceedings of the Conference held in Edinburgh 10–12 July 2000* (BAR International Series 1220) (Oxford) 115–124.

Gauthier, P. (1995). "Du nouveau sur les courses aux flambeaux d'après deux inscriptions de Kos," *Revue des études grecques* 108: 576–585.

Gauthier, P., and M. B. Hatzopoulos. (1993). *La loi gymnasiarchique de Beroia* (Meletemata 16: Athens).

Gerling, J. (2006). "The idea of peace as Coubertin's vision for the modern Olympic movement: Development and pedagogic consequences," *Information Letter of the International Pierre de Coubertin Committee* 1:31–38.

Gleason, M. W. (1995). *Making Men: Sophists and Self-Presentation in Ancient Rome* (Princeton, NJ).

Golden, M. (1985). "*Pais*, 'child' and 'slave'," *Antiquité classique* 54: 91–104.

————. (1998). *Sport and Society in Ancient Greece* (Cambridge).

————. (2000). "Demosthenes and the social historian," in I. Worthington, ed., *Demosthenes: Statesman and Orator* (London) 159–180.

Gorn, E. J. (1986). *The Manly Art: Bare-knuckle Prize Fighting in America* (Ithaca, NY).

Griffith, M. (2006). "Horsepower and donkeywork: Equids and the ancient Greek imagination," *Classical Philology* 101: 185–246, 307–358.

Gurwal, R. (1995). *Actium and Augustus: The Politics and Emotions of Civil War* (Ann Arbor, MI).

Guttmann, A. (1988). *A Whole New Ball Game* (Chapel Hill, NC).

Habicht, C. (1991). "Was Augustus a visitor at the Panathenaia?" *Classical Philology* 86: 226–228.

Hall, A. S., and N. P. Milner (1994). "Education and athletics at Oenoanda," in D. French, ed., *Studies in the History and Topography of Lycia and Pisidia in Memoriam A. S. Hall* (Ankara) 7–47.

Hall, N. (1980). "Slaves' use of their 'free' time in the Danish Virgin Islands in the later eighteenth and early nineteenth century," *Journal of Caribbean History* 13: 21–43.

Hallett, C. H. (2005). *The Roman Nude: Heroic Portrait Statuary 200 BC–AD 300* (Oxford).

Hammond, M. (1979–1980). "A famous exemplum of Spartan toughness," *Classical World* 75: 97–109.

Hansen, W. (2000). "The winning of Hippodameia," *Transactions of the American Philological Association* 130: 19–40.

Hatzfeld, J. (1919). *Les trafiquants italiens dans l'Orient hellénique* (Paris).

Hemingway, S. (2004). *The Horse and Jockey from Artemision: a Bronze Equestrian Monument of the Hellenistic Period* (Berkeley, CA).

Herrmann, H.-V. (1988). "Die Siegerstatuen von Olympia: Schriftliche Überlieferung und archäologischer Befund," *Nikephoros* 1: 119–183.

Hersey, L. (1998). *Elsie!—An Authorized Biography of Elsie Wayne* (Saint John, NB).

Herz, P. (1997). "Herrscherverehrung und lokale Festkulture im Osten des römischen Reiches (Kaiser/Agone)," in H. Cancik and J. Rüpke, eds., *Römische Reichsreligion und Provinzialreligion* (Tübingen) 239–264.

Himmelmann, N. (1971). *Archäologisches zum Problem der griechischen Sklaverei* (Mainz).

Hirsch, E. (1997). "'Olympic Games' on the Drehberg in Anhalt-Dessau in the Age of Goethe," *Nikephoros* 10: 265–288.

Hodkinson, S. (2004). "Female property ownership and empowerment in classical and Hellenistic Sparta," in T. J. Figueira, ed., *Spartan Society* (Swansea) 103–136.

Homoth-Kuhs, C. (2005). *Phylakes und Phylakon-Steuer im griechisch-römischen Ägypten: Ein Beitrag zur Geschichte des antiken Sicherheitswesens* (*APF* Beiheft 17: Munich).

Hope, V. M. (1998). "Negotiating identity and status: The gladiators of Roman Nîmes," in R. Laurence and J. Berry, eds., *Cultural Identity in the Roman Empire* (London) 179–195.

———. (2000). "Fighting for identity: The funerary commemoration of Italian gladiators," in A. E. Cooley, ed., *The Epigraphic Landscape of Roman Italy* (London) 93–113.

Hopkins, K., and M. Beard (2005). *The Colosseum* (London).

Hornblower, S. (2000). "Thucydides, Xenophon and Lichas: Were the Spartans excluded from the Olympic Games from 420 to 400 B.C.?" *Phoenix* 54: 212–225.

———. (2004). *Thucydides and Pindar* (Oxford).

Hornum, M. B. (1993). *Nemesis, the Roman State, and the Games* (Leiden).

Horsmann, G. (2001). "Sklavendienst, Strafvollzug oder Sport? Über-legungen zum Charakter der römischen Gladiatur," in H. Bellen and H. Heinen, eds., *Fünfzig Jahre Forschungen zur antiken Sklaverei an der Mainzer Akademie 1950–2000. Miscellanea zum Jubiläum* (Stutt-gart) 225–241.

Hubbard, T. K. (2003). "Sex in the gym: Athletic trainers and peda-gogical pederasty," *Intertexts* 7: 1–26.

———. (2005). "Pindar's *Tenth Olympian* and athlete-trainer peder-asty," in B. C. Verstraete and V. Provencal, eds., *Same-Sex Desire and Love in Greco-Roman Antiquity and in the Classical Tradition of the West* (Binghamton, NY) 137–171 (= *Journal of Homosexuality* 49.3/4).

Hunt, A. S., and C. C. Edgar (1942). *Select Papyri* 1 (Cambridge, MA).

Hunt, P. (1998). *Slaves, Warfare and Ideology in the Greek Historians* (Cambridge).

Hunter, R. (2004). "Poems for a princess," in M. Fantuzzi and R. Hunter, *Tradition and Innovation in Hellenistic Poetry* (Cambridge) 83–88.

Hupfloher, A. (2006). "Kaiserkult in einem überregionalen Heilig-tum: Das Beispiel Olympia," in K. Freitag, P. Funke, and M. Haake, eds., *Kult-Politik-Ethnos: Überregionale heiligtümer im Span-nungsfeld von Kult und Politik. Kolloquium, Münster, 23–24. November 2001* (Stuttgart) 239–263.

Jacobs, M. S., and R. K. Winter, Jr. (1971). "Antitrust principles and collective bargaining by athletes: Of superstars in peonage," *Yale Law Journal* 81: 1–29.

James, B. (2001). *The New Bill James Historical Baseball Abstract* (New York).

Jones, A. H. M. (1940). *The Greek City from Alexander to Justinian* (Oxford).

Jones, C. P. (1990). "A new Lycian dossier establishing an artistic con-test and festival in the reign of Hadrian," *Journal of Roman Archaeol-ogy* 3: 484–488.

Kah, D., and P. Scholz, eds. (2004). *Das hellenistische Gymnasion* (Berlin).

Kajava, M. (2002). "When did the Isthmian Games return to the Isthmus? Rereading *Corinth* 8.3.153," *Classical Philology* 97: 168–176.

Kayser, F. (2000). "La gladiature en Égypte," *Revue des études anciennes* 102: 459–478.

Kennedy, J. H. (2005). *A Course of Their Own: A History of African American Golfers* (Lincoln, NE).

Kennell, N. M. (1988). "*Nerōn periodonikēs*," *American Journal of Philology* 109: 239–251.

———. (2001). "'Most necessary for the bodies of men': Olive oil and its by-products in the later Greek gymnasium," in M. Joyal, ed., *In Altum: Seventy-five Years of Classical Studies in Newfoundland* (St. John's, NF) 119–133.

Kertész, I. (1991). "Schlacht und 'Lauf' bei Marathon-Legende und Wirklichkeit," *Nikephoros* 4: 155–160.

———. (1999). "New aspects in the connections between Macedonia and the ancient Olympic Games," in *Ancient Macedonia 6, Papers Read at the Sixth International Symposium held in Thessaloniki, October 15–19, 1996* (Thessalonica) 579–584.

———. (2003). "Studies on ancient sport history," *Acta Antiqua Academiae Scientiarum Hungariae* 43: 47–58.

———. (2005). "When did Alexander I visit Olympia?" *Nikephoros* 18: 115–126.

King, Jr., M. L. (1964). *Why We Can't Wait* (New York).

King, W. (1995). *Stolen Childhood: Slave Youth in Nineteenth-Century America* (Bloomington, IN).

Kitroeff, A. (2004). *Wrestling with the Ancients: Modern Greek Identity and the Olympics* (New York).

Klose, D. O. A. (1997). "Zur Entstehung der Preiskronen: Das Beispiel der Aktischen Spiele," *Jahrbuch für Numismatik und Geldgeschichte* 47: 29–45.

———. (2004). "Festivals and games in the cities of the East during the Roman Empire," in C. Howgego, V. Heuchert, and A. Burnett, eds., *Coinage and Identity in the Roman Provinces* (Oxford) 125–133.

Knoepfler, D. (1979). "Contributions à l'épigraphie de Chalcis, 2," *Bulletin de correspondance hellénique* 103: 165–188.

Koch-Harnack, G. (1983). *Knabenliebe und Tiergeschenke: Ihre Bedeutung im päderastischen Erziehungssystem Athens* (Berlin).

König, J. (2000). "Athletic Training and Athletic Festivals in the Greek Literature of the Roman Empire." (Diss. Cambridge).

———. (2001). "Favorinus' Corinthian Oration in its Corinthian context," *Proceedings of the Cambridge Philological Society* 47: 141–171.

———. (2005). *Athletics and Literature in the Roman Empire* (Cambridge).

Kosmetatou, E. (2004a). "Bilistiche and the quasi-institutional status of Ptolemaic royal mistress," *Archiv für Papyrusforschung* 50: 18–36.

———. (2004b). "Constructing legitimacy: The Ptolemaic *Familiengruppe* as a means of self-definition in Posidippus' *Hippika*," in B. Acosta-Hughes, E. Kosmetatou, and M. Baumbach, eds., *Labored in Papyrus Leaves: Perspectives on an Epigram Collection Attributed to Posidippus (P. Mil. Vogl. VIII 309)* (Washington, DC) 225–246.

Kosmopoulou, A. (2001). "'Working women': Female professionals on classical Attic gravestones," *Annual of the British School at Athens* 96: 281–319.

Kurke, L. (1993). "The economy of kudos," in C. Dougherty and L. Kurke, eds., *Cultural Poetics in Archaic Greece: Cult, Performance, Politics* (Cambridge) 131–163.

Kyle, D. G. (1983). "Directions in ancient sport history," *Journal of Sport History* 10.1: 7–34.

———. (1984). "Solon and athletics," *Ancient World* 9: 91–105.

———. (1998a). "Games, prizes and athletes in Greek sport: Patterns and perspectives (1975–1997)," *Classical Bulletin* 74: 103–127.

———. (1998b). *Spectacles of Death in Ancient Rome* (London).

———. (2003). "'The only woman in all Greece': Kyniska, Agesilaus, Alcibiades and Olympia," *Journal of Sport History* 30: 183–203.

———. (2007a). "Fabulous females and ancient Olympia," in G. P. Schaus and S. R. Wenn, eds., *Onward to the Olympics: Historical Perspectives on the Olympic Games* (Waterloo, ON) 131–152.

———. (2007b). *Sport and Spectacle in the Ancient World* (Malden, MA).

Lafaye, G. (1896). "Gladiator," in C. Daremberg and E. Saglio, eds., *Dictionnaire des antiquités grecques et romaines d'après les textes et les monuments* (Paris) 2.2, 1563–1599.

Lämmer, M. (1982/1983). "Der sogenannte Olympische Friede in der griechischen Antike," *Stadion* 8/9: 47–83.

———. (1986–1987). "Die Aktische Spiele von Nikopolis," *Stadion* 12/13: 27–38.

Langenfeld, H. (1991). "Artemidors Traumbuch als sporthistorische Quelle," *Stadion* 17: 1–26.

Lapini, W. (1994). "Note testuali sulla 'Αθηναίων πολιτεία della pseudo-Senofonte," *Rivista di filologia ed istruzione classica* 122: 129–138.

Larmour, D. H. J. (1999). *Stage and Stadium: Drama and Athleticism in Ancient Greece.* (*Nikephoros* Beiheft 4: Hildesheim).

Le Dinahet, M.-T. (2001). "Image de l'enfance à l'époque hellénistique: La valeur de l'exemple délien," in G. Hoffman and A. Lezzi-Hafter, eds., *Les pierres de l'offrande: Autour de l'oeuvre de Christoph W. Clairmont* (Kilchberg) 90–106.

Lee, H. M. (1997). "The later Greek boxing glove and the 'Roman' caestus: A centennial reevaluation of Jüthner's 'Über antike Turngeräthe'," *Nikephoros* 10: 161–178.

———. (2000). "Venues for Greek athletics in Rome," in S. K. Dickison and J. P. Hallett, eds., *Rome and Her Monuments: Essays on the City and Culture of Rome in Honor of Katherine A. Geffcken* (Wauconda, IL) 215–239.

———. (2001). *The program and schedule of the ancient Olympic Games* (*Nikephoros* Beiheft 6: Hildesheim).

Legras, B. (1999). *Néotês: Recherches sur les jeunes grecs dans l'Égypte ptolémaïque et romaine* (Geneva).

Lendon, J. E. (2000). "Gladiators," *Classical Journal* 95: 399–406.

Lennartz, K. (1998). "The exclusion of the Central Empires from the Olympic Games in 1920," in R. K. Barney, K. Wamsley, S. G. Martyn, and G. MacDonald, eds., *Global and Cultural Critique: Problematizing the Olympic Games* (London, ON) 69–74.

Lennartz-Lohrengel, B., and K. Lennartz (2005). "Von Pheidippides zum Spartathlon," *Nikephoros* 18: 315–322.

Lens Tuero, J. (2004). "Una dimensión ideológica del *Alejandro* de Eurípides," in J. A. López Férez, ed., *La Tragedia griega en sus textos: Forma (lengua, estilo, métrica, crítica textual) y contenido (pensamiento, mitos, intertextualidad)* (Madrid) 307–316.

Leschhorn, W. (1998a). "Die Verbreitung von Agonen in den östlichen Provinzen des römischen Reiches," *Stadion* 24: 31–57.

———. (1998b). "Griechische Agone in Makedonien und Thrakien: Ihre Verbreitung und politisch-religiöse Bedeutung in der römischen Kaiserzeit," in U. Peter, ed., *Stephanos Nomismatikos: Edith Schönert-Geiss zum 65. Geburtstag* (Berlin) 399–415.

Levine, P. (1985). *A. G. Spalding and the Rise of Baseball: The Promise of American Sport* (New York).

Lewis, N. (1982). *The Compulsory Public Services of Roman Egypt* (Papyrologica Florentina 11: Florence).

Lewis, S. (2002). *The Athenian Woman: An Iconographic Handbook* (London).

Leyshon, G. A. (1991). Review of Fried (1991), *Aethlon* 8.2: 151.

Llewellyn-Jones, L. (2003). *Aphrodite's Tortoise: The Veiled Woman of Ancient Greece* (Swansea).

Llewellyn Smith, M. (2004). *Olympics in Athens 1896: The Invention of the Modern Olympic Games* (London).

Long, A. A. (2002). *Epictetus: A Stoic and Socratic Guide to Life* (Oxford).

Mactoux, M.-M. (1988). "Lois de Solon sur les esclaves et formation d'une société esclavagiste," in T. Yuge and M. Doi, eds., *Forms of Control and Subordination in Antiquity* (Leiden) 331–354.

Mann, C. (2002). "Griechischer Sport und römische Identität: Die *certamina athletarum* in Rom," *Nikephoros* 15: 125–158.

Mari, M. (1996). "Le Olimpie macedoni di Dion tra Archelao e l'età romana," *Rivista di filologia ed istruzione classica* 126: 137–169.

Maróti, E. (1998). "Zur Regelung der Sportwettkämpfe der *Sebasta* in Neapel," *Acta Antiqua Academiae Scientiarum Hungariae* 38: 211–213.

Martin, D. E., and R. W. H. Gynn. (2000). *The Olympic Marathon: The History and Drama of Sport's Most Challenging Event* (Champaign, IL).

Matthews, V. J. (1979). "Sulla and the games of the 175th Olympiad (80 B.C.)," *Stadion* 5: 239–243.

———. (2000). "Sex and the single racehorse: A response to Cameron on equestrian double entrendres in Posidippus," *Eranos* 98: 32–38.

Maul-Mandelartz, E. (1990). *Griechische Reiterdarstellungen in agonistischem Zusammenhang* (Frankfurt am Main).

McDaniel, P. (2000). *Uneven Lies: The Heroic Story of African-Americans in Golf* (Greenwich, CT).

McKeown, N. (2002). "Seeing things: Examining the body of the slave in Greek medicine," in T. Wiedemann and J. Gardner, eds., *Representing the Body of the Slave* (London) 29–40 (= *Slavery and Abolition* 23.1).

Merkelbach, R. (1975). "Der griechische Wortschatz und die Christen," *Zeitschrift für Papyrologie und Epigrafik* 18: 101–148.

Miller, M. C. (1997). *Athens and Persia in the Fifth Century B.C.* (Cambridge).

Miller, Stephen G. (2000). "Naked democracy," in M. P. Flensted-Jensen, et al., eds., *Polis and Politics. Studies in Ancient Greek History Presented to Mogens Herman Hansen on His Sixtieth Birthday, August 20, 2000* (Copenhagen) 277–296.

———. (2004). *Ancient Greek Athletics* (New Haven, CT).

———. (2005). *Arete: Greek Sports from Ancient Sources* (3rd edition: Berkeley, CA).

Milner, N. P. (1991). "Victors in the Meleagria and the Balbouran elite," *Anatolian Studies* 41: 23–62.

Miranda, E. (1992/1993). "Testimonianze sui Kommodeia," *Scienze dell'Antichità* 6/7: 69–88.

Mitchel, F. (1973). "Lykourgan Athens: 338–322," in C. G. Boulter, D. W. Bradeen, A. Cameron, J. K. Caskey, A. J. Christopherson, G. M. Choen, and P. Topping, eds., *Lectures in Memory of Louise Taft Semple. Second Series* (University of Cincinnati Classical Studies 2: Norman, OK) 163–214.

Mitchell, S. (1993). *Anatolia: Land, Men and Gods in Asia Minor. I. The Celts in Anatolia and the Impact of Roman Rule* (Oxford).

Moreau, A. (1999). "Le discobule meurtrier," in A. Moreau, *Mythes grecs I. Origines* (Montpellier) 127–146.

Moretti, L. (1953). *Iscrizioni agonistiche greche* (Rome).

Morgan, M. G. (1975). "Three non-Roman blood sports," *Classical Quarterly* 25: 117–122.

Mouratidis, J. (1996). "On the origin of the gladiatorial games," *Nikephoros* 9: 111–134.

Müller, S. (1995). *Das Volk der Athleten: Untersuchungen zur Ideologie und Kritik des Sports in der griechisch-römischen Antike* (Bochumer Altertumswissenschaftliches Colloquium Band 21: Trier).

Munn, M. (2006). *The Mother of the Gods, Athens, and the Tyranny of Asia: A Study of Sovereignty in Ancient Religion* (Berkeley, CA).

Musti, D. (2000). "Un bilancio sulla questione dei *Nikephoria* di Pergamo," *Rivista di filologia ed istruzione classica* 128: 257–298 (= D. Musti, ed., *Nike: Ideologia, iconografia e feste della vittoria in età antica* [Rome 2005] 93–147).

———. (2005). "*Isopythios, isolympios* e dintorni," in D. Musti, ed., *Nike: Ideologia, iconografia e feste della vittoria in età antica* (Rome) 149–172.

Nagel, R. (1999). "Polynices the charioteer: Statius, *Thebaid* 6.296–549," *Échos du monde classique* 43: 381–396.

Newby, Z. (2005). *Greek Athletics in the Roman World: Victory and Virtue* (Oxford).

Nicholson, N. (2005). *Aristocracy and Athletics in Archaic and Classical Greece* (Cambridge).

Nielsen, T. H. (2007). *Olympia and the Classical Hellenic City-State Culture* (Hist. Fil. Medd. Dan. Vid. Selsk. 96: Copenhagen).

Nieto Ibáñez, J.-M. (2003). "Galen's treatise 'Thrasybulus' and the dispute between 'paidotribes' and 'gymnastes'," *Nikephoros* 16: 147–156.

Nigdelis, P., and D. Stephani. (2000). "*Nea epitymbia mnēmeia monomachōn apo tē Beroia,*" *Tekmēria* 5: 87–107.

Nisetich, F. (2005). "The poems of Posidippus," in K. Gutzwiller, ed., *The New Posidippus: A Hellenistic Poetry Book* (Oxford) 17–64.

Nutton, V. (1973). "The chronology of Galen's early career," *Classical Quarterly* 23: 158–171.

Oakley, J. H. (2000). "Some 'other' members of the Athenian household: Maids and their mistresses in fifth-century Athenian art," in B. Cohen, ed., *Not the Classical Ideal: Athens and the Construction of the Other in Greek Art* (Leiden) 227–246.

Padgett, J. M. (2000). "The stable hands of Dionysos: Satyrs and donkeys as symbols of social marginalization in Attic vase painting," in B. Cohen, ed., *Not the Classical Ideal: Athens and the Construction of the Other in Greek Art* (Leiden) 43–70.

Papakonstantinou, Z. (2003). "Alcibiades in Olympia: Olympic ideology, sport and social conflict in classical Athens," *Journal of Sport History* 30: 173–182.

Papastolou, I. A. (1989). "Monuments de combats de gladiateurs à Patras," *Bulletin de correspondance hellénique* 113: 351–401.

Patterson, O. (1982). *Slavery and Social Death* (Cambridge, MA).

Petermandl, W. (1997). "Überlegungen zur Funktion der Altersklassen bei den griechischen Agonen," *Nikephoros* 10: 135–147.

Plass, P. (1995). *The Game of Death in Ancient Rome: Arena Sport and Political Suicide* (Madison, WI).

Pleket, H. W. (1975). "Games, prizes, athletes and ideology," *Arena* (= *Stadion*) 1: 49–89.

———. (1992). "The participants in the ancient Olympic Games: Social background and mentality," in W. Coulson and H. Kyrieleis, eds., *Proceedings of an International Symposium on the Olympic Games* (5–9 September 1988) (Athens) 147–152.

————. (1998a). "Mass sport and local infrastructure in the Greek cities of Asia Minor," *Stadion* 24: 151–172.

————. (1998b). "Sport and ideology in the Graeco-Roman world," *Klio* 80: 315–324.

————. (2000). "The infrastructure of sport in the cities of the Greek world," *Scienze dell'Antichità* 10: 627–644.

————. (2001). "Zur Soziologie des antiken Sports," *Nikephoros* 14: 157–212.

————. (2004). "Einige Betrachtungen zum Thema 'Geld und Sport'," *Nikephoros* 17: 77–89.

Poliakoff, M. B. (1986a). "Deaths in the pan-Hellenic games: Addenda et corrigenda," *American Journal of Philology* 107: 400–402.

————. (1986b). *Studies in the Terminology of the Greek Combat Sports* (2nd edition: Meisenheim).

————. (1987). *Combat Sports in the Ancient World: Competition, Violence and Culture* (New Haven, CT).

————. (1989). "Guilds of performers and athletes: bureaucracy, rewards and privileges," *Journal of Roman Archaeology* 2: 295–298.

Pomeroy, S. B., S. M. Burstein, W. Donlan, and J. T. Roberts (1999). *Ancient Greece: A Political, Social and Cultural History* (New York).

Potter, D. S. (1994). Review of T. E. J. Wiedemann, *Emperors and Gladiators, Journal of Roman Studies* 84: 229–231.

————. (1998). *Gladiators: Sports and Entertainment in the Roman World,* an illustrated video lecture (Institute of Mediterranean Studies, Cincinnati, OH).

Pritchard, D. (2003). "Athletics, education and participation in classical Athens," in D. Phillips and D. Pritchard, eds., *Sport and Festival in the Ancient Greek World* (Swansea) 293–349.

Raubitschek, A. E. (1988). "The panhellenic ideal and the Olympic Games," in W. J. Raschke, ed., *The Archaeology of the Olympics: The Olympics and Other Festivals in Antiquity* (Madison, WI) 35–38.

Rausa, F. (2004). "I luoghi dell'agonismo nella Roma imperiale: L'edificio della Curia Athletarum," *Mitteilungen des Deutschen Archäologischen Instituts, Römische Abteilung* 111: 537–554.

Reynolds, J. (2000). "New letters from Hadrian to Aphrodisias: trials, taxes, gladiators and an aqueduct," *Journal of Roman Archaeology* 13: 5–20.

Rieger, B. (1999). "Die Capitolia des Kaisers Domitian," *Nikephoros* 12: 171–203.

Rigsby, K. J. (1986). "Notes sur la Crète hellénistique," *Revue des études grecques* 99: 350–360.

Ritti, T., and S. Yilmaz (1998). "Gladiatori e *venationes* a Hierapolis di Frigia," *Accademia nazionale dei Lincei. Memorie* 10: 445–542.

Rizakis, A. (1984). *"Munera gladiatoria* à Patras," *Bulletin de correspondance hellénique* 108: 533–542.

Robert, L. (1930a). "Pantomimen im griechischen Orient," *Hermes* 58: 106–122.

———. (1930b). "Études d'épigraphie grecque XXI–XXXI," *Revue de philologie* 4: 25–60.

———. (1937). *Études anatoliennes: Recherches sur les inscriptions grecques de l'Asie Mineure* (Paris).

———. (1939). "Inscriptions grecques de Phénicie et d'Arabie," in *Mélanges syriens offerts à René Dussaud par ses amis et ses élèves* (Paris) 729–738.

———. (1940). *Les gladiateurs dans l'Orient grec* (Paris).

———. (1960). *Hellenica* 11–12 (Paris).

———. (1967). "Sur des inscriptions d'Ephèse: Fêtes, athlètes, empereurs, épigrammes," *Revue de philologie* 41: 7–84.

———. (1968). "Les épigrammes satiriques de Lucillius sur les athlètes: Parodie et réalités," in O. Reverdin, ed., *L'épigramme grecque* (Entretiens sur l'antiquité classique 14: Vandoeuvres) 181–291.

———. (1974). "Un citoyen de Téos à Bouthrôtos d'Épire," *Comptes rendus de l'Académie des Inscriptions et Belles-Lettres:* 508–529.

———. (1982). "Une vision de Perpétue, martyre à Carthage en 203," *Comptes rendus de l'Académie des Inscriptions et Belles-Lettres:* 228–276.

———. (1984). "Discours d'ouverture," in *Praktika tou 8° Diethnous Synedriou Hellenikēs kai Latinikēs Epigraphikēs Athena, 3–9 Oktabriou 1982* I (Athens) 35–45.

Robertson, B. G. (2000). "The scrutiny of new citizens at Athens," in V. Hunter and J. Edmondson, eds., *Law and Social Status in Classical Athens* (Oxford) 149–174.

Romano, D. G. (1990). "Philip of Macedon, Alexander the Great and the ancient Olympic Games," in E. C. Danien, ed., *The World of Philip and Alexander* (Philadelphia) 63–79.

Roos, P. (1985). "Alexander I in Olympia," *Eranos* 83: 162–168.

Roueché, C. (1993). *Performers and Partisans at Aphrodisias in the Roman and Late Roman Periods* (*Journal of Roman Studies* Monograph No. 6: London).

Roy, J. (1998). "Thucydides 5.49.1–50.4: The quarrel between Elis and Sparta in 420 B.C., and Elis' exploitation of Olympia," *Klio* 80: 360–368.

Rühfel, H. (1984a). *Das Kind in der griechischen Kunst: Von der minoisch-mykenischen Zeit bis zum Hellenismus* (Mainz).

———. (1984b). *Kinderleben im klassischen Athen* (Mainz).

Rühl, J. K. (1997). "The Olympian Games at Athens in the year 1877," *Journal of Olympic History* 5.3: 26–34.

Rühl, J. K., and A. Keuser (1997). "Olympic Games in 19th century England with special consideration of the Liverpool Olympics," in R. Naul, ed., *Contemporary Studies in the National Olympic Games Movement* (Frankfurt am Main) 55–70.

Rumscheid, J., and F. Rumscheid (2001). "Gladiatoren in Mysala," *Archäologischer Anzeiger*: 115–136.

Rutherford, I. C. (2004). "Theoria and the Olympic Games: A neglected aspect of ancient athletics," in M. Kaila, G. Thill, H. Theodoropolou, and Y. Xanthacou, eds., *The Olympic Games in Antiquity: Bring Forth Rain and Bear Fruit* (Athens) 171–183.

Sammons, J. T. (1988). *Beyond the Ring: The Role of Boxing in American Society* (Urbana, IL).

Santi Amantini, L. (1996). "Olimpiadi e imperatori romani," in C. Stella and A. Valvo, eds., *Studi in onore di Albino Garzetti* (Brescia) 361–375.

Sayar, M. H. (2000). *Die Inschriften von Anazarbos und Umgebung 1: Inschriften aus dem Stadtgebiet und der nächsten Umgebung der Stadt* (Bonn).

Scanlon, T. F. (1997). *Olympia and Macedonia: Games, Gymnasia and Politics* ("Dimitria" Annual Lecture, 1996: Toronto).

———. (2002). *Eros and Greek Athletics* (Oxford).

———. (2005a). "Death and the discus in Greek and Hindu myth," *Nikephoros* 18: 219–233.

———. (2005b). "The dispersion of pederasty and the athletic revolution in sixth-century BC Greece," in B. C. Verstraete and V. Provencal, eds., *Same-Sex Desire and Love in Greco-Roman Antiquity and the Classical Tradition of the West* (Binghamton, NY) 63–85 (= *Journal of Homosexuality* 49.3/4).

Scarborough, J. (1971). "Galen and the gladiators," *Episteme* 5: 98–111.

Schade, G. (2006). "Die Oden von Pindar und Bakchylides auf Hieron," *Hermes* 134: 373–378.

Schmidt, S. (1993). "Das Bild des Berufsathleten in medizinischen Schriften der klassischen Antike," in R. Renson, T. González Aja, G. Andrieu, M. Lämmer, and R. Park, eds., *Sport and Contest. Proceedings of the 1991 International ISHPES Congress* (Madrid) 297–305.

Schubert, P. (1990). *Les archives de Marcus Lucretius Diogenes et textes apparentés* (Bonn).

Schulze, C. (2004). "Roman games and Greek origins in Dionysius of Halicarnassus," in S. Bell and G. Davies, eds., *Games and Festivals in Classical Antiquity. Proceedings of the Conference held in Edinburgh 10–12 July 2000* (BAR International Series 1220) (Oxford) 93–105.

Schumacher, L. (2001). *Sklaverei in der Antike: Alltag und Schicksal der Unfreien* (Munich).

Schwarz, A. (2004). *The Numbers Game: Baseball's Lifelong Fascination with Statistics* (New York).

Senn, A. E. (1999). *Power, Politics, and the Olympic Games* (Champaign, IL).

Serghidou, A. (1997). "Corps héroïque et expérience du moi servile dans la tragédie," *Échos du monde classique* 41: 391–420.

Severson, K. (2006). "At 190 m.p.h., who needs a spare tire?" *New York Times* (14 June) p. F1.

Shapiro, H. A. (2000). "Modest athletes and liberated women: Etruscans on Attic black-figure vases," in B. Cohen, ed., *Not the Classical Ideal: Athens and the Construction of the Other in Greek Art* (Leiden) 315–337.

Shipley, G. (1987). *A History of Samos 800–188 BC* (Oxford).

Siewert, P. (1990). "Die Namen der antiken Marathonläufer," *Nikephoros* 3: 121–126.

———. (1992). "The Olympic rules," in W. Coulson and H. Kyrieleis, eds., *Proceedings of an International Symposium on the Olympic Games (5–9 September 1988)* (Athens) 113–117.

Simri, U. (1980). "The development of female participation in the modern Olympic Games," *Stadion* 6: 187–218.

Sinn, U., ed. (1996). *Sport in der Antike: Wettkampf, Spiel und Erziehung im Altertum* (Würzburg).

Slater, W. J. (1990). "Orchestopala," *Zeitschrift für Papyrologie und Epigrafik* 81: 215–220.

Slater, W. J., and D. Summa (2006). "Crowns at Magnesia," *Greek, Roman, and Byzantine Studies* 46: 275–299.

Slowikowski, S. (1989). "Alexander the Great and sport history: A commentary on scholarship," *Journal of Sport History* 18: 70–78.

Smith, A. M. (2005). *44 Scotland Street* (Edinburgh).

Smith, Z. (2000). *White Teeth* (New York).

Solomon, M. (1983). "Villainless quest: Myth, metaphor and dream in 'Chariots of Fire'," *Communication Quarterly* 31: 274–281.

Spivey, N. (1999). "Kings and colossi," *Times Literary Supplement* no. 5017 (28 May 1999): 10.

———. (2004). *The Ancient Olympics* (Oxford).

Stallings, A. D. (1996). "'The time you won your town the race': *A Shropshire Lad* and the Modern Olympics," *Classical Outlook* 73: 113–116.

Stirpe, P. (2005). "Concomitanze di feste greche e romane con grandi feste panelleniche tra l'età ellenistica e la prima età imperiale," in D. Musti, ed., *Nike. Ideologia, iconografia e feste della vittoria in età antica* (Rome) 227–280.

Stroyer, J. (1890). *My Life in the South* (3rd edition: Salem, MA).

Stuller, J. (2000). "Holding the bag," *Hemispheres* (October): 68–74.

Stump, A. (1994). *Cobb* (Chapel Hill, NC).

Sugden, J. (1996). *Boxing and Society: An International Analysis* (Manchester).

Sumi, G. S. (2002). "Spectacles and Sulla's public image," *Historia* 51: 414–432.

Sweet, W. O. (1987). *Sport and Recreation in Ancient Greece* (Oxford).

Szastyńska-Siemion, A. (1981). "*Dapana* und *ponos* bei Pindar," in E. G. Schmidt, ed., *Aischylos und Pindar* (Berlin) 90–92.

Thompson, D. J. (2005). "Posidippus, poet of the Ptolemies," in K. Gutzwiller, ed., *The New Posidippus: A Hellenistic Poetry Book* (Oxford) 269–283.

Thuillier, J.-P. (1996). *Le sport dans la Rome antique* (Paris).

———. (1998). "Le *cirrus* et la barbe: Questions d'iconographie athlétique romaine," *Mélanges de l'École française de Rome. Antiquité* 110: 351–380.

———. (2004). "La nudité athlétique, le pagne et les Étrusques," *Nikephoros* 17: 171–180.

Toews, M. (2004). *A Complicated Kindness* (Toronto).

Tracy, S. V., and C. Habicht (1991). "New and old Panathenaic victor lists," *Hesperia* 60: 187–236.

van Nijf, O. (1999). "Athletics, festivals and Greek identity in the Roman east," *Proceedings of the Cambridge Philological Society* 45: 176–200.

———. (2001). "Local heroes: Athletes, festivals and elite self-fashioning in the Roman east," in S. Goldhill, ed., *Being Greek under Rome: Cultural Identity, the Second Sophistic and the Development of Empire* (Cambridge) 306–334.

———. (2003a). "Athletics and *paideia:* Festivals and physical education in the world of the Second Sophistic," in B. E. Borg, ed., *Paideia: The World of the Second Sophistic* (Berlin) 203–228.

———. (2003b). "Athletics, *andreia* and the *askêsis*-culture in the Roman east," in R. M. Rosen and I. Sluiter, eds., *Andreia: Studies in Manliness and Courage in Classical Antiquity* (*Mnemosyne* Supplement 238: Leiden) 263–286.

———. (2004). "The Roman Olympics," in M. Kaila, G. Thill, H. Theodoropolou, and Y. Xanthacou, eds., *The Olympic Games in Antiquity. "Bring Forth Rain and Bear Fruit"* (Athens) 187–213.

———. (2005). "*Aristos Hellenôn:* Succès sportif et identité grecque dans la Grèce romaine," *Métis* 3: 271–294.

Veeck, B., with Linn, E. (2001) [1962]. *Veeck as in Wreck* (Chicago).

Vial, C. (2003). "À propos des concours de l'Orient méditerranéen à l'époque hellénistique," in F. Prost, ed., *L'Orient méditerranéen de la mort d'Alexandre aux campagnes de Pompée: Cités et royaumes à l'époque hellénistique. Actes du colloque international de la SOPHAU, Rennes, 4–6 avril 2003* (Rennes) 311–328.

Vickers, M. J. (1997). *Pericles on Stage: Political Comedy in Aristophanes' Early Plays* (Austin, TX).

Ville, G. (1981). *La gladiature en Occident des origines à la mort de Domitien* (Rome).

Vollgraff, W. (1901). "Inscriptions de Béotie," *Bulletin de correspondance hellénique* 25: 259–378.

Wallner, C. (1997). *Soldatenkaiser und Sport* (Frankfurt am Main).

Weeber, K.-W. (1994). *Panem et Circenses: Massenunterhaltung als Politik im antiken Rom* (2nd edition: Mainz).

Weiler, I. (1981). *Der Sport bei den Völkern der Alten Welt: Eine Einführung* (Darmstadt).

———. (1983). "Einige Bemerkungen zu Solons Olympionikengesetz," in M. P. Händel and W. Meid, eds., *Festschrift für Robert Muth zum 65. Geburtstag am 1. Januar 1985 dargebracht von Freunden und Kollegen* (Innsbrucker Beiträge zur Kulturwissenschaft 22: Innsbruck) 573–582.

———. (1996). "Physiognomische Überlegungen zu *mens sana in corpore sano*," in C. Klodt, ed., *Satura Lanx: Festschrift für Werner A. Krenkel zum 70. Geburtstag* (Hildesheim) 153–168.

———. (2004a). "Theodosius I. und die Olympischen Spiele," *Nikephoros* 17: 53–75.

———. (2004b). "The predecessors of the Olympic movement, and Pierre de Coubertin," *European Review* 12: 427–443.

Weir, R. (2004). *Roman Delphi and Its Pythian Games* (BAR International Series 1306: Oxford).

Welch, K. (1998). "Greek stadia and Roman spectacles: Asia, Athens and the tomb of Herodes Atticus," *Journal of Roman Archaeology* 11: 117–145.

———. (1999). "Negotiating Roman spectacle architecture in the Greek world: Athens and Corinth," in B. Bergmann and C. Kondoleon, eds., *The Art of Ancient Spectacle* (New Haven, CT) 125–145.

———. (2001). "Recent work on amphitheatre architecture and arena spectacles," *Journal of Roman Archaeology* 14: 492–498.

West, W. C. (1990). "M. Oulpios Domestikos and the athletic synod at Ephesus," *Ancient History Bulletin* 4: 84–89.

Wiedemann, T. E. J. (1992). *Emperors and Gladiators* (London).

Wiggins, D. K. (1977). "Good times on the old plantation: Popular recreations of the black slave in antebellum South, 1820–1860," *Journal of Sport History* 4: 260–284.

———. (1995). "Sport and popular pastimes: Shadow of the slavequarter," in D. K. Wiggins, ed., *Sport in America: From Wicked Amusement to National Obsession* (Champaign, IL) 51–68.

———. (1997). *Glory Bound: Black Athletes in a White America* (Syracuse, NY).

Willcock, M. M. (1995). *Pindar: Victory Odes* (Cambridge).

Williams, C. A. (1999). *Roman Homosexuality: Ideologies of Masculinity in Classical Antiquity* (Oxford).

Wilson, P. (2002). "The musicians among the actors," in P. Easterling and E. Hall, eds., *Greek and Roman Actors: Aspects of an Ancient Profession* (Cambridge) 39–68.

Winkler, M. M., ed. (2004). *Gladiator: Film and History* (Oxford).

Winter, E. (1998). "Die Stellung der frühen Christen zur Agonistik," *Stadion* 24: 13–29.

Wistrand, M. (1992). *Entertainment and Violence in Ancient Rome: The Attitudes of Roman Writers of the First Century A.D.* (Göteborg).

Young, D. C. (1984). *The Olympic Myth of Greek Amateur Athletics* (Chicago).

———. (1988). "The riddle of the rings," in S. J. Bandy, ed., *Coroebus Triumphs: The Alliance of Sport and the Arts* (San Diego) 257–276.

———. (1996a). *The Modern Olympics: A Struggle for Revival* (Baltimore, MD).

———. (1996b). "First with the most: Greek athletic records and 'specialization'," *Nikephoros* 9: 175–198.

———. (2004). *A Brief History of the Olympic Games* (Oxford).

———. (2005). "Evangelis Zappas: Olympian sponsor of modern Olympic Games," *Nikephoros* 18: 273–288.

Zirin, D. (2005). *What's My Name, Fool? Sports and Resistance in the United States* (Chicago).

SOURCE INDEX

I. TEXTS

2. INSCRIPTIONS

191 no. 191: 74
214–215 no. 257: 75

SEG
7.825: 152n121
8.531: 67, 157n81
13.258: 42
20.661–664: 151n115
22.354: 72
27.261: 40, 67, 152n1
43.381.Bback.98: 36, 40, 67, 152n1
44.501: 157n79
45.1127: 116
47.1742: 77
47.2247: 161n47
48.736: 124

49.815–818: 86
49.1504: 35
49.1755: 77
50.546: 149n85
50.1163: 78
*SIG*³
314: 146n46
577: 36
578: 36
880: 88
1066: 149n80
1073: 162n61

TAM 2.470: 63, 67

ZPE 7 (1971) 155–156: 67

3. PAPYRI

BGU 2.466: 67, 157n74

PAmh. 2.124: 67, 157n76
PBerl. Leihgabe
  39: 157n80
  39.107: 67, 157n74
P. Cairo Zeno
  59060: 153n11
  59061: 153n11
  59098: 153n11
  59296: 153n12
  59488: 153n12
PDiog. 47: 67, 157n80
PLondon
  137: 31
  1158: 150n97
  1178: 150n97, 151n109
POxy.
390: 67, 157n74
  466: 151n111

1266: 63, 67
2082: 18
2707: 93
PRyl.
  15: 75
  121: 65, 67
  224a: 67, 157n74, 157n80
PSakaon 94: 63, 67
PSI
  364: 153n12
  1100: 67
PStrasb.
  791: 67, 157n74
  847: 67, 157n74
  848: 67, 157n74

SB
  6.9406: 67, 157n74, 157n80
  16.12495: 67, 157n74

GENERAL INDEX

Abrahams, Harold, 68, 69
Achaean League, 81
Acrisius, 73
acrobats, 160n29
Acropolis, Athenian, 44
Actia, 80, 82
actors, 93, 102
Adeimantus, 56
Aegina, 24, 29
Aelian, 58
Aelius Tertius, P., 36
Agathos Daimon, 72, 96
age, 13, 25, 61, 120
age classes, 26, 27, 119–120, 130,
    151n101. See also *paides; ageneioi*
ageneioi, "beardless youths," 32,
    120, 150n101
Agesilaus, 11, 12, 120
Agis, 11
agōnes, "contests," 77, 78, 92, 93,
    94, 96, 163n74
agōnothetai, "sponsors or managers
    of contests," 55, 78, 83, 86, 87,
    152n121
agoranomoi, "market overseers," 63
Agrippa, 81
Agyrium, 58
Ajax, 76

akoniti, "without dust" (used for an
    uncontested victory or walk-
    over), 12
Alcibiades, 6, 7, 9, 11, 48, 154n28
Alcimedon, 28
aleiptai, "anointers, oilers," 58,
    148–149n74, 155n57
aleiptos, "undefeated," 78
Alexander I, 16, 117, 146n40
Alexander III (the Great), 8, 17, 22,
    44, 81, 118, 133
Alexandria, 29, 43, 92, 147n52
Ali, Muhammad, 50
Altis, 81, 116, 122, 124, 126
amateurs, 55, 110, 134, 135, 142
Ammonius, 63
amphitheaters, 71, 77, 87, 88, 90,
    91, 92, 98, 159n21
amphorae (Panathenaic prize), 25,
    44, 135, 146n45. See also vases
Amycus, 51
Anacreon, 13
Anaxilas, 7, 8
Ancyra, 86
Andocides, 7
andres, "men" (athletes), 120, 121
Androsthenes, 72
Anicius, L., 80